Betsy Bonaparte

Betsy Bonaparte

Helen Jean Burn

The Maryland Historical Society

Baltimore, Maryland 21201

Library of Congress Cataloging-in-Publication Data
Burn, Helen Jean.
    Betsy Bonaparte / Helen Jean Burn.
    p. cm.
    Includes bibliographical references and index.
    ISBN-13: 978-0-9842135-0-4
    ISBN-10: 0-9842135-0-3
      1. Bonaparte, Elizabeth Patterson, 1785–1879. 2. Bonaparte, Elizabeth Patterson, 1785–1879—Marriage. 3. Bonaparte, Elizabeth Patterson, 1785–1879—Family. 4. Jerome Bonaparte, King of Westphalia, 1784–1860. 5. Bonaparte, Jerome Napoleon, 1805–1870. 6. Heirs—Case studies. 7. Napoleon I, Emperor of the French, 1769–1821—Family. 8. Bonaparte family. 9. Women—Maryland—Baltimore—Biography. 10. Baltimore (Md.)—Biography. I. Title.
    DC216.95.B629B87 2010
    943'.5906092—dc22
    [B]

                        2010013246

ISBN-13: 978-0-9842135-0-4
Manufactured in the United States of America. The paper used in this book meets the minimum requirements of the American National Standard for Information Sciences Permanence of Paper for Printed Library Materials, ANSI Z39. 48-1984.

Publication of this work was made possible
by the generous support of
Robert Brent, provided in honor of Hallie Dame,
and the
Friends of the Press at the Maryland Historical Society.
Grateful thanks are also extended to the late
Georgia L. Linthicum
for her kind support of this publication.

Contents

List of Illustrations

Illustrations follow page 132
All illustrations courtesy the Maryland Historical Society

12. Jerome Bonaparte in uniform.
[XX-5-52]. 1805.

13. Napoleon Bonaparte.
[154-158-3]. Jean-Baptiste Isabey, 1806.

14. Jerome Napoleon "Bo" Bonaparte.
*[Z24-1135]. Patterson-Bonaparte Collection, Acc. 76562,
Prints and Photographs Division, PP70, box 1.*

15. / 16. Two Views, Jerome Napoleon Bonaparte House, c. 1910.
*[Subject Vertical File – Baltimore City Homes].
[Patterson-Bonaparte Collection PP70].*

17. Susan May Williams.
[XX-5-76]. George d'Almaine, 1856.

18. Jerome Napoleon Bonaparte Jr. at West Point.
[Z24-1828 VF]. Prints and Photographs Division.

19. Jerome Napoleon Bonaparte Jr., French army officer.
[XX-5-73]. Prints and Photographs Division.

20. Charles Joseph Bonaparte.
[pvf]. Prints and Photographs Division.

21. Charles Joseph and Ellen Channing Day Bonaparte.
[Z24-01046]. Prints and Photographs Division.

PREFACE

*I*n Baltimore there is a large old cemetery called Green Mount. It used to be rural, but long ago the city engulfed it. Somewhere near the middle of those grassy hills there is a solitary marble tomb on a plot empty of other graves. On the face of the tomb you can read a woman's name, her birth and death dates, and the words: *"After life's fitful fever she sleeps well."*

If you say her name to people today, you'll find most of them never heard of her, yet during her lifetime she was one of the most famous women in America, possibly second only to her friend Dolley Madison. She was clever and so witty that people repeated her sharp remarks for decades, and she was so beautiful they used to say when she was in a room, it was impossible to look at anyone else.

She dined with President Jefferson and danced with the Duke of Wellington not long after he had defeated Napoleon at Waterloo. Her marriage was performed by a bishop, confirmed by a pope, and challenged by an emperor. When she was young she felt very poor, but she forced herself to learn how to handle money, getting advice from men who knew how it was done, among them multimillionaire John Jacob Astor.

At least a half-dozen novels were published based on her life. There was an off-Broadway play and two Hollywood movies. None of these entertainments gave a good answer to the question: *Why was her life a fitful fever?*

The answer is revealed in the things she saved through the

years: hundreds of letters, love notes, books with her opinions jotted in the margins, some twenty notebooks, souvenirs of all kinds, invitations, dance programs, dinner menus, and calling cards—all the treasured mementoes that marked key events in her life. While most of the women who lived prior to modern times left no record, this one saved everything. It was only after the death of her grandson (a member of President Theodore Roosevelt's cabinet) that these things became available for study by way of a bequest to the Maryland Historical Society.

Now at last we can begin to understand the fitful fever that was the life of Betsy Bonaparte.

Betsy Bonaparte

Chapter 1

Let No Man Tear Asunder

In the parlor of a large townhouse within sight of Baltimore's inner harbor, a group of the town's leading people gathered. It was Christmas Eve 1803, and the occasion was a marriage to be performed by Bishop John Carroll, who had been specifically chosen by the bride's father to perform this ceremony.

Carroll had misgivings about it, but because of his nature and training, the concern he felt would have been carefully concealed. During his childhood, higher Catholic education was not available in the colonies, so when he was twelve his family sent him from his home in Maryland to St. Omer's, Flanders, to be trained for the priesthood. Now, at sixty-seven, he was the highest prelate of the Catholic Church in the United States. Those who knew him said he was dignified yet simple, pious but not austere. They said to his courtesy was joined a rare goodness of heart, and the portraits of him reveal that in the gently curving mouth and the warm gaze.

He had fulfilled his pastoral responsibility by interviewing the young couple. The bride-to-be was a Protestant whose parents were well known to him. She had been baptized in the local First Presbyterian Church, which had been founded by some of her relatives, and her father was a trustee there.[1]

The groom was a French naval officer, handsome, well-mannered, and beautifully dressed. His ignorance of English was not an impediment to the interview, since at St. Omer's John Carroll had learned to speak perfect French. Further, the bishop knew that the young man was Catholic, although perhaps not as well versed in the faith as he should have been. The groom was supposed to be on duty, traveling home to France from his ship in the West Indies by way of the United States. To elude the British blockade he had planned to sail incognito on a neutral vessel, but on his way to charter a ship at Philadelphia, he passed through Baltimore and fell wildly in love. He was determined to marry as quickly as possible.[2]

Christmas Eve was a holy night, so having a wedding in the procathedral of St. Peter, especially with a Protestant, might have appeared unseemly. On the other hand, the bridal family's residence was a spacious double dwelling, the family home adjacent to the counting house for the father's shipping business. Hence the nuptials could take place there.[3]

More than the required number of witnesses were present, among them the mayor of Baltimore, James Calhoun; Pierre Jean Marie Sotin, French vice-consul for the port; and a collection of family and friends, including the Revolutionary War hero Commodore Joshua Barney and the bride's maternal uncle General Sam Smith, also a war hero and now a U.S. Senator.[4]

The bishop began by saying that they had come together for the celebration of matrimony. He said the proper publication had been made for three days in case anyone knew of a legitimate impediment. He acknowledged the presence of the witnesses and sprinkled holy water upon the couple. Then he said to the groom, *"Jerome, vis accipere Elizabeth hic praesentem in tuam ligitimam uxorem juxta ritum sanctae Matris Ecclesiae?"* Jerome, wearing a heel-length purple coat lined in white satin, with his hair powdered and silver buckles on his shoes, gave the required reply, *"Volo."*[5]

Elizabeth, or Betsy as her family called her, also gave her affirmation. Unlike the groom, she was dressed simply. Her father's early privations even now impelled him to practice thrift like a religion, and later Betsy said the dress wasn't even new, she'd worn it before; but the muslin was of fine texture and richly embroidered. Nevertheless it was clear Jerome had already introduced her to the Paris fashions of the Consulate period, for beneath it was but a single garment, and one of the guests said, "All the clothes worn by the bride might have been put into my pocket."[6]

The criticism however did not extend to her person. Although almost nineteen, she was petite, only four feet eleven, and she had fair skin, even features, large hazel eyes, and dark auburn hair. People said she had the ancient Grecian look much admired at the time, and that her arms and shoulders were as exquisitely formed as those of a classical statue. It was common for people to gather on the street to watch her getting out of a carriage, and spectators would collect outside a home where she was attending a party. One woman remarked, "I think I never beheld a human form so faultless." Others claimed Betsy was so beautiful it was impossible to look at anyone else when she was in the room.[7]

Now the bishop joined the right hands of bride and groom saying, "*Ego conjungo vos in matrimonium. In nomine Patris, et Filii, et Spiritus Sancti. Amen.*"

A wedding supper followed the ceremony. Bishop Carroll sat on the groom's right for the meal but then returned the few blocks to his home adjacent to the procathedral of St. Peter. Before he slept he entered the marriage record:

> *With license, I this day joined in holy matrimony, according to the rites of the holy Catholic Church, Jerome Bonaparte, brother of the First Consul of France, and Elizabeth Patterson, daughter of Wm. Patterson, Esq., of the City of Baltimore, and his wife.*
> *John, Bishop of Baltimore.*[8]

The day after Christmas he expressed his concern in a letter to one of his friends,

> *You will have heard before this, of my having officiated in uniting Jerome Bonaparte to Miss Patterson, on Saturday. I wish well to the young lady, but cannot help fearing that she may not find all the comforts hereafter, which she promised herself.*[9]

His words were prophetic.

Chapter 2

The Patriarch

$\mathcal{T}$he wealthiest man in the wedding party was the bride's father. President Thomas Jefferson said he was the second richest man in Maryland, and perhaps in the country. Ordinarily that would assure good fortune for a marriage, but William Patterson's nature and convictions put him inevitably into conflict with both his daughter and her husband.[1]

He was a small spare man of dark complexion, with great determination in his look. He was said to be brief of speech, but strong in intelligence, sagacity, and power. His portraits show the intense, piercing eyes of a man molded by a stark childhood. He was born in 1752 at Rossgarrow near Milford in County Donegal, Ireland. His family's roots were in England, but his father farmed land in Donegal and was connected to other Pattersons there, cousins living at Fox Hall near Rathmelton. Yet it seems clear that William's family could not provide for all six of their sons. One took off for Jamaica and another went to North Carolina.[2]

As for William, he was sent alone from Ireland to America at the age of fourteen. When he arrived in Philadelphia in April 1766 he went to work as an apprentice in the counting house of another Irishman, Samuel Jackson, who was in the shipping business. At that time Philadelphia, the third largest town in the colonies after New York and Boston, was heavily engaged in trade with Europe, South America, and especially the West Indies. In addition to importing and exporting goods, Jackson in cooperation with other merchants built a new vessel almost every year.[3]

A traveler describing Philadelphia some years later said the Quaker-dominated business climate gave "a tone to the manners of the people different from what is to be found in most places of equal extent." He added, "They are industrious and sober, and, though sufficiently commercial, they do not conduct their business in the same dashing style which is done by some commercial cities; but confine themselves within bounds, and secure what they gain."[4]

In his later business dealings, Patterson matched the Quaker description. He was industrious and sober, confined himself within bounds, and secured what he gained. In the autobiographical sketch that prefaces his will, he said of his experience in Jackson's shipping firm, "This gave me an early knowledge and attachment to that business, a passion that has followed me through life." Nevertheless his years of apprenticeship in Philadelphia were painful for him. He was poor and he had no friends, perhaps because his childhood training had given him a grim view of society. He said, "In early life in Philadelphia, I experienced considerable inconvenience in not being able to find young people suitable for companions; they were almost all more or less tainted with folly and vice, and did not seem to suit my turn of mind." Consequently he sought the company of men much older than himself and filled his solitary hours with books.

By the time the American Revolution loomed, he was twenty-two years old, had thoroughly learned the shipping business, saved some money, and cultivated profitable friendships with older men of substance. He realized there was going to be a great need for powder and arms, because over the years the Mother Country had taken precautions to prevent these commodities from being brought into the colonies. So in 1775 he invested all his savings into shares of two vessels and their cargoes, bound from Philadelphia to France for the sole purpose of returning with powder and arms, and he sailed with them. One of the ships got back to Philadelphia in March 1776 with a shipment of munitions "in a most critical time," he recalled, "when it was said that General Washington, then before Boston with the Army, had not powder sufficient to fire a salute."

On his way home Patterson stopped in the West Indies at the island of St. Eustatius and encountered there business acquaintances who persuaded him to remain. "Statia," as he called it in his will, was experiencing enormous prosperity. Its Dutch owners, having found their trade brought to a standstill by the blockades of warring Britain and France, had declared the place a free port. The island's area was only seven square miles, most of it taken up by two volcanic peaks, but its roadstead could accommodate two hundred vessels. This roadstead was usually filled with ships come to take advantage of the island's excellent facilities for transshipment. Goods from Europe, especially the vital arms, powder, and ammunition, could be warehoused at St. Eustatius and then re-embarked for the shorter haul north to the colonies. There the British navy prowled, but the shippers could evade the blockade by posing as coastal traders and slipping into one of the many smaller rivers to off-load their cargoes.

The island's governor, Johannes de Graaff, was so hospitable to Americans that his superiors in the Netherlands reprimanded him lest he provoke retaliation from Britain or France. While Patterson was at St. Eustatius, Governor de Graaff infuriated the British by firing the first ceremonial salute to acknowledge formally the red-and-white-striped flag of the Continental Congress, flown by the incoming vessel *Andrew Doria*. The Royal Navy, watching from neighboring St. Kitts, considered this recognition of the colonial traitors extremely offensive. London's pressure upon de Graaff's superiors in the Netherlands intensified.[5]

That salute occurred on November 16, 1776. Patterson had been at St. Eustatius eight months and was already building the foundation for his fortune. But here, as in Philadelphia, he was dismayed by the folly and vice of his associates. He preferred to live among religious people of what he termed *correct principles*.

> *No one came there to settle for life; all were in quest of fortune, to retire and spend it elsewhere; character was little thought of. Of course it required the utmost circumspection and caution to steer clear of difficulties. A kind superintending Providence, in this, as in*

many other concerns of my life, enabled me however to surmount
every difficulty, young and inexperienced as I was then.

Among the difficulties he felt compelled to surmount was gambling. Shortly after his arrival in St. Eustatius, he spent an evening with a family he thought suited his turn of mind, only to learn that their whist game had been played for a substantial sum of money. He had come out well ahead, but he refused the proffered winnings.

After eighteen months at St. Eustatius he found that Britain had made it impossible for the Dutch government to protect Americans and their trade any longer, so he moved to the French island of Martinique, where he continued his operations in ships and cargoes. He spent a year there, then decided to leave the West Indies and establish himself in a permanent home and place of business. Although he'd lost over half his holdings to storms and British capture, the profits remained substantial. His net fortune amounted to a hundred thousand dollars in gold, paper money, and merchandise, comparable to a million in contemporary money.[6]

In addition to his financial gain, he'd learned lessons he would continue to practice, and to judge others by, for the rest of his life:

A merchant possessing a fortune should never put more at risk than one half what he is worth and should he have the misfortune to lose that half, which is more than probable, he ought to retire immediately from business, for it is fifty to one that he will lose the other half, and be left a beggar. Want of this precaution has been the cause of many failures after people have made fortunes, but unfortunately merchants consider themselves entitled or rather disgraced, unless they will trade, not only up to their capital, but as far beyond it as they can obtain credit. What better is this than a Gambler staking his money on games of chance, and doubling his bets every time he wins? It is true that chance may favor him for a time; "luck," however, as it is termed by the thoughtless, must change, and he is soon broke and ruined. And such is the fate of Merchants who make use of all their Capital and Credit in Commerce in the Shipping line.

In July 1778, armed with these mercantile convictions, he packed his cash and merchandise into a couple of fast-sailing vessels and headed north. He did not return to Philadelphia. Instead he chose a newer settlement, one with certain advantages and much less competition. He chose Baltimore.[7]

Geography had determined the placement of this town far up the Chesapeake Bay, deep into a fertile countryside where crops could be grown and then shipped out. On the west side of the upper bay, the Patapsco River splits into three branches. The northwest branch ends in a small basin. At its 1729 founding, Baltimore Town bordered this basin. On the south side of the basin, later called the inner harbor, was Smith's Hill, so named because it had been described by the original white explorer of Maryland, John Smith. Along the west edge of the basin ran a trail that became the coastal road between north and south.[8]

From Charleston, South Carolina, the road (known now as U.S. Rte. 1) trekked north over long stretches of rough ground, wound among the trees of deep forests, and ferried over rivers and bays to link the colonies. In Virginia it touched Norfolk and Alexandria, then crossed over the Potomac to head through countryside to the Maryland capital, Annapolis. Continuing north, the trail bent around the Baltimore basin, then rose northeast over low hills, to cross the stream that marked the town's eastern boundary and make its way to Philadelphia, New York, and eventually Boston. This boundary stream, named Jones Falls, was deep enough to accommodate ships, although they could not turn around until a turning basin had been made. Farther upstream, mills used the water falling down from higher ground to grind wheat into flour and later to power machines that made sailcloth. Hence, with a busy road and water for transportation and mills, the town was laid out within reach of everything needful.

In the early years the streets were named after the Maryland colony's proprietor, Charles Calvert, Lord Baltimore. Charles and Calvert Streets ran north and south; Baltimore Street stretched from the Great Road on the west to Jones Falls on the east. There a market was built, called Marsh Market because of the swampy ground along the stream, and town folk commonly omitted the name of Baltimore Street and instead referred to it as Market Street. Beyond Jones Falls, the land continued eastward along the Patapsco River to a nearby settlement called Fell's Point. There the water was much deeper than that of the Baltimore basin, and in time Fell's Point became a site for shipbuilding and a mooring place for ocean-going ships. Yet it was to Baltimore Town's encircled basin that men with the most money came. Their investments would enable Baltimore to expand, absorb Fell's Point, and for a time surpass both Philadelphia and Boston.

At first the northern rim of the basin was a winding lane called Water Street, but gradually part of the shore was filled in, so that when Patterson arrived in 1778, Water Street was a block north of the shore. He bought lots between Water and Market streets, within sight of the harbor. There he built a pair of large brick houses, numbers 18 and 20 South Street. One building would be the counting house for his shipping business, the other would be his town home. More profits were to be made. True to his economic principles, Patterson invested only half his money in shipping. The other half he put into real estate, some of it bought on favorable terms after Maryland confiscated the property of Loyalists who sided with Britain during the war.[9]

Eventually he owned a dozen residences, most of them country estates; one was thirty miles west of town and exceeded two thousand acres. He enjoyed the security that land ownership gave him. Although he bought, sold, and rented out town lots, houses, stores, and warehouses, he never parted with the suburban and country properties. He left them to his sons, explaining in his will: "I have thought it better to leave them Real Estate than money or stocks, the two latter being too easily parted with, whilst the former is more likely to stick by them, and is the last thing that young people think of selling after everything else is disposed of."

Now that Water Street was no longer the edge of the basin, the new waterside became known as Pratt. Reaching southward

from Pratt Street into the basin were piers named for their owners: among them, Smith's Wharf, Spear's Wharf, and Buchanan's
Wharf. Those three families were already well established in Baltimore when Patterson arrived. John Smith and James Buchanan
had come to town two decades earlier; their relatives William Smith
and William Spear arrived soon after. They built warehouses, stores,
and homes on the streets surrounding the north shore of the basin.
William Spear's thousand-foot pier had the distinction of a bakery
on the end, where he made ship's bread and sold it directly to vessels in the harbor. People said when the wind was right the aroma
of baking bread pervaded the town.

Smith's Hill, on the south side of the basin, gave the town's
merchants a lookout point. From a tower built on the crest, a lookout
could see far down the Patapsco to a point of land where another
lookout could discern ships coming up the Chesapeake Bay. Ship-
owners designed company flags such as the "S & B," signifying the
Smith and Buchanan Company, or the white flag with conjoined
blue letters "WP," indicating a vessel belonging to William Patterson. When the more distant lookout sighted a ship, he raised
the appropriate flag to signal the Smith's Hill lookout who in turn
raised a duplicate flag visible to the merchants in their counting
houses across the basin. By the time the ship moored in Baltimore,
unloading crews and warehouse space would be ready.[10]

Understandably, devout William Patterson praised the Providence that had led him to this place. His will states: "My family
was of the Episcopal Church, the established religion of Ireland,
in which I was born and brought up with great care and attention,
and from the religious impressions which I then received, I am,
under the guidance of a Divine and kind Providence, indebted
for my future conduct and success in life."

When he settled in Baltimore there was a well-established
Episcopal Church a short distance from his home. Nevertheless, he changed his affiliation: he became a Presbyterian. That
choice enabled him to enter an association of businessmen active
in every phase of the town's commerce and politics. They served

as magistrates, commissioners, and wardens of the port. They were connected to one another by their faith, mutual enterprises, and by serpentine intermarriages. Within ten months of his arrival in town, Patterson's own marriage gave him a place among them. On May 15, 1779, he was wed at First Presbyterian Church to Dorcas Spear, daughter of the man with the bakery on his wharf, and sister, cousin, or in-law to more than two dozen Spears, Smiths, and Buchanans.[11]

These Presbyterians were part of a distinct element of migration into the colonies. Their history was unique, as were the characteristics borne in upon them by their collective experience. British historians call them "Ulster Scots"; in America they came to be known as the "Scots-Irish." They were tough, adventurous, and outspoken. So were their women, and dealing with women was something for which William Patterson's life had not prepared him.

Chapter 3

Dorcas Spear Patterson

*W*illiam Patterson's wife Dorcas was descended from participants in the great Scots-Irish migration to the New World. Oddly, the genealogy charts for her mother and grandmother contain more than birth and death dates: they add a bit of descriptive commentary. For her mother Elizabeth Galbraith Spear a note says, "All of her daughters were women of great beauty." Regarding the marriage of Elizabeth's parents, the chart remarks, "All five daughters of Captain John Galbraith and his wife Dorcas Smith were beautiful and talented." [1]

Unfortunately, that's all we know about the women of the family, but regarding the men we know much more. The general outline of their history is a matter of record—a record that sheds light on the behavior of these men for generations to come and, by implication, something about the nature of their women.

Some understanding of the family may be gained by exploring the family's British heritage. There had been conflict between the Irish and the English for centuries. After each military victory, titles and choice Irish lands were given to Englishmen. Yet beyond Dublin and its surroundings the invaders had a weaker hold. Outside of this center lay most of Ireland, whose peasants, according to historian James Leyburn, "spoke no English and lived wretchedly poor agricultural lives." He adds, "Their culture, like their background and poverty, made them resemble the Highlanders of

Scotland, and civilized Englishmen regarded them, as they did the Highlanders, as little better than savages." [2]

Queen Elizabeth I tried to colonize the provinces of Leinster and Munster by driving out the Irish and planting English farmers, but she failed. Few of her subjects wanted to leave England, and the displaced Irish kept coming back. When Elizabeth died without an heir in 1603, her Stuart cousin James VI of Scotland united the two realms by ascending the throne as James I of England. Along with the crown he inherited the Irish "troubles," but James understood that you couldn't entice people to move unless you offered them something of an enticement. James looked for colonists in the harsh and impoverished countryside of Lowland Scotland, where farmers said all their produce went into three shares, "ane to sow, ane to gnaw, and ane to pay the laird witha'." [3]

The Reformation had brought to Scotland a strict Calvinist Church. The Presbyterian kirk promoted rigorous personal discipline, and outlawed all frivolity, yet their religion was one of the things that made the Lowland Scots so appealing to King James. As Protestants, they might counter-balance the Catholicism of the Irish. Further, James perceived the Lowlanders to be more governable. Instead of living in remote mountain glens, they were settled within reach of villages and towns, and they had proven themselves amenable to management by their betters.

King James had at his disposal thousands of acres in the nine northern counties of Ireland known as Ulster. His plan was to give large grants of this land to Scottish lairds, who could then lease parcels to their tenants on inexpensive terms. King James set aside ten percent of the Irish properties for the London guilds so they could bring in skilled workers to advise the tenants. Among the invited guilds were the mercers, drapers, merchant tailors, and haberdashers. Best of all, relocation would be less arduous. Unlike the horrendous voyage to America, the trip to Northern Ireland was but a skip; at some points in Western Scotland, Eire was only twenty miles across the water. James reasoned that this was a winning situation all around (except, of course, for the Irish). The opening of Ulster in 1610 was a chance for the Lowlanders to escape their poverty and improve their lives, and the Plantation of Ulster was a success. In the first thirty years, 50,000 Scots moved in and they kept on coming. Twenty years later that number had doubled.[4]

The Scots worked hard and made the land productive. With the guidance of the guilds, their crops of flax became exportable linen and the fleece of their sheep became wool cloth. Eventually, however, their success did them in. By the final years of the century, English competitors promoted the passage of the 1699 Woolens Act, which drastically restricted exports and virtually destroyed the Ulster cloth industry. At the same time the Scots' landlords began shortening the terms of their leases. Previously, immigrants had farmed the land on long leases, typically thirty-one years; the leases were renewed so regularly that a family could live on the same parcel for generations. But now that these lands had been well developed, landlords began offering expiring leases to the highest bidder.

In addition, there were threats to the Ulster Scots' Presbyterian faith. The established church for the whole of Ireland—the Church of England—had been taken over by an intolerant Puritanism. The Test Act, originally aimed at Catholics, was broadened to turn Presbyterian ministers out of their pulpits. The Test Act also sought to invalidate the marriages they had performed, forbid the education of children in that faith, and unseat all Presbyterian officials above the level of constable.

Now, however, having experienced a degree of self-determination, the Ulster Scots were no longer so amenable to management from outsiders. In addition, their faith, though strict, was to a degree democratic. In every parish ministers and laymen sat on the governing body and voted. They sent representatives to a regional Presbytery, and men chosen from this body went to a national assembly. In church the humblest tenant had a right to express an opinion, and if one were accused of anything, a fair hearing was guaranteed.

Perhaps even more important, the Ulster Scots were literate. The Scottish kirk, in its reaction against Catholicism's use of priests as interpreters and intermediaries between God and man, had decreed that its communicants be educated so they could read the Scriptures. When in 1718 the members of an Ulster community wrote to the governor of Massachusetts requesting permission to settle in his colony, only thirteen of the 319 applicants were unable to sign their names.[5]

These people read more than the Scriptures. They read about the New World in broadsides, pamphlets, and letters from the colonies, and the mass movement that became known as the Great Scots-Irish Migration began. It lasted from 1717 until the start of the American Revolution. During those six decades, over 200,000 Ulstermen sailed to America.[6]

Their experience in Ulster had not only fostered in them a hatred of interfering governments, it had also toughened them, forced them to become resourceful, and made them willing to take risks. Those without passage money would sacrifice from four to seven years of freedom by signing articles of indenture, knowing that at the end of their term they would be supplied with whatever was necessary for a start in the New World.

Invitations to migrate were going out from several of the North American colonies, but for many Ulstermen the religious tolerance described in the publications of William Penn were particularly appealing. Also, for those who migrated under articles of indenture, the Pennsylvania legislature had specified the end-of-term rewards: two suits of apparel, a new axe, a grubbing hoe, a weeding hoe, and William Penn's gift of fifty acres of land. Hence the Pennsylvania colony exerted a powerful appeal for immigrants from Ulster.

After they arrived at Philadelphia, they moved out into the countryside. One of the earliest groups settled in Lancaster County, along the Susquehanna River, where they found good soil, lumber, and abundant game for meat. Nevertheless, they remained bitterly distrustful of authority and hence prickly and contentious. Pennsylvania's provincial secretary, James Logan, wrote that "a settlement of five families from the North of Ireland gives me more trouble than fifty of any other people." And Logan was an Ulster Scot himself.[7]

Another aspect of the Ulstermen's nature was their clannishness. The Lancaster County group consisted of closely associated families, a practice of the Scots-Irish immigrants noted by historian David Hackett Fischer.[8] This practice persisted and was enhanced among the Pennsylvania immigrants. In a pattern that would be repeated later by successive waves of immigrants arriving in America from numerous countries, members of a community or family would depart for the New World and then later be joined by those they had left behind. As Sir Walter Scott observed in *The Heart of Midlothian*, "Perhaps one ought to be actually a Scotchman to conceive how ardently, under all distinctions of rank and situation, they feel their mutual connexion with each other . . . the feelings of kindred and relationship are more widely extended; and, in a word, the bonds of patriotic affection . . . have more influence on men's feelings and actions."[9]

The people of this network established farms and businesses in Pennsylvania, and several of the men served in public offices. At the same time, they worked closely together. Sam Smith's store sold the Spear and Buchanan wheat and milled flour. Together they provided supplies to the newer immigrants who continued to pour in and surge through Lancaster County.

By 1750, original migrant Sam Smith, now aging, turned over the family enterprise to his son John. He sold off his property in Lancaster County, bought land around Carlisle, and opened a store there in western Pennsylvania. When he moved, a cohort of cousins moved with him. Some of the group remained behind, but since in the preceding generation James Buchanan had married Elisabeth Spear and John Buchanan had married Dorcas Galbraith, all elements of the familial clan were represented on the frontier.

Settlement in the West proved dangerous due to the French and Indian Wars, so in 1759 the migrants moved again, this time to the port of Baltimore, where some of the Buchanans were already settled. John Smith brought with him his aged parents, his wife, and the first six of what was to become their eleven children, as well as cash and goods amounting to the equivalent of forty thousand dollars in the later American money.[10]

Two years after the Carlisle group arrived in Baltimore, the clan was enlarged again with the arrival of William Smith and William Spear. Along with the continuing connectedness, these people maintained their innate contentiousness as well, especially when the colonists' troubles with the Mother Country increased. Their experience with the English back in Ulster made the Scots-Irish automatic American patriots. A Hessian captain, fighting on the British side in 1778, wrote: "Call this war by whatever name you may, only call it not an American rebellion; it is nothing more or less than a Scotch Irish Presbyterian rebellion." It was reported that King George III himself characterized the revolution as "a Presbyterian war." Jonathan D. Sergeant, member of the Continental Congress from New Jersey, stated that the Scots-Irish of Pennsylvania were "the most God-provoking democrats on this side of Hell." [11]

The contentiousness and hard-won success in the historical background of the Patterson and Spear families would eventually appear in the tensions that resulted when William Patterson's severe, cautious, and low-key conservatism encountered his wife's familial daring and contentiousness.

We know very little about Patterson's wife, except that she was sufficiently educated to homeschool Betsy until the age of ten and in the process turn the little girl into a prodigy. Yet from the time of her marriage Dorcas Spear Patterson seems to have followed the rule that a lady gets her name in print only three times in her life: birth, marriage, and death. We have enough information about William Patterson to know that this is what he would have expected of his wife.

Dorcas's sister Margaret Spear was different, in part because the husband she chose was different.[12]

Among the six children John Smith brought from Carlisle to Baltimore was the grandson and namesake of "Old Sam." This grandson, who as a child had seen and been inspired by soldiers in the French and Indian War, became General Sam Smith and eventually married Dorcas Spear Patterson's sister Margaret. One man described Margaret as "beautiful and imperious." Another said she was "beautiful and high-spirited." She must have been outspoken as well, for Albert Gallatin wrote his wife from Washington, "Mrs. Smith is here and hates the place."[13]

Throughout the sixty years of Sam Smith's career as business-man, soldier, and politician, Margaret was her husband's compan-ion, partner, and hostess. There are references to her hospitality, both in Baltimore and in Washington. A traveler visiting Baltimore in 1785 wrote: "We dressed ourselves at two o'clock and at three went to Colonel Smith's to dinner. I was introduced to his lady, a genteel, elegant woman. We had a very elegant dinner, and a most agreeable company. We sent for a violin in the evening and had a most agreeable dance. At ten we walked downstairs to an elegant sideboard instead of a formal supper."[14]

That word *elegant* comes up often in descriptions of the Spear-Smith-Buchanan women, to such an extent that some observers were critical. One elderly woman recalling her childhood in Bal-timore said the Spears were showoffs; they had what she termed "too much *side*." She also objected to their clinging to the tartans of their Ulster-Scottish heritage.[15]

Much later, when a misguided business partner bankrupted Sam Smith, Margaret helped bail him out, using nine thousand dollars of her own money, apparently an endowment William Spear provided for each of his daughters.[16]

Another Spear woman, Anne or "Nancy," never married. She was highly intelligent, wrote descriptive letters, and had skill in money management. Nancy stayed with the Smiths in Washington during the months when Congress was in session. She was keenly interested in politics and spent her time in the congressional gallery listening to the legislators at work. William Patterson rebuked her for this behavior in his will. He left her an annuity of one hundred dol-lars a year, "but on this express condition that she shall never, after my death, attend any of the sessions of Congress, at Washington or elsewhere; for this annuity is solely intended to provide against the calls and infirmities of old age, and not for the gratifications of folly or ambition."[17]

Like her sisters, Dorcas also had money from her father, but according to the laws of the time, it was controlled by her husband. On her deathbed she asked him to divide her money equally among their children. Patterson refused. He gave it all to his sons and none to his sole surviving daughter, Betsy. One of her brothers, George, felt this injustice so keenly that he gave her his share.[18]

When it comes to the role of women, Patterson's attitude was the prevailing one, which was patriarchal. Similar views were expressed by such diverse men as Napoleon and Thomas Jefferson. Jefferson liked women who were "gentle, feminine, and yielding." He wrote to his daughter Martha on her marriage: "The happiness of your life depends now on the continuing to please a single person. To this all other objects must be secondary; even your love to me." Many women supported this restriction of the proper place and behavior of women. In 1842, Mrs. A. S. Graves wrote: "Descent into ruin is usually commenced with the false education, the indolence, and the luxurious habits of the female sex." [19] Emperor Napoleon's view was even harsher:

> *We treat women too well, and in this way have spoiled everything. We have done every wrong in raising them to our level. Truly, the Oriental nations have more mind and sense than we in declaring the wife to be the actual property of the husband. In fact nature has made woman our slave. . . .Woman is given to man that she may bear him children . . . consequently she is his property, just as the fruit tree is the property of the gardener.*[20]

While Patterson's attitude toward women was typical of the time, his behavior toward his sons was much more tolerant. He described himself as being in his early years "young and inexperienced," so apparently he could forgive them for that. The description of his plan to leave the sons land as well as other assets suggests he found the improvidence of young men not only expected, but acceptable, and he took steps to protect them from themselves.

When it came to females, however, what he expected was complete obedience, and this became clear in his later dealings with his daughter Betsy.

After the 1779 marriage of Dorcas Spear and William Patterson, the newly built house on South Street began to fill with what would become a family of thirteen children. The first three, who were sons, presented their father with no particular problem. He planned to run each of them through his counting house and eventually launch them into the management of the shipping, insurance, banking, iron works, rope-walk, and other ventures that would make up the firm of William Patterson & Sons. The fourth child was a daughter, Elizabeth. She exhibited none of the traits that marked William Patterson's identity and convictions, at least not in her early years. Instead she displayed the nature of her mother's family: she was adventurous, contentious, outspoken, and tough.

Betsy baffled her father, but had he considered Dorcas Spear's life, he would have understood his daughter's behavior. Betsy adored her mother. For decades after Dorcas's death, wherever she traveled she carried mementos of her, among them Dorcas's teapot and a lock of her hair. Dorcas's life—married at seventeen to a man ten years older, giving birth to thirteen children, half of them dying young, including all of her daughters but one, and then dying herself—filled Betsy with grief and rage.

She saw that sad story all around her. Her Aunt Margaret lost four of her children in early childhood. Diaries and letters written by women in the early and mid-nineteenth century confide the fear that came into the world with each new baby. Mothers counseled their daughters not to love the little one too much until they were sure he or she would survive. The young mothers' lives were at risk as well. There was no remedy for the postpartum infections known as "fevers" beyond strewing straw on the cobbled streets to quiet the sound of wagon wheels while the patient lay dying.[21]

Although Betsy knew her father expected her to become the

obedient homemaking wife of some local merchant whose business interests would mesh nicely with those of William Patterson & Sons, she was determined never to follow that path. She chose another, one that put her on a direct collision course with her father, her brothers, and in some respects the whole town of Baltimore.

Chapter 4

The Belle of Baltimore

$\mathcal{B}$etsy was born Elizabeth Spear Patterson on February 6, 1785. Apparently the arrival of a female child after the births of three boys was greatly celebrated, because an artist was commissioned to paint the toddler posed on her mother's lap.[1]

When she was three, several years after the War for Independence ended, Baltimore may have provided her with a vivid early memory. An immense parade passed near her home on its way around the basin to Smith's Hill to commemorate Maryland's ratification of the new nation's federal Constitution. Thousands of laborers, sailors, ship captains, and merchants marched cheering through the streets. At the center of the parade was a horse-drawn cart bearing the replica of a warship named *The Federalist*, fifteen feet long, fully rigged, and commanded by naval veteran Joshua Barney. On the summit there was a ceremony to rename the site "Federal Hill" in honor of the occasion. A feast followed, with a bonfire, fireworks, and plenty of drinks. Sometime during the festivities, Barney had the little boat dragged down to the water and launched. Then he sailed down the Patapsco into the Chesapeake Bay, all the way to the Potomac River and up to Mount Vernon, where he presented the ship to George Washington as a gift from the town.[2] The retired general wrote his thanks to Baltimore.

I pray you, gentlemen, to accept the warmest expressions of my sensibility for this specimen of American ingenuity, in which the exactitude of the proportions, the neatness of the workmanship, and the elegance of the decorations, which make your present fit to be preserved in a cabinet of curiosities, at the same time that they exhibit the skill and taste of the artists, demonstrate that Americans are not inferior to any people whatever, in the use of mechanical instruments, and the art of ship-building.[3]

Not long after, Betsy could have seen the great man himself. When he was unanimously chosen to be the first president of the United States, Washington passed through Baltimore on his way from Mount Vernon to the seat of government in New York. A delegation of leading citizens, no doubt including her father and uncles, rode their horses south on the Great Road to escort Washington into town. Cannons were fired, there was a banquet, and the new president was put up for the night at a local inn.[4]

These events hint at the town's vitality. There were some 1,200 houses in the vicinity of the basin, and several hundred more over at Fell's Point. Not only the shipping business was thriving, but also shops, coffee houses, and even a theater. A visitor from London said, "Baltimore is now a very considerable place, but, in the course of a few years, when these elegant homes are finished, it will be one of the first towns in America."[5]

Baltimore's women were praised as well. Several authors said they were the most beautiful in the country.[6] Baron de Closen, aide-de-camp to the Comte de Rochembeau, commented: "Permit me to remark that, for my taste, the ladies of Baltimore are more charming than the rest of the fair sex in America. . . . They enchant by their freshness and the brilliant vivacity of their eyes. One may see many of them with svelte, perfectly proportioned figures, with beautiful little white, dimpled hands; with dainty exquisite feet."[7]

Eventually Betsy would be numbered among those beautiful women of Baltimore, but as the Pattersons' celebrated first daughter, she did not remain the center of attention for long. Soon two more brothers were born, followed by two sisters, so that by the time she was nine years old, she was one of eight children, and the family continued to expand.

In addition she was part of a much larger clan, because her

extended family included many more youngsters among the Smiths, Spears, Buchanans, and others. She was also related to the prestigious Nicholas family of Virginia, because two of Sam Smith's sisters had married brothers George and Wilson Cary Nicholas. Later this connection would have an effect on Betsy's life and even on Washington politics during the administration of Thomas Jefferson.

Now, however, Aunt Margaret and Uncle Sam, with their half-dozen children, lived nearby and both families were growing larger. These children and their other cousins shared family events, and all went to the same church.

Being related to Sam Smith must have added a touch of excitement to the children's lives. He was tall, lean, and handsome. People said his voice reverberated across a parade ground. During the Revolution he was an officer in the Maryland Line, a unit praised by Washington early in the war for their rear guard action during the costly retreat from Long Island. Later, when British ships tried to sail up the Delaware to the rebels' capital at Philadelphia, Captain Smith repulsed them with a heroic defense at Fort Mifflin. He served with distinction for five years, but then financial concerns forced him to give up the inadequate salary of an officer and return to Baltimore to manage his family's shipping business. Still, he remained in the militia, continued to recruit and train men for Washington's army, and rose to the rank of major general.[8]

One Sunday in September when Betsy was nine years old, worship at First Presbyterian Church was interrupted by a courier who entered and approached Smith with orders from the Maryland governor. President Washington had asked the governors of Virginia, Maryland, and Pennsylvania to muster their militias and have them march immediately to counteract an uprising known as the Whiskey Rebellion. It had been set off by Treasury Secretary Alexander Hamilton's imposition of federal excise taxes on distilled spirits. Since the production of liquor was central to the economy of western sections of the mid-Atlantic states, the farmers there had clashed with officials. They abused tax collectors, disrupted court sessions, and seized the U.S. mails.[9]

A large body of these rebels was reported to be marching on the arsenal at Frederick, Maryland, intent on getting the arms and ammunition stored there. Although excise taxes were unpopular in commercial centers like Baltimore, resolving the constitutional question of whether federal laws were binding was essential to the survival of the republic. Smith didn't hesitate. He left the church service at once and ordered the drums to beat. The militia assembled from around the region to muster on the parade ground, and a mass of concerned citizen gathered there as well. A newspaper editor described the scene:

> *A more warlike appearance, perhaps, our town has not exhibited since the year '76, than it did yesterday, in consequence of an express from the Governor to General Smith. The militia of this town were requested to meet on the parade, near the old Theatre, at 4 P.M. They met accordingly and General Smith, in a short but energetic address, informed them of the object of their meeting. . . . "It is not," he said, "against an enemy that we have to march, but a set of men more daring than the rest, a lawless banditti, who set themselves up to govern."* [10]

Smith went on to ask, "Shall we permit them to seize our arms and give us laws, or shall we keep our arms and give laws to ourselves?" After a moment, he called for three hundred volunteers to go with him to Frederick. Nearly three times that number stepped forward. After an exhausting and ill-equipped march, the Baltimore force found the danger in Frederick had evaporated, or perhaps had existed only as a rumor. Even the larger army, massed farther west at Cumberland under Washington's command, had difficulty finding rebels. At length, two of the ringleaders were arrested and convicted of treason, but the president pardoned them. Still, the situation had provided lessons about the country's readiness to defend itself, and later Sam Smith would make good use of those lessons when he set about defending Baltimore against a major British attack during the War of 1812.

After the excitement of these events, life in town must have settled back into its daily routine. For Betsy that routine meant close and unremitting supervision by her father. Perhaps it was William Patterson's early separation from his parents that impelled him to make certain his own children were kept close. The living arrangement, with his home at Number 18 South Street and his counting house at Number 20, facilitated this supervision. His unmarried children, even sons who had reached their twenties, were always required to be home and in their beds early.

> *I always considered it a duty to my family to keep them as much as possible under my own eye, so that I have seldom in my life left home whether on business or pleasure. . . . And ever since I had a house it has been an invariable rule with me to be the last up at night, and to see that the fires and lights were secured before I retired myself; from which I found two advantages: one was that there was little or no risk of fire under my own roof, and the other that it induced my family to keep regular hours.*[11]

For the first few years, while her older brothers were sent to school, Betsy was taught at home by her mother. During this time she learned to read and loved it. She began collecting books of her own, and saved many of them all her life. From the start, she engaged in an active dialogue with them, writing in the margins: "True." Or, "That's a lie!" In one she wrote "Do not write in your books!" But she continued to do so. The French traveler Moreau de St. Méry said that at a very early age she had memorized all of La Rochefoucauld's *Maxims*. When they met she was only ten, but she borrowed from him a book by salon doyenne Mme. de Staël. Another writer said she was thoroughly familiar with Edward Young's "Night Thoughts," some ten thousand lines of blank verse.[12] Even after she started going about in society she remained obviously bookish. Rosalie Stier Calvert, a Belgian married to a descendant of Maryland's founder, Lord Baltimore, wrote to her mother: "She is a most extraordinary girl, given to reading Godwin on the rights of women, etc., in short, a modern *philosophe*."[13]

We have no letters written by Betsy in her early years, but letters to her from her young cousins make them all seem like typical teens. During a congressional session in Washington, nineteen-year-old Elizabeth Smith wrote to Betsy about the social life there. She begins by chiding Betsy: "We all agree here that you should be whipt for giving your handsome rosettes for Sophia's shawl that she wore at least six or seven times, especially Miss Spear and myself." Then she chats about several young men, one of whom she describes as "your little man" and goes on to describe a social event.

> *I was at the George-Town ball on Tuesday where I danced a great deal with R. G. [Robert Gilmor] & other beaus, the suppers are very elegant and good. I of course thought of you when I was eating the grapes and jellies. R. G. standing behind me remarked how much you would enjoy them. . . . You ask what other beaus we have, it would take me three days to give you a list of them, the room is always full & every time the door opens a new face enters, which is the reason my letters are so short.*

To that letter another cousin, Smith Nicholas, added a flowery postscript.

> *However elegant the above composition—however ingenious its author—however interesting the subject yet still I most solemnly declare that all these were incapable of arresting my attention away for a moment—no madam each thought, each idea, were immoveably fixed upon the pleasing tho' dangerous, perhaps delusive contemplation of an absent object, brought to my recollection by the address of this letter—at the bare recital of that name ten thousand inexpressible sensations crowd impetuously upon me—driven by their irresistible force, those objects which but a moment before had occupied the conspicuous part of reflections, are now hurried into one common oblivion.*[14]

Apparently Betsy was already attracting male attention. Yet something else had happened to her that would change her life from the typical to the distinctive: at ten years of age she had been propelled into a new and irresistibly appealing direction when she was sent to a French school.

There had been a French element in Baltimore ever since

the 1756 expulsion of the Acadians from Nova Scotia by the British. They were welcomed and settled in a section that became known as Frenchtown. A second influx came after the French Revolution ignited a slave revolt in the West Indies. In 1792 the state legislature authorized refugees from Santo Domingo to come to Maryland, and the next year thirteen boatloads of French-speaking people arrived at Fell's Point. They were well educated, some had been planters and owned slaves, but they went to work as barbers, hairdressers, dressmakers, dancing instructors, and shopkeepers.[15]

One of the refugees was a widow named Madame Lacomb, reputed to be an aristocrat who had fled to the West Indies from Revolutionary France in fear for her life. At 36 South Street she opened a boarding school for girls. The school was patronized by well-to-do families, so when Betsy was enrolled she found among her classmates many students she already knew. Some of them were her cousins, or cousins of her cousins, such as the three Hollins girls, Ann, Sarah, and Mary, who were the children of one of her Uncle Sam's sisters. Another pupil, Mary Chase, was the daughter of a signer of the Declaration of Independence who had become an associate justice on the Supreme Court. Mary, Louisa, Emily, and Elizabeth Caton were there too; they were the granddaughters of Charles Carroll of Carrollton, who outranked William Patterson as the *first* richest man in Maryland.[16]

Patterson, aware of the importance of business contacts, may have been impressed by the clientele. Perhaps an even stronger inducement for placing his daughter in the school was its proximity to his home: Betsy would be a day student, not a boarder, and hence under his roof where his children belonged. So she was enrolled at the nearby Madame Lacomb's.

In the view of the old lady mentioned earlier, who was so critical of the Spears and their *side*, Betsy was "spoiled by that French school her mother sent her to." Apparently what Madame Lacomb did was teach Betsy to read and speak French, along with how to behave in the loftiest levels of society. She may also have shared with her students memories of her life in pre-revolutionary France. She may even have imparted an aristocratic distaste for middle-class Baltimore and its merchants.[7]

What's certain is that somewhere in her early life, Betsy developed a longing to inhabit a realm where people had titles. Several of her fellow students exhibited the same trait. Three of the Caton girls and Betsy's cousin Mary Buchanan Smith eventually went to England and married men with titles—a couple of dukes, a lord, and a baron.[8]

One way or another, when Jerome Bonaparte, brother of the future emperor, came to town several years later, Betsy was ready to meet and fall in love with a handsome Frenchman who had impressive connections.

Chapter 5

"I Just Love Beautiful Things"

*I*n mid-July 1803 the Norfolk, Virginia *Herald* reported the arrival of several French gentlemen from Martinique. The leader of the group was a black-haired naval officer of average height who appeared to be between twenty and thirty years of age. He said his name was Monsieur d'Albert, and he brought with him a complete entourage. Soon word spread that this young man was Jerome Bonaparte, brother of Napoleon, first consul of France, and an officer in the French navy. His companions were his naval aide Lieutenant Meyronnet; his secretary Alexandre Le Camus; a physician; and Jean-Jacques Reubell, who was an army officer and son of a high-ranking official in the French government. There was also at least one servant and probably several more.[1]

The group stirred gossip from the start. It was rumored that while in town Bonaparte paid court to a young woman named Miss Sarah Wheeler, but she was said to have rejected his advances. Several days later the *Herald* reported the group had chartered Walker's packet and sailed for Baltimore. That was inaccurate. Bonaparte had sent his luggage to Baltimore with a servant and dispatched his lieutenant to Philadelphia; then with the others, he set out for Washington City and the French embassy located in nearby Georgetown.[2]

Although it was not well known outside the French navy, the young officer's departure from Martinique had been the result of a mistake he'd made in the West Indies. While on patrol in command of the brig *l'Epervier*, he had encountered a ship he didn't recognize. When his signal for the other vessel to identify itself was not obeyed, he ordered one of his cannoneers to fire a warning shot. Unfortunately the shot struck the rigging of the other ship, which turned out to be British. Worse, the attack took place at a most precarious time, when Britain and France—after ten years of war—were enjoying a tenuous accord called the Peace of Amiens. [3]

When Jerome made port and described the incident to his commanding officer, the man was appalled. Rear Admiral Villaret-Joyeuse feared this action could reignite the war. He ordered young Bonaparte to sail immediately for France and report the event to his brother. He added: "Now, my dear Jerome, I beg you to consider the inevitable dangers you expose yourself to with the slightest delay. If war breaks out, the superior naval forces of the enemy will go to nearly any means of retaliation. . . . Thus there is not one minute to waste in your departure." [4]

It is a question whether the admiral was more afraid of the British or of the man now at the head of the French government. The shadow of Napoleon had hovered over every aspect of Jerome's naval career. The promotions he received, from midshipman to ensign to commander of a brig, were made over a matter of months, with the elder Bonaparte's approval and, on occasion, at his behest. Jerome's orders came to him headed: "Instructions for Citizen Jerome Bonaparte having to do with carrying out the instructions of the first consul, which have been transmitted by the Minister of Marine." [5]

Jerome was comfortable with this nepotism. He considered himself entitled to higher rank. Frédérick Masson, who wrote a dozen books about the Bonapartes, concluded that in regard to Napoleon, his siblings "consider everything which comes to them from him as their due; they haven't the slightest idea of considering themselves under obligation to him. . . . If you don't press them too closely they would say that they have become what they are by their own efforts." [6]

Though theoretically only one of the three consuls who ruled France, Napoleon was actually a dictator. He hadn't hesitated to quell a protest with "a whiff of grapeshot," and as a result many Frenchmen who'd lived through the Reign of Terror admired him for the stability he brought to the country. At the same time, others feared the power he wielded. Yet, unlike many of his countrymen, Jerome was not afraid of his brother. He was also not afraid of his commander or anybody else in the navy. So he quickly decided to pursue a course that differed from his orders, and this was entirely in keeping with Jerome's nature.

According to people who knew the Bonapartes well, Jerome as the youngest child had been coddled and in effect spoiled all his life, even though the family as a whole had endured difficult times. The mother, Letizia Ramolino, had been married at fourteen, bringing as her dowry a mill, an oven for baking bread, and thirty-one acres of land outside the town of Ajaccio, Corsica. Her husband, Carlo Buonaparte, had dropped out of law school before finishing his course but became a lawyer anyway, and was notorious in Ajaccio as the spendthrift who celebrated passing the bar examination by throwing a party that cost twice his annual income. [7]

Carlo and Letizia had thirteen children, though only eight survived early childhood. When Jerome was born in November 1784 he joined a family of four brothers—Joseph, Napoleon, Lucien, and Louis—ranging in age from seventeen to six, and three sisters—Elisa, Pauline, and Caroline, ages seven, four, and two. Letizia was not well educated, but it was possible for her children to go to good schools because during the period between the births of her two eldest, Genoa ceded Corsica to France, and that made them eligible for education at French schools. Second brother Napoleon, who in early childhood amused himself by drawing pictures of soldiers on the walls of their home, went to a military academy. At the time of Jerome's birth, he had just left the preparatory school at Brienne for the military college in Paris. Eldest brother Joseph was in Paris with their father, Carlo, whose illness had forced him to seek help from French physicians. Carlo never made it back to Corsica; early in 1785 he died in the care of family friends, the Permons. He had owned an olive orchard, a couple of small vineyards, and the family house in Ajaccio, but he left many debts. At the time of his death, his last child, Jerome, was only four months old.

Fortunately, the widow was a superb manager. With the help of her half-brother Joseph (later the Abbé Fesch), Letizia was able to raise her family, even in the midst of the unrest caused by the rebellion against France led by Pasquale Paoli. By the time the revolt made their life in Ajaccio too dangerous, Napoleon was in a position to get the family out of Corsica to safety in Marseilles. There the two older brothers gave what little help they could afford, but the rest of the Bonapartes remained so poor that Letizia and her daughters had to take in laundry. Jerome, now eight years old, simply ran the streets of the city.

Gradually, however, Napoleon was rising in the world. He was an artillery captain at the siege of Toulon, where his work earned him the rank of brigadier. The next year he was promoted to general and put in charge of the Army of the Interior, which included Paris and made him responsible for keeping the peace there. By the time Napoleon got around to checking on Jerome, he discovered the boy was utterly uneducated. He accused him of being a *petit polisson*, an illiterate little urchin, and enrolled him in a top-notch school. That didn't turn out well, for Jerome did not like to study.

Napoleon was baffled. In his own teens he'd read every book he could find and written hundreds of pages of analysis on everything, from what Alexander the Great thought about the strategic importance of Egypt to the battle tactics of Julius Caesar. He admired the conqueror of Gaul so much that when a priest told him Caesar was burning in hell, he lost his faith. And he could not comprehend why this kid brother was interested in no branch of study whatsoever.[8]

What the boy enjoyed at his school was meeting the girls of the associated female academy, learning how to talk to them and dance with them. In addition, Napoleon had married an aristocrat, so that when Jerome spent time with his sister-in-law Josephine de Beauharnais and her friends, he observed how well-born women liked to be treated. From then on, Jerome was always described as courtly and well mannered. Further, he was so handsome, good natured, and generous that women began to find him lovable.

As far as Napoleon was concerned Jerome had learned nothing useful, so he hired a tough tutor and instructed him to be very hard on the boy. What the general didn't understand was that his own growing power and his well-known closeness to his family made people reluctant to offend any Bonaparte. The tutor's teaching lacked muscle and had little effect.

By Jerome's fifteenth birthday, Napoleon had risen to first consul of France and was living in the Tuilleries Palace. He took Jerome to live with him there where he could keep an eye on him. Further, he put the unregenerate *polisson* into a regiment of guards. Jerome loved that, especially the military uniform, but soon he got into a duel with a fellow guardsman. The quarrel was over a woman, and his opponent was apparently the better shot. Jerome took a lead ball in the chest.

Military campaigns often took Napoleon away from Paris. When he got back from one of them, he found a pile of bills waiting to be paid. Upon investigation he found that a youth matching Jerome's description had been shopping in Paris jewelry stores and telling the merchants to send the bills to the palace. One item struck Napoleon as particularly offensive. It was an elaborate traveling case with a complete shaving set: razors, shaving pots, combs for the moustache, and various toiletry items made of gold, mother of pearl, silver, and ivory. It cost ten thousand francs. Napoleon raged, "But you have no beard, you don't even need to shave!" Jerome responded, "I know, but I just love beautiful things." [9]

While the conqueror had been off campaigning, Bonaparte family friends, the Permons, were supposed to keep an eye on Jerome. On his return Napoleon sarcastically confronted Madame Permon. "You brought him up well while I was far off. I find him willful, and willful in bad things." After a moment he admitted Jerome's problems were not all the fault of the Permons. He said, "The

Signora Letizia spoils him so totally that I doubt much whether he will mend where he now is."

Mme. Permon, who like other women found Jerome endearing, replied, "He is an excellent lad, all warmth of heart and good sentiments." She went on to suggest that maybe he ought to go into the navy, and she assured Napoleon the youth would return to them a naval hero.[10]

The idea made sense. Napoleon took care of his family, and he expected his family to assist him. The other brothers were helping. Joseph, a lawyer like their father, served as a military procurement officer. The politically active Lucien had played an important role in Napoleon's rise to power, and even young Louis helped by serving as Napoleon's military aide. At the same time, Napoleon had a serious problem he'd been unable to solve: the British navy remained a severe threat to his operations. He desperately needed someone in the family to learn naval warfare. Jerome's courage was unquestioned; he had certainly been brave when facing a dueling pistol. So the first consul put the seventeen-year-old into the navy and ordered his commander to make him work "like a very cabin boy." Later he wrote to Jerome with advice:

> I'm glad to hear you are getting used to the life of a sailor. There's no better career in which to win a name for yourself. Go up aloft, get to know every part of the ship; and when you come back from your voyage, I hope to hear that you are as active as any powder-monkey. . . . Make up your mind that you are going to be a sailor. I hope you have already learned to keep your watch, and box the compass.

In the summer of 1803, after several promotions and not much action, Jerome found himself facing real danger. He'd been ordered to sail home at a time when the British were patrolling not only the Caribbean but also the Atlantic, and his description had been distributed throughout the fleet.[12] Rather than risk capture, he had decided to travel to America as "M. d'Albert" and then go home incognito on an American merchant vessel. From Norfolk, he ordered his aide Meyronnet to go to Philadelphia and charter a ship, while Jerome himself went to Washington to get the cash he needed from the French chargé d'affaires, Louis André Pichon.

As soon as Pichon got the news he wrote to his superior in Paris, Minister of Foreign Affairs Talleyrand.

> *I received this morning, to my great astonishment, a letter from Citizen Jerome Bonaparte which informs me that he is arrived at Portsmouth, opposite Norfolk, in a pilot boat which will bring him as soon as he gets over the fatigue of his voyage, on his way to Philadelphia to embark for France. He remarks that he wishes to be incognito. I expect him daily.*[13]

Pichon's next letter two days later was much longer. He reported that Jerome had arrived with Citizen Reubell, son of the director of that name, and Citizen Le Camus, a young Creole of Martinique whom he introduced as his secretary. Pichon had called upon Jerome at his inn to offer him whatever assistance he might need in this country. Bonaparte told him he'd chartered a ship of four hundred tons, for the sum of $10,000, that would be ready to leave Philadelphia on August 3rd. Pichon reported:

> *Yet in spite of these arrangements Citizen Bonaparte had a new idea; he had learned that the United States were outfitting frigates in Washington for the Mediterranean and in consequence he made me two proposals: (1) to ask the American government to lend him a frigate, or (2) to ask passage to Spain on the first one to be sent to Europe.*

Pichon knew these requests would be refused. Borrowing a frigate was out of the question and giving passage to a French officer and especially to the brother of the first consul would be a violation of the neutrality of the United States. Nevertheless Jerome insisted, so Pichon had gone to President Jefferson's secretary of state James Madison to make the request. He did not mention the name of Bonaparte, but Madison, though small, slight, and looking unwell, was often described as the cleverest man among the nation's early leaders. He asked if this person was a military officer. When Pichon answered in the affirmative, Secretary Madison told him it was impossible to do so, that a similar request had been made by an English naval officer, Captain Murray, several days before and it had been refused. The chargé went on:

> The Citizen Bonaparte, after many hesitations, decided not to leave; the sailing of the vessel was put off to the 11th to give him time to decide. I had urged him several times, in the strongest terms, to leave as I was sure that this was the best opportunity that could be had. He persists in waiting the orders of the First Consul.[14]

For Jerome to remain in the United States while awaiting orders from Napoleon meant a delay of months. Any trip across the Atlantic and back took a minimum of eight weeks, and much longer if the wind and weather were not favorable. Pichon, though desperate for advice from Talleyrand, was forced to wait as well. In the meantime, the chargé felt obliged to supply the consul's brother with whatever funds he could spare. So Jerome, with thousands of dollars in spending money from the legation's coffer, set off for Baltimore to look up an old friend, the legendary sailor Joshua Barney.

∾

The tales about Barney went all the way back into his childhood, starting at the age of ten, when he came home from school and told his father he wasn't going back any more. He'd learned all the instructor could teach him, he could write a good hand and had mastered arithmetic, and what he wanted to do now was go to sea. His father refused and put him to work for a series of shopkeepers, but after a year of that, Joshua prevailed. He was allowed to sign on with a Chesapeake Bay pilot, where he learned to navigate and handle the sails. He did well and eventually was apprenticed to a relative who captained a small brig in the Liverpool trade. On their second voyage, after a storm in the Atlantic battered them so badly that the ship began to leak, the captain fell ill and died. The first mate had quit just before they embarked, so young Joshua the apprentice took over, sailed the ship safely into port, disposed of the cargo advantageously, got repairs made, had a series of adventures, and—to the astonishment of the boat's owner—sailed back into Baltimore with a profit. He was sixteen.[15]

At the onset of the American Revolution he was seventeen, so he went into the Continental navy, serving as mate on some vessels and captaining others himself. On the occasion of that first salute to a revolutionary naval vessel at St. Eustatius, Barney was first mate of the *Andrew Doria*. As the war continued, he fought in about two dozen engagements. He was captured by the British six times, escaped twice, and on other occasions was exchanged for British prisoners. His most spectacular victory came as commander of the *Hyder Ally* when he defeated the much larger and more heavily armed *General Monk*. Barney maneuvered in such a way that the other ship could not aim a broadside at him, and he confused the opponent by shouting prearranged false orders to his helmsman. In just twenty-six minutes the *Monk* struck her colors. Barney's casualties were four killed and eleven wounded. The British lost three times as many, including all of their officers except for one midshipman.[16]

Barney spent part of the war in Amsterdam, and from that time on he always cursed in Dutch, because it sounded so forceful and nobody outside of Holland knew what he was saying. When the war ended, the new United States was in no financial condition to maintain a navy, so he spent a few years in the shipping business and then joined the maritime service of France, where he rose to the rank of *chef de division*, or commodore. He enjoyed Paris. One of the stories about him claims that Queen Marie Antoinette was so delighted with him that she kissed him at a public function, and then all of her ladies-in-waiting followed suit. After that event, a song became popular that went, "Barney, leave the girls alone!" [17]

After the French Revolution he continued his dealings with France through commercial ventures and spent time in Paris and in the West Indies. Somewhere in his travels he encountered Jerome

Bonaparte, and apparently they discussed their mutual interest in the opposite sex, because Barney told Jerome that the most beautiful women in America lived in his hometown, Baltimore.

As a result, in late July 1803 Jerome and his entourage turned up at Barney's house on Charles Street. Barney, though now forty-four, was as energetic as ever. His portrait by Rembrandt Peale shows his even features, cleft chin, brilliant black eyes, and the jaunty air that was characteristic of him. He welcomed the Frenchmen, invited them all to stay in his home, and commenced to show them a good time. He took them to other cities and to various summer resorts.[18]

The Philadelphia ship had sailed without Jerome, but it took Lieutenant Meyronnet to France with letters from Jerome to the Bonapartes. While waiting for replies to this correspondence, Jerome enjoyed himself. In the *Times* a local gossip reported:

> *Extract of a Letter from Baltimore, in America, dated August 20, 1803. Bonaparte's brother Jerome is now here, living in high style; he has engaged seven rooms in the first inn in town for himself and suite, dashes about in an English curricle, and has ordered a public ball to be given on his account monthly. Where all the money is to come from to pay such expenses is problematical. I should not like to be his banker.* [19]

His "banker" was Pichon, who—based on Jerome's repeated requests for money—estimated that young Bonaparte was spending a stunning thousand dollars a week. When the legation funds were gone, Jerome found other "bankers." There is evidence that one of his sources was the Dupont family of Delaware, one of whom he apparently helped to bankrupt.[20]

In the late summer there were horse races at several locations around Baltimore. One of them was at Govanstown, north of the city, and it was there that Jerome encountered the most beautiful woman he'd ever seen. According to one account, she was wearing a buff-colored silk dress and a hat with long ostrich plumes. The writer said, "Her pure Grecian contours, her exquisitely shaped head, her large dark eyes, a peculiarly dainty mouth and chin, the soft bloom of her complexion, beautifully rounded shoulders and tapering arms, all combined to form one of the loveliest types of womanhood." [21]

Jerome wanted this woman. After all, he just loved beautiful things and found them irresistible. He tried to speak to her, but she turned away—they had not been introduced. Barney warned him off. He explained she was the daughter of the president of the Bank of Maryland, one of the richest merchants in America, and a rigid man who would brook no foolishness. A swift temporary dalliance of the kind Jerome was accustomed to was out of the question. As for a serious relationship, what would the first consul say? [22]

Various accounts say Jerome later met Betsy formally at a ball given in the Baltimore home of Justice Samuel Chase, who had built a three-story brick mansion on a downtown Baltimore square. People later said that when they danced together there, her necklace caught on the buttons of Jerome's uniform, and this meant they would be entwined forever. An addendum to that legend says William Patterson had forbidden his daughter to attend the event and had moved her out to his two-hundred-acre Springfield estate for good measure, but she slipped away and rode the thirty miles to Baltimore. [23]

Betsy herself years later told another story, one involving Jerome's friend Jean-Jacques Reubell, who'd come to Norfolk with him, and one of her own best friends, Henrietta Pascault. She spoke about it at a dinner party in the home of former Secretary of the Treasury Albert Gallatin, whose son James recorded the occasion in his diary:

> *Madame Bonaparte was very witty and made father laugh. She told us how she first met her husband, Jerome Bonaparte. . . . She was invited to dine with an old Frenchman, the Marquis de Poléon [Louis Pascault], who had escaped with his family from San Domingo during the massacre of that island. . . . All the beauties of Baltimore were invited to the dinner . . . the Catons, etc. She was looking out of the window overlooking the drive with M. de*

Poléon's eldest daughter. "We saw two young men approaching the house. Mlle Pascault exclaimed, pointing to the tall one, 'That man will be my husband!' I answered, 'Very well, I will marry the other one.' Strangely enough, we both did as we said. Henrietta Pascault married Reubell, son of one of the three Directors, and I married Jerome Bonaparte." [24]

At another time Betsy confirmed that account in a letter to her friend Alexandre Gortchakoff when she told him she had been introduced to Jerome by Mrs. Louis Pascault.[25]

The Pascault-Reubell wedding did take place in Baltimore that summer, with Jerome, Joshua Barney, and Jerome's physician Dr. Garnier signing the guest book. [26] So maybe all of the stories were true: the first sighting at the races, the entanglement at the ball, and the young girls' resolutions. Whatever the circumstances of the meeting, Jerome was smitten, and he lost all interest in going home.

Chapter 6

"Trust Not His Honor!"

*I*n the fall of 1803 the two powerful men on the fringe of Betsy and Jerome's story, Napoleon and Thomas Jefferson, had a great deal on their minds. Earlier, President Jefferson had learned that the Louisiana Territory and some land in Florida no longer belonged to ineffectual Spain, but were now owned by powerful France. Napoleon had secretly gotten the territories from Spain when he was contemplating some sort of American empire for himself. For Jefferson the prospect of Napoleon's troops lining the far bank of the Mississippi was alarming, and already the westerners, collectively known as Kentuckians, were protesting the potential closing of the port of New Orleans to U.S. cargoes.

Apparently France's troubles in the West Indies, with their tropical epidemics, a slave uprising, and a fruitless military campaign, had cast a pall over Napoleon's American plans. He also needed money for his war against Britain, so he was willing to have Talleyrand talk business with Jefferson's emissaries regarding the possible sale of Louisiana.[1]

At the time, half the inhabitants of the United States lived within fifty miles of the Atlantic Ocean, but population in the West was growing. With this purchase Jefferson, for about three cents an acre, could double the nation's size and guarantee the safety of the vital Mississippi River with uninterrupted access to the port of New Orleans. Napoleon, however, could change his mind, so there was no time to wait for congressional approval. Jefferson gave the go-ahead, and his envoy in Paris, Robert Livingston, completed the arrangements. Jefferson had already sent off Lewis and Clark on a cross-country trek to find out what he was buying. Now he set about getting approval for his extra-constitutional exercise of power. The Senate ratified the deal on October 20, 1803.

After the brief Peace of Amiens, Napoleon was at war again. It wasn't Jerome's fault; among the causes for the outbreak were Napoleon's attempts to keep British goods from coming into Europe and his continued harassment of British shipping. The first consul's victories on land continued, but he remained unable to cope successfully with the British at sea, so the idea of emulating his hero Julius Caesar by slipping across the English Channel to conquer Britain appealed to him. On the coast facing England, a French army began to gather troops, horses, supplies, wagons, and barges for an invasion. Day after day the British kept watch and lit bonfires in case the invasion came after dark. By the end of the year the London *Times* estimated that more than 300,000 defenders were on guard along the country's eastern coast. Strangely, some of America's funding for the Louisiana deal was obtained through London bankers, with the approval of their government, so in effect, Britain was financing Bonaparte's invasion.[2]

Meanwhile, Jerome mounted his own campaign. He rented a place on South Street not far from William Patterson's home and counting house. Neither the merchant's wealth nor his reputation for keeping a tight rein on his family deterred young Bonaparte, who paid a call on Patterson and asked for his daughter's hand in marriage. His suit was refused. Undaunted, he sent the Spanish minister to the U.S., Yrujo, Marquis de Casa, to plead for him. Yrujo himself had wedded an American, Sally Kean, hence he was sympathetic to the marriage. Further, the Spaniard hated Napoleon and might have enjoyed causing him trouble. But that intervention was also ineffective.

While he tried to change Patterson's mind, Jerome visited the family often. It was a busy household. Patterson himself, now fifty-one, was deeply involved in business, not just shipping, but banking, insurance, real estate, and several other ventures. Dorcas

Spear Patterson, now forty-two, was at this time the mother of a family of eleven. There were three young men in their early twenties, William, Robert, and John, although John was spending most of his time in Virginia at the home of U.S. Senator Wilson Cary Nicholas. (Mrs. Nicholas was the sister of Sam Smith, and and therefore John's aunt, and John would eventually marry one of her daughters.) Also residing at the Patterson house were two teenage boys, Joseph and Edward, and four youngsters: Margaret, ten and a half; George, seven; Caroline, five; and Henry, three. One baby girl had died at the age of two, but now Dorcas had another baby, Octavius, a year old. Although Patterson owned slaves, eighteen-year-old Betsy as the oldest sister was no doubt required to help care for the younger children.

Jerome seemed to enjoy this family's company, and apparently they enjoyed his. In a letter to his lawyer a short time later Patterson said that during Jerome's constant visits to his house, he "always conducted himself with the utmost delicacy and propriety." Apparently Dorcas grew fond of Jerome, because a year later when she gave birth to her last child, she named her Mary Ann Jeromia, and Jerome and Mary Caton were named the godparents.[3]

In spite of the early refusals, Jerome's campaign seemed to be going well. On August 23 a woman in Baltimore wrote to a friend in Philadelphia, "You are not singular in your observations of Miss P—she is at present quite the Town talk. Mama was there yesterday and she thought the family appeared very much delighted with the match."[4]

Joshua Barney persisted in his attempts to persuade Jerome to be less insistent. Barney had been to Paris, he'd met Napoleon, and he had misgivings about the situation. In September he succeeded in luring Jerome away to Philadelphia, where a great fuss was made over the brother of Napoleon.[5]

In late September Chargé Pichon encountered the party at Lancaster, Pennsylvania, as they were on their way home from Philadelphia. By now he despaired of ridding himself of Jerome and suspected he'd be blamed for this mess that could ruin his

career. In addition, Jerome's reputation was raising questions. During a carriage ride he had been accused of improper advances that
caused members of the woman's family to challenge him to a duel.
Somehow that had quieted down and been passed off as rumor.
There's no doubt, however, that he got two letters from a former
mistress. Her name was Eugénie Vermigli, and she wrote from
Paris asking for money and urging him to fulfill his "obligation to
render service" to her.[6]

For Pichon, there was one glimmer of hope. A storm-damaged
French warship, the *Poursuivante*, had laid up at Baltimore for
repairs. Its commander, Admiral Willaumez, invited Jerome to sail
home with him when the repairs were finished. Jerome expressed
no interest; he continued to await orders from his brother. Still,
when Jerome and Barney went to the capital in October, Pichon
dutifully took them, along with Willaumez, to see the president.
Jefferson welcomed them cordially and invited them to come back
the next day to dine with him. Pichon reported to his superiors that
Jerome had behaved well during these visits.[7]

While he was with Jerome, Pichon seized the opportunity
to explain all the reasons this marriage was far from a good idea.
Jerome listened, and Pichon believed he'd finally succeeded in
changing Jerome's mind. But through all this, Jerome never stopped
thinking about Betsy. He wrote her several times from Georgetown
in October to keep her up to date on his activities in the capital.
He said the road was bad, Miss Spear was always frightened, and
the weather was very cold. He told her how much he loved her and
how desperately he missed her.[8]

As soon as he got back to Baltimore he went to the county
courthouse and got a marriage license. He also began inviting
people to the wedding, suggesting that Minister Yrujo come to Baltimore on the second of November to be in time for the ceremony
on the third.[9]

Patterson was getting pressure from all sides. When he insisted
Betsy reconsider her enthusiasm for this Frenchman, she declared
she would rather be the wife of Jerome Bonaparte for an hour than

that of any other man for a lifetime. She was supported by the Spears, who were perhaps intrigued by the glamour of the situation. General Sam Smith, now in the Senate, was on Betsy's side as well. Certainly close ties with those in power in France would be beneficial for U.S. trade and security: as recently as the Adams administration the country had for a time been on the brink of war with France. Personally, too, General Smith may have had some motivation. Two years earlier Smith had approached President Jefferson to request a diplomatic post, but received no reply. He didn't give up. In the fall of 1802 there were rumors that both the American ministers to Britain and to France planned to resign, so Smith asked his brother-in-law Senator Wilson Cary Nicholas to intercede for him with fellow Virginian Jefferson for one of the posts. Smith felt his wealth and his business experience qualified him, but Nicholas pointed out that a diplomatic position demanded very different skills. Apparently disheartened, Sam let the matter drop. Now, however, there may have been in the back of his mind the thought: What if my niece became a member of Napoleon's family?[10]

Patterson, ever a cautious man, consulted his lawyer, Alexander Dallas. He asked Dallas to draw up a detailed prenuptial contract that would protect Betsy in case the marriage encountered difficulties. In addition he asked his brother-in-law, Sam Smith, to call upon the president and Mr. Madison for letters in support of the marriage. On October 28 Madison wrote to Robert Livingston, U.S. minister to France. He gave a summary of the events following young Bonaparte's arrival at Newport, culminating in the impending marriage. He pointed out that these events "were not without importance," and added that Livingston should be aware of the circumstances in order to be able to give explanations in accord with the truth and to prevent erroneous impressions.

> *I follow, therefore, my own sense of propriety, as well as the wishes*
> *of the friends of the young lady, in informing you that her parents*
> *have had no share in promoting this distinction of their daughter,*
> *and that their station in society and their independence of fortune*

place their acquiescence in it far above any suspicion of indelicate considerations. Mr. Patterson the father, is a man of the fairest character, of real respectability, of very great wealth, perhaps near a million dollars, and has received sufficient proofs of the esteem and confidence of his fellow citizens. By marriage he is connected with a very important family in Maryland, to which you are not a stranger; Mrs. Patterson being the sister of Mrs. Smith, the wife of General Smith, well known in our public councils and at present a Senator of the United States, and himself also of a very respectable family.[11]

While this letter went on its way, Patterson addressed another matter of concern. He was puzzled about Jerome's age; apparently the young man hadn't been forthcoming about it. So while Jerome was in Washington paying his respects to officials and dining with the president, Patterson asked Sam Smith to see if he could find out exactly how old Jerome was.

On October 26 Smith wrote to say he'd visited Jerome and they had talked for two hours. When he asked Bonaparte about his age, the young man said he had just passed twenty-one, but that by his commission he appeared to be twenty-two. He said no one under twenty-one could be a lieutenant in the French navy, so when he had left France fifteen months past, being then under age, they advanced the year by one. "If this is true," Smith wrote, "his commission will prove it," adding:

I am informed that Pichon has actually refused to attend his marriage, has declared that the match will give great offense and that therefore he dare not be any part in it. Of course he will not be a witness to the contract. . . . Pichon told me no marriage made under twenty-five . . . in France was valid. . . . the positive law of France would be in favor of annulling the marriage.[12]

Patterson also asked Dallas to research marriage law. On November 3 the lawyer wrote a detailed and complex analysis. He concluded that marriages, on principles of general law, were governed by the laws of the country in which the marriage took place and were then accepted in other countries. Maryland law stipulated that anyone over the age of twenty-one and those who are younger but have parental consent can make a valid marriage. "Therefore the marriage of Mr. Bonaparte, according to the laws of Maryland, would be here valid, to every intent and purpose; and even in France it would not be void, though it might be voidable, if the parties should hereafter go within the jurisdiction of France." Dallas also called upon Pichon, who confirmed that the old law of 1792 in France had been replaced by the new Civil Code in February 1802, which stipulated that no one under the age of twenty-five could marry without the parental consent.[13]

Patterson concluded this ground was too shaky. On November 16 he informed Mr. Dallas that the engagement had been broken off.

> *A variety of circumstances led to this step, and I could never reconcile it to reason or my own feelings to suffer my D_____ to marry leaving it in the power of Mr. B_____ or any of his Family to annul the marriage, the moment the parties might arrive in France. Indeed it would appear that by the Laws of France the thing would have been void of itself, and required no Ceremony or legal process to set it aside. This was the great leading motive with me, and I reasoned constantly with my D_____ to convince her of the danger. Some circumstances of no great importance occurred before the Day appointed came round, which gave us an opportunity of putting an end to the Business, and greatly relieved my mind. It was done by letter from my D_____ to Mr. B_____ declaring that under existing circumstances she could not consent to their marriage.*

Patterson added that he had assured young Bonaparte that if he obtained the consent of his mother so as to render the marriage legal in France, there would be no further objection to the match. He concluded by saying he was very much indebted for Dallas's friendship and trouble in this affair, and he begged him to accept "the enclosed fee in the line of your profession."[14]

The circumstance of no great importance that occurred before the planned wedding date and gave an opportunity to put an end to the business, was probably the following anonymous letter sent to Patterson.

> *Is it possible, sir, you can so far forget yourself, and the happiness of your child, as to consent to her marrying Mr. Bonaparte? If you knew him, you never would, as misery must be her portion—he who but a few months ago destroyed the peace and happiness of a respectable family in Nantz by promising marriage, then ruined, leaving her to misery and shame. What has been his conduct in the West Indies? There ruined a lovely young woman who had only been married for a few weeks. He parted her from her husband, and destroyed that family! And here, what is his conduct? At the very moment he was demanding your daughter in marriage he ruined a young French girl, whom he now leaves also in misery! His conduct at Nantz and in the West Indies has already reached his brother's ears, and he dares not appear before him! His voyage to this country proves it! He now wishes to secure himself a home at your expense until things can be arranged for his return to France, when rest assured he will be the first to turn your daughter off, and laugh at your credulity! Nothing that can be done will be binding on him; and if you knew his moral character of dissipation, you would never! no, never! even with the approbation of his family, trust your daughter to him. Then take advice in time and break off everything before it is too late. Let nothing on earth tempt you to such an union! What is here said may be depended upon, and much more might be said, for, without exception, he is the most profligate young man of the age. Demand seriously of Miss Wheeler, and you will there find he has already demanded her in marriage with the same intentions! . . . Trust not his honor! There never was any in his family!* [15]

The writer of that letter remains unknown, but it certainly appears to have been from an insider. Who but a member of Jerome's entourage would have known such details regarding not only France, but the West Indies and Norfolk? It is possible someone close to Jerome, despairing of changing his mind and fearing the effect of Napoleon's reaction on Jerome and on his friends, turned to William Patterson for help.

In any case, the marriage was called off and the gossip spread quickly. Rosalie Stier Calvert wrote her mother that Jerome Bonaparte had been courting Miss Patterson,

> *but her parents refused to consent to the marriage. The young lady threatened to run away with him, [so] they gave in. The date was set and preparations made, but the evening before the wedding she was driven off to one of her relatives in Virginia under a chaperone's custody. I don't know how this story will end.*[16]

There's no record of where Patterson sent Betsy. It's possible she was taken to the family's Virginia connections, the Nicholas clan. Her brother John was already at Wilson Cary Nicholas's place "Mount Warren" on the James River. She also may have gone to a Nicholas home in Richmond. There Dorcas Patterson's niece Mary Spear was married to Philip Norborne Nicholas, and two years later Betsy wrote to Miss Eliza Monroe at Paris, reminding her of "the acquaintance I formerly had the pleasure of cultivating with you and your amiable family during my stay in Richmond."[17]

Jerome went to New York, and no doubt Patterson felt the situation had been cleared up, because after a time Betsy was allowed to return home. Though neither had written to the other during Betsy's banishment, somehow Jerome came back to Baltimore within a week of her reappearance in town.[18]

The marriage was rescheduled. Maybe Patterson despaired of being able to keep his wayward daughter a prisoner indefinitely, while for Dorcas the possibility of losing the love of her eldest girl forever may have been too dreadful to accept. There's also evidence that Patterson extracted Jerome's promise not to leave this country until he had obtained Napoleon's approval.[19]

In addition Patterson had on hand lawyer Dallas's proposed prenuptial contract. It stated that if any doubts were raised respecting the validity of said marriage either in Maryland or France, Jerome would perform any and every act necessary to remove such doubts, and to render the marriage in all respects valid. Further, upon Jerome's death one third of his property real and personal would come to Elizabeth Patterson, and further benefits were added for any issue from the marriage. If for any cause whatsoever a separation should take place, those same property divisions would continue to apply. Patterson also guaranteed that upon his own death, his daughter would receive a share of his estate equal to that given to his other children.[20]

The marriage went ahead on Christmas Eve, with the prenuptial being signed by the participants before the ceremony and witnessed by several members of the wedding party, including the mayor of Baltimore. Although a number of invitees were absent, among them Minister Yrujo, Dr. Garnier (who pleaded illness), and of course Pichon, all seemed well once the contract had been signed. At the wedding supper there must have been many toasts and much joyful celebration.

Nevertheless the joy was unfounded. The guests did not know that even in America the marriage was invalid. Jerome had concealed from everyone the truth about his age. A few weeks before, on his November 15 birthday, he had become just nineteen years old.

Chapter 7

A Capital Scandal

The newlyweds set about enjoying themselves and decided the best place to do that would be Washington City. The government had moved there only three years before, but already the place was becoming known for its suppers, dances, card games, and horse racing. Getting there, though, was a challenge, and once there, going about in town was another.

The French engineer and Revolutionary War veteran Major Pierre Charles l'Enfant had planned the new seat of government for a very large population. He designed spacious squares and wide avenues radiating out from central points, a plan both elegant and potentially spectacular. The man was a genius, but like many such men he did not get on well with others. He resisted compromise, refused to give a copy of his plan to the District of Columbia commissioners who were in charge, and had his crew pull down the early phase of construction for a large private home of whose placement he disapproved.

George Washington, who had hired him, said, "Men who possess talents which fit them for peculiar purposes are almost invariably under the influence of untoward dispositions, or a sottish pride, or possessed of some other disqualification by which they plague all with whom they are concerned; but I did not expect to meet with such perverseness in Major l'Enfant as his late conduct exhibited." So Washington fired him. For the remainder of his life this brilliant engineer, tall and thin, dressed in a high-buttoned military coat and army boots, and carrying under his arm a roll of papers relating to his claim, prowled the halls of the Capitol seeking redress for his injury and refusing every compensation offered. At length he died and was buried in the garden of a local benefactor.[1]

Others took over the work on what was becoming a town of three or four thousand people scattered over what one visitor tactfully called a place of "magnificent distances." Before and during his presidency, Thomas Jefferson gave some of his attention to the town's practical concerns, such as fire safety, the height of the buildings, and the lack of funds to complete the work and concluded the whole project must be cut back. So, even after years of work, many structures remained unfinished and the broad avenues were still unpaved, which meant clouds of dust in dry weather and deep mud in wet. The largest building was the white stone house of the president, called optimistically his "palace." In 1804 it still had temporary wooden steps, a leaky roof, and wings containing a wine cellar, coal and wood bins, and privies, while the surrounding grounds were an unimproved waste.[2]

Because of the expansive original plan, the existing buildings were so widely spaced that travelers got lost in the forest going from one part of town to another. A writer described the not-uncommon plight of several congressmen returning from a dinner party, losing their way and traveling "until daybreak in their carriage weaving through bogs and gullies in search of Capitol Hill, only a mile away." An attaché at the British Embassy during the Jefferson administration said: "In going to assemblies one had sometimes to drive three or four miles within the city bounds, and very often at the risk of an overturn, or of being what is termed 'stalled,' or stuck in the mud, when one can neither get backward or forward, and either loses one's shoes or one's patience." But the capital's wilderness was not without benefit, as another British envoy claimed the sport shooting was excellent. "I put up a covey of partridges about 300 yards from the Capitol."[3]

The sessions of the Senate and the House of Representatives convened after the fall harvest and adjourned before spring planting, so the Washington season could be as short as four or five months, and the nation's elected representatives had difficulty finding the temporary lodging they needed. Nearby Georgetown had inns, but in Washington City lodging was harder to find. It is estimated that in 1804 there were six small hotels and one inn, places that were relatively expensive and often fully booked. There were, however, some ten boarding houses, and many legislators preferred them.[4]

Year-round government employees could rent a room in one of the modest private dwellings among the connected brick homes called "row houses." There were also a number of upscale dwellings, some belonging to longtime residents of the neighborhood, others to upper-level administration staffers such as Secretary of the Treasury Albert Gallatin. Even Chargé Pichon and his wife Emelie had a private house.[5]

Usually the government's workday ended around 4:00 P.M., and in the beginning there was nothing to do during leisure time. Early on, the population of year-round government employees and part-time officials was swelled by visitors. Wives of legislators from distant states sometimes left their children at home in the care of others and set off for the capital with their husbands, while some of those with marriageable daughters brought them to town, seizing this opportunity for exposure to a crop of politically minded bachelors. Perhaps the dreariness of the situation and the difficulties regarding travel and lodging drove the residents and visitors to intensified revels. Soon, owners of homes were entertaining throughout the winter. One hostess "attended or hosted sixty-one teas, nineteen dinners, four parties, and one ball" during the 1803–1804 winter season.[6]

For entertainment people attended the legislative sessions, especially if an interesting topic was being debated. Everywhere people played cards, and in the larger buildings there were dances or performances by traveling theatrical companies. The higher officials established a regular schedule for dinners and assemblies. Accordingly, there was a detailed protocol for paying calls and the use of personal cards. The result was a busy social season that was in certain respects more Old World than New. Hence the newlyweds' decision to travel there.

Throughout that winter of 1803–1804 the weather was bitterly cold. Rosalie Calvert wrote her mother that they could cross the Potomac on horseback and travel about Washington by sleigh. "One night as we were returning home we met another sleigh, the road was narrow, our horses were lively, and in passing the other too fast, we overturned in several feet of snow." [7]

When Betsy and Jerome set out for the capital not long after their wedding, Baltimore was also buried in snow. A local paper reported:

> *Our city, especially market street, exhibited a lively scene yesterday and to-day, from the incessant passing of sleighs and four!!!! Sleighs and two! And sleighs and one! The younger part of our city patriots were, as is customary on such occasions, troublesome and dangerous with their snowballs. Madame Bonaparte, we understand, was thrown at and struck by a ball; for the perpetrator of which, it is said, her husband offered a reward of five hundred dollars. The evil certainly requires a remedy, and several lads, we learn, have been taken up by the constables.* [8]

Going south the forty miles to the District of Columbia was a rough trip in any season. During the presidency of John Adams, his wife Abigail and her party got lost after leaving Baltimore and wandered around for two hours until a slave working in a field showed them the way. She wrote that "woods are all you see until you reach the *city*, which is only so in name." [9]

The public coach, called a "stage" because the trip was broken into stages, left Baltimore at four in the morning, and after eight miles arrived at another branch of the Patapsco River. At that site there were barges that could take in one crossing a large vehicle loaded with passengers, along with its horses, but smaller boats had to make several trips. From time to time the passengers had to get out and walk if the road went up a steep hill. The route was partially cleared. Trees had been felled, but the stumps often remained, so that a large conveyance with eight to ten passengers had to weave from side to side to avoid them. Occasionally, as Rosalie Calvert found, the vehicle turned over in a deep rut.

At eight in the morning the stage stopped for breakfast at an inn in the midst of a dense forest. The next fifteen miles continued through more forest, but at length the coach stopped at another inn for mid-day dinner. By the last stage of the journey, the road was somewhat better. If it rained, though, the trip grew increasingly uncomfortable. The passengers were obliged to unroll and let down the heavy leather curtains, which made the interior of the coach dark and oppressively hot. But if all went well, the trip ended in Georgetown during the late afternoon, having taken twelve hours to travel forty miles.[10]

Jerome would have refused public travel. For himself and Betsy, he would have begged, borrowed, or bought on credit a private carriage. And that's what he did: an observer later reported that Jerome came to Washington in "a beautiful carriage and six horses, but later it was discovered that it belonged to his friend, Commodore Barney." If Jerome was unable to provide another conveyance for his entourage of companions and servants, they probably took the stage.[11]

Yet even in the best possible vehicle, the trip was never easy. This time, there was an accident. From Washington, Sam Smith wrote to William Patterson in Baltimore to describe what happened.

> Betsy's great presence of mind and firmness of character preserved her last night. Coming in after night, the coachman was thrown from the box. Mr. Bonaparte jumped out, but could not stop the horses. They went on, but regularly. Finding her danger increased, she opened the door, and jumped out into the snow, without receiving any injury.[12]

No doubt Patterson was glad the outcome was good, but he had something else on his mind. He'd received another anonymous letter.

Sir, this is to inform you as a friend that you must be aware of your son-in-law, as you may now term him Bonaparty, for he has made his brags and boastings, before his marriage that he would get married to your daughter and then he would leave her and go home to his brother in France. This he has told in public company before several; and likewise that when he goes to France, he will still be a single man, and she may then go to the devil for all he cares; and I and many others you may be assured must think the same—certainly of such a French fop of a fool. So therefore, as a friend, I warn you of him in time, as he has declared the above.

Your friend,

A Frenchman[13]

And still there had been no word from the Bonapartes in response to the letters Jerome sent to France with his lieutenant Meyronnet. Patterson decided to write to Robert Livingston, the American ambassador in Paris.

I can assure you with truth that I never, directly or indirectly countenanced or gave Mr. Bonaparte the smallest encouragement to address my daughter; but on the contrary, resisted his pretensions by every means in my power consistent with discretion. Finding, however, that the mutual attachment they had formed for each other was such, that nothing short of force and violence could prevent their union, I with much reluctance consented to their wishes.

Patterson went on to enlist Livingston's help in putting the best possible direction on the situation by reconciling Mr. Bonaparte's family to the match. He enclosed letters from the president and the secretary of state, and asked the ambassador "if you think it proper" to furnish them to the first consul. He asked that Livingston let him know whether this marriage was likely to meet with approval there. Then he commenced to wait for an answer, which did not come for months.[14]

Patterson's shipping business was international in scope. He had well-established contacts around Europe and often sent his own sons to foreign cities to supervise shipments of goods, exchange rates, and money transfers. Now, in his frustration over the lack of news, he decided to send his son Robert to Paris to see if he could find out what was going on.

Meanwhile the newlyweds were basking in Washington City's social season. There's no proof of where they stayed. Jerome's name appears in the records of the Union Tavern at Georgetown (along with that of Talleyrand, Alexander von Humboldt, and Louis Philippe, later a king of France) but there is no mention of Jerome's "lady," so that entry may relate to one of his earlier visits to see Pichon. Betsy had relatives in Washington, the Nicholas family of Virginia, her uncle Sam Smith, and his brother Robert, who was secretary of the navy. Both Smiths brought their families with them, and Robert had a house on Capitol Hill, so Betsy had several aunts in town. These women were about to be embarrassed.[5]

The problem was the Paris fashions that Jerome knew so well and enjoyed so much. Those fashions reflected the environment of a dramatically post-revolutionary nation. When the French threw off the Old Regime, they also rejected everything connected with it. They instituted a new calendar, numbering the years in Roman numerals from the start of their new republic; and the old months of the Julian calendar were given new names that described the seasons, such as "Floreal" for April and "Thermidor" for July. Ranks were thrown out along with the heads of guillotined aristocrats, so now every man's title was "Citizen." Even clothing was transformed. Men replaced the former knee breeches and silk hose with trousers. The towering coiffeurs and bouffant dresses of Marie Antoinette and her ladies were gone as well. The new fashion looked back to the austerity of the ancient Greeks and Romans who had helped inspire the recent political changes. Women's hair was pulled back into a graceful Psyche knot; caps were replaced by bandeaus, and high-heeled shoes by flat slippers. Although the Athenian law that a woman could wear only one garment was not reinstated, dresses did become slim, sheer, and revealing. Waistlines were raised to support the breasts, sleeves were short enough to show the arms, and necklines low enough to offer (as one writer described it) "an ample sample."[16]

Somehow, perhaps when Betsy's banishment to Virginia had driven him off to New York, Jerome had managed to get her some stunning jewelry and a Parisian-style wardrobe. Consequently, when the young Bonapartes' arrival in Washington City was marked by parties given in their honor, Betsy was ready with garments in the latest Paris fashions. Unfortunately the fashions of Paris had not yet been embraced by the new American elite. Already a Georgetown paper had warned of the destructive tendencies of "the fair sex in the higher circles to sacrifice decency at the shrine of fashion." Some thought that immodest attire posed a real threat to civil society itself.[17]

Margaret Bayard Smith, wife of the publisher of the local *National Intelligencer,* wrote to her sister:

> *Since my last letters, we have been at a large and splendid ball at Mr. Robt. Smith's, a dining party at Md'm Pichon's, a card party at Mrs. Gallatin's. . . . Mrs. Smith's was by far the most agreeable. . . . But of Mad'm* _____ [Bonaparte] *I think it no harm to speak the truth. She has made a great noise here, and mobs of boys have crowded around her splendid equipage to see what I hope will not often be seen in this country, an almost naked woman. An elegant and select party was given her by Mrs. Robt. Smith; her appearance was such that it threw all the company into confusion, and no one dar'd look at her but by stealth; the shutters being left open, a crowd assembled around the windows to get a look at this beautiful little creature, for everyone allows that she is extremely beautiful. Her dress was the thinnest sarcenet and white crepe without the least stiffening in it, made without a single pleat in the skirt, the width at the bottom being made of gores; there was scarcely any waist to it and no sleeves; her back, her bosom, part of her waist and her arms were uncover'd and the rest of her form visible. She was engaged the next evening at Madm P's [Pichon], Mrs. R. Smith and several other ladies sent her word, if she wished to meet them there, she must promise to have more clothes on.*[18]

Rosalie Calvert also gave her opinion: "Madame Bonaparte wears dresses so transparent and tight that you can see her skin through them. No chemise at all." She was also critical of a diplomat's wife. "Mrs. Merry, the new English Ambassadress, is very fat and covers only with fine lace two objects which could fill a fourth of a bushel!" [19]

Anthony Merry and his wife were used to the rigid protocol of the London court, where rank was all-important. They found quite disconcerting President Jefferson's deliberately Americanized manners, which at times led him so far as to greet company while wearing his bathrobe and slippers. Even more disconcerting was Jefferson's refusal to abide by the proper precedence: an ambassador's wife outranked other guests and should be personally taken in to dinner on the president's arm. Instead, this man ignored Mrs. Merry and led into the dining room at various times Mrs. Madison, Mrs. Gallatin, and even Jerome Bonaparte's wife! Mrs. Merry refused to attend any more presidential dinners. [20]

The British "ambassadress" did however decide to go to the fancy dress ball that Robert and Sam Smith sponsored for their niece and her husband. The *National Intelligencer* called this event "the most numerous and brilliant affair which has ever met in this district," and the chief executive himself was going to be there. Mrs. Merry, determined to achieve the preference she was entitled to, put herself into her most elegant dress and donned her best jewels. "For a few golden moments," a writer says, she "seemed to be the center of attention. Then things started going downhill for her. . . . Elizabeth Bonaparte put in an appearance, wearing a gown of dampened muslin that clung to her body, and in an instant everyone forgot about Mrs. Merry." [21]

The Merrys remained deeply offended and the diplomatic scandal assumed historic, if whimsical, proportions. Betsy herself seems to have remained unrepentant while the criticism continued for months. Even then, the censures were blended with admiration. A local woman said of this "pretty little Duchess of Baltimore":

She outshines all the Ladies here for the splendour and elegance of her dress; even Mrs. M [Madison] cannot sport Diamonds and pearls in such profusion. The evening I saw her, she was dressed very plain, at least that part of her body that was covered at all. She exposes so much of her bosom as modesty would permit, & I think rather more. Her back was laid bare nearly half way down to the bottom of her waist. . . .The state of nudity in which she appeared attracted the attention of the Gentlemen, for I saw several of them take a look at her bubbies while they were conversing with her. [22]

About this time, the American painter Gilbert Stuart set up a studio in Washington City. He had a rare ability to capture, not just the likeness, but the personality of a subject as well. He did this in part by getting his sitters to talk about themselves. During his early sessions with the first president, Stuart had difficulty getting him to talk. At length it occurred to him to ask the general to explain battle tactics, and after that the old warhorse talked continuously. Stuart's portraits of Washington became famous, including the image now appearing on the U.S. one-dollar bill.

When word spread that Gilbert Stuart had opened a painting room in town, all the Washington locals with a spare hundred dollars tried to get on his schedule. Soon he had more commissions than he could complete, but he had to continue accepting them. He was supporting his wife and nine children, and his financial problems were severe. In addition, he suffered mood swings, depression, and frequent extreme irritability. He refused to allow a picture to be viewed until he was satisfied with it, and the slightest critical comment enraged him. When General Knox, George Washington's secretary of war, offended him during a sitting, Stuart refused to give up the picture and used it at home as the door of his pigsty.[23]

When Jerome and Betsy appeared in his studio, he was intrigued by the young bride's remarkable beauty. An art historian described the painter's reaction:

The effect of Elizabeth Patterson on Stuart was instantaneous; never before had he ventured to paint three heads on one canvas—

an idealized front-face, deep-cut Grecian profile, and tip-tilted three-quarter face, each conveying the clear girlish skin, pink lips, white neck, and curiously elfin eyes of his radiant subject. His sketches delighted him, and were finished not as portraits, with the addition of three separate draperies, but to represent angelic heads floating in cloudy heavens.[24]

Betsy said later these portrait studies were the only pictures that looked like her; the other paintings she had done "could have been any other woman." She also said the reason she looked so happy in these likenesses was because Jerome was holding her hand the whole time.

Jerome posed for Stuart too, but his effect on the painter was different. The youngest Bonaparte's manner tended to be arrogant, and something he said set Stuart off. One story is that Jerome objected to the cloudy heavens in place of clothing on his wife. Whatever it was, the painter was furious, refused to finish the pictures, and ordered the couple out of his studio. In later years Jerome's portrait was seen on the floor of the artist's workroom, and when a student apologized for stepping on it, Stuart said, "You needn't mind, it's only a damned French barber."

It took years to get Betsy's portrait study back from Stuart. At one point he got so tired of requests for the picture he said if he was bothered about it again, he would put rings through the nose and give it to any tavern-keeper who would hang it up. Eventually Betsy's childhood friend, the art patron Robert Gilmor, persuaded the artist to give him the picture, and he returned it to Betsy's father, who left it to her in his will.[25]

While all this was going on, back home in Baltimore William Patterson received from his son Robert a series of reports on the situation in Paris. The news was very good.

Chapter 8

An American in Paris

$\mathcal{R}$obert Patterson arrived in Paris on March 11, 1804, and immediately went to see Ambassador Livingston. The next day he wrote
his father to say the American representative was doing everything in
his power to support Betsy's marriage. He had reassured the consul's
brothers and other highly placed persons that Jerome Bonaparte
could not have made a more respectable connection, and that to
consider annulment of the marriage "would be scandalizing the
most sacred of human engagements."

Robert went on to say that apparently the Bonaparte family
expected Jerome to live in the United States as an American citizen. The consul's elder brother Joseph consulted Mr. Livingston
about the best place for Jerome to reside, and talked about making
provision for him by investing a large sum of money in American
funds, not to give Jerome access to it, but to derive from it an annual
income sufficient to live on. However, Robert warned, we must be
cautious.

> *Bonaparte is of a very irritable temper, and as he is at present*
> *highly incensed with his brother, he might, were he here, take*
> *some violent measures with him. Still, Mr. Livingston thinks he*
> *will after a while become better satisfied with the union; and as*
> *he has by his conduct hitherto uniformly endeavored to impress*
> *on the world the highest idea of his moral character, he will not*
> *lightly, in this present affair, do anything to impeach or bring that*
> *character in question.*

Robert concluded that, for the present, it would be much

better for the couple to remain in America, but should Jerome be directed to return to Paris, Betsy ought to accompany him. In the worst possible situation—that is, the failure of Napoleon to acknowledge the marriage—"she would have asylum in the house of our Minister."[1]

Since the eldest Bonaparte, Joseph, was technically head of the family and hence the logical spokesperson for them, Robert tried to call upon him at the Hôtel de Marbeuf, his Paris mansion in the Faubourg St. Honoré. He was not admitted; he was told M. Bonaparte was out of town.

Two days later Robert wrote again to say that now he had even more satisfying information. On returning to his rooms that morning he had found a note from another Bonaparte brother, Lucien. Since Robert did not speak French, he took the communication to Paul Bentalou, a Patterson family friend who had been born in Toulouse, was a captain in Pulaski's cavalry regiment during the American Revolution, and was now living in Paris with his French wife. Bentalou told him the note said that Mr. and Mrs. Lucien Bonaparte were extremely desirous of having the pleasure of seeing Mr. Patterson, brother-in-law of M. Jerome. They would both be at home the whole morning in hopes he would have the goodness to call on them. Robert and Paul went together to Lucien Bonaparte's residence, and later each of them sent William Patterson a detailed account of the meeting.[2]

Upon their arrival Lucien took them into a private room. With Paul Bentalou acting as interpreter, Lucien told Patterson that although the first consul was displeased with the marriage, his mother and the rest of the family were not. The meeting lasted two hours, and during that time Lucien tried to explain Napoleon's attitude. "Placed on the lofty ground on which he stands as the first magistrate of a great and powerful nation, all his actions and ideas are directed by a policy with which we have nothing to do." He went on to say that the rest of the Bonapartes still remained plain citizens, but from all they had learned of the young lady's character and the respectability of her friends, the family felt "highly gratified with the connection." He said the Pattersons should not feel hurt by the displeasure of the consul; Lucien himself had had a similar experience: "Although of an age to be my own master, and occupying distinguished places under the government, I have also, by my late marriage, incurred his displeasure, so that Jerome is not alone." He stated his conviction that when we marry, "we are to consult our own happiness and not that of another."

During the rest of the meeting, Lucien and Robert discussed the family's plans for Jerome. Lucien repeated the information about investing in funds so that the young couple could live on the interest. He asked for specifics regarding what would be required. They wanted him to become a permanent resident of the United States and in fact to become a citizen. When Robert pointed out that citizenship required seven years and a renunciation of all titles of nobility and all allegiance to other countries, Lucien said, *"Very well, Jerome must do all that."* He contended that France was yet on a tempestuous sea, while Jerome was moored in a safe harbor, and he must adopt *"the plain and uncorrupted manners of your incomparable nation."* He insisted that Jerome "must positively change his mode of living, and must not, as he has hitherto done, act the part of a prince of royal blood."

Gradually it came out that the family wanted to have permanent capital secured in America. Lucien said they had "already applied for purchase of the newly created funds for the Louisiana acquisition, and found that they were above par." Paul Bentalou assured him that they would be able to make the purchase under par from Americans now living in Paris who were having financial difficulties. Lucien felt that his family would invest enough capital to earn an income of $15,000 a year to cover the young couple's living expenses. He also suggested that, as a well-known businessman, William Patterson might be willing to be appointed to hold the investments in trust for Jerome.

Lucien then told them that dispatches for Jerome had been sent from Paris yesterday. Lucien said of them that "the Consul, as Consul, directed his Minister to tell the Chargé d'affaires in the

United States to express his displeasure to Jerome, which must be considered as simply a matter of form; but by the same conveyance, Jerome will receive from his family comfortable letters such as all of you wish for." As the meeting ended, he asked for a likeness of Madame Jerome to share with the rest of his family, and invited Robert and Paul to visit him again. Robert told his father, "I was highly flattered by the attention shown me. He observed at parting, that he should expect to see me every three or four days, and if I disappointed him, he would be obliged to quarrel with me."

After that Robert made another attempt to see Joseph Bonaparte. Lucien had explained that technically the members of the family were not supposed to receive anyone until after he had been officially received by Napoleon. Still Patterson tried again, and again was told that Joseph was not at home.

A few days later Robert's hopes were revived. Joseph had indeed been out of town; he'd been staying at another Bonaparte property called Malmaison, and had now returned. He and his wife welcomed Patterson to their Paris mansion for dinner, but it turned out to be a strange affair. They were pleasant and friendly, but Jerome's marriage was never mentioned. The omission was so marked that Robert hesitated to bring it up.[3]

When he went to see Lucien again to get an explanation, he found that his only satisfactory Bonaparte contact had left town. There was a rumor that he'd fled in exile to Italy. And still, despite all the gossip in Paris, no one seemed to know Napoleon's response to Jerome's American marriage.

What Patterson and his friend Bentalou did not know was the reason for Joseph's absence from the city. He had been at Malmaison to give support to his troubled and at times distraught brother. For several years Napoleon had been the target of murder attempts sponsored by royalists who sought the restoration of the Bourbon monarchy. Recently there'd been an increase in these attacks. Among them was an ambush and abortive attempt to kidnap the first consul. Several of the supposed ringleaders had been seized, but the attacks continued. The most frightening was a bombing aimed at catching the first consul on his way to attend the opera. It missed him, but there were dozens of casualties among bystanders. Napoleon decided to strike fast and hard to put a stop to these plots. He sent a team across the border into Bavaria to kidnap the royalist Duc d'Enghien on suspicion of implication in the assassination schemes. The raid was successful, and the captors brought their prey into France. The duke was denied counsel, not told the evidence against him, and not allowed to call witnesses in his defense. He was tried, found guilty, and executed in a matter of days.[4]

Nevertheless, Napoleon now had more distractions than ever to take his attention from Jerome's situation. Despite his boast that he was going to raise the French flag over the Tower of London, his expeditionary force on the coast was kept ashore by the British navy. Further, putting d'Enghien in front of a firing squad on very flimsy evidence had stirred up international fury. Even Fouché, his own minister of police said, "It was more than a crime—it was a mistake." Not only had this murder intensified the royalist plots, it also spread what was equally painful to Napoleon: more of the sort of criticism that countered his carefully promoted image of high moral standards.

That was important to him for a specific reason. The plots against him had brought to the forefront of his attention the realization that, even though he had conquered most of Europe, he had no heir to carry on the empire he was building. His supporters in the French legislature saw the need to give permanence to the regime so that opponents would realize that even if Napoleon were assassinated, this government would continue. A plan was devised to make Napoleon *Emperor of France,* a hereditary title that could be assumed by Napoleon's son, if he should have one or legally adopt one. Alternatively, he could designate one of the male offspring of someone else in his family to succeed him.

There was a national plebiscite to confirm the plan. The vote was 3,572,329 in favor and 2,569 against. Napoleon would be proclaimed emperor, and by the end of the year he was going to be formally crowned by the pope. That meant the peccadilloes of his siblings would take on increased seriousness as the actions of a *royal* family, and it was imperative for all the Bonapartes to adhere to the highest levels of behavior, at least in public.

The prospective emperor had some cleaning up to do among his siblings and started by making an example of Lucien. His offense was the marriage he'd mentioned to Robert Patterson. A widower, Lucien had lived for several years with a woman named Alexandrine Jouberthon, and the previous May she had borne him a son. He loved her, so he married her in spite of his brother's disapproval. Napoleon had no objection to affairs, long-term mistresses, or even a multitude of mistresses, but marriage into a soon-to-be royal family was quite another thing, especially when he had planned for Lucien to strengthen the empire by marrying the widowed Queen of Etruria. Lucien's refusal to forsake this woman whom Napoleon considered a tramp made the offense enormous, and wiped out the younger brother's past contributions to Napoleon's success. Napoleon's rage was so great that Lucien found it necessary to flee the country.

There were even more derelictions within the family. One of the nation's new laws stated that a widow could not marry until a year and six weeks after her husband's death. Napoleon's favorite sister Pauline was widowed when her husband, General Victor Leclerc, died in a yellow fever epidemic, but she married again several months short of the prescribed mourning period. She had fallen in love with an Italian, Prince Camillo Borghese, or possibly with the famous Borghese diamonds, so she tied the knot too swiftly and found herself out of her older brother's favor.

As for Jerome, his crime was frolicking around America while his country needed him. When word finally came that the reason for Jerome's defection was a *woman*, the crime became virtually unforgivable.

Chapter 9

Running the Blockade

*N*one of the most recent Bonaparte news from Paris had reached Baltimore when, on March 19, 1804, Jerome wrote to his mother:

> *My letters by which I have announced to you my marriage, have no doubt reached you, my good Mama. It is news which will astonish you, but when you know my wife I hope you will approve of my choice. It is in this essential epoch of a man's life, my dear Mama, that one is drawn to it as to a destiny that cannot be avoided or foreseen. Assuredly I have not foreseen mine and I have not avoided it. I have given you some more particular details in my last letters, which are without doubt under your eyes. I will not speak of it further and I will await the occasion of presenting to you a dear wife and one who deserves to be it. I send you her portrait.*
>
> *M. de Maupertuis who has passed the winter with me, will deliver it to you, and as his intention is to return, if by chance I should still be in America, will bring me news of you and of your approval of my marriage; without which I could not be happy.*
>
> *Adieu, my good Mama, I embrace you with all my heart.*
>
> J. Bonaparte
>
> [P.S.] *I learn that Lucien is traveling, Paulette is at Rome, Louis at the waters; in your letters recall their brother Jerome to their thought and present to them the regards of my wife.*[1]

William Patterson had also gotten no information. The letters written by Robert and Paul Bentalou in mid-March did not reach

Baltimore until late May, and by mid-May William was writing again for news from Europe. The letter he had written to Ambassador Livingston at Paris on February 10 was not answered until June 20, and then it had to be sent across the ocean. Even then, all the letter said was that the Bonaparte family's plans might no longer include setting up Jerome in America.[2]

Most worrisome was the silence of Napoleon, along with the lack of orders for Jerome. For several months after the wedding, Chargé Pichon and Admiral Willaumez tried every argument to get Jerome to sail home on the admiral's repaired ship, *Poursuivante.* In response Jerome used several excuses: he was waiting to hear from his brother, he had promised his father-in-law not to leave America until he'd heard from his family, and so on. Finally out of patience, the admiral ordered the young lieutenant to get on board. Jerome angrily refused, saying he took orders from no one. Willaumez gave up and sailed for home the fourth week in March.

Finally, in April, Jerome heard from his superior in Paris by way of a hand-delivered letter brought to him by his aide, Lieutenant de Vaisseau Meyronnet. In this communication, dated February 18, Minister of Marine Denis Decrès relayed Napoleon's orders. There was no reprimand for the failure to come home in the chartered ship that had brought Meyronnet to France; apparently not traveling in a merchant ship that could be seized by Britain was a prudent enough choice. But now he must immediately make the voyage home in a French warship. Decrès said it was his brother's formal intention that under no pretext was Jerome's return to France to be accomplished on anything other than a French ship of war.

> You must, as soon as you receive this new letter, embark on this frigate in your grade of Lieutenant de Vaisseau, and fulfill all the functions following your rank, during the crossing. If the frigate "Poursuivante" is no longer in the United States, you must seize the occasion of the first frigate, well armed, to return here, as it will be against the instructions of the First Consul that you should let slip any such occasion, and that you should think of prolonging

> *your stay in the United States at this time, when great preparations*
> *for war are being made.*

Decrès added that the contents of this letter were being made known by the Lieutenant Meyronnet, whom the first consul ordered sent to the United States in order to bring Jerome back home.[3]

Meyronnet had left Philadelphia the previous August, so he had not known about the marriage that took place in December. Therefore the urgency of the minister of marine's order was simply a response to Jerome's absence from naval duty. There was no mention of Betsy, hence no ruling that she could not travel with him. Jerome decided he would find the nearest French frigate and order its captain to make room for him and his wife.

There was no French warship at Baltimore, so the couple set out for New York. On the way they enjoyed themselves. Philadelphia was always a good place to visit. From there they went across New Jersey to New York. A newspaper reported that Jerome Bonaparte and his lady arrived at New York City "in a coach and six, followed by his Secretary and Surgeon in a curricle and four, with numerous out-riders." [4]

They stayed in a home belonging to Mr. Magnitot, a former prefect of Santo Domingo, now living in the United States. The place had been rented for them by Victor Du Pont, and it was near Victor's town house in Greenwich Village. The young Bonapartes announced that they expected to spend several weeks in the city, so the Du Ponts planned a number of social events to entertain them. At one party they invited more than a hundred people to a dance at their home. Madame Victor Du Pont confided in a letter that she was worried about the expense and about the capacity of her house to accommodate so many. She praised Betsy; she was "as beautiful as an angel" and spoke French very well. Jerome, she added, had excellent horses, an impressive carriage, and servants in expensive livery, but she suspected that Jerome's showy equipage was designed to fix attention on his bank account.[5]

Since no French vessels had arrived at New York, the Bonapartes went back to Baltimore. After three days word came that two warships were anchored in New York harbor. The *Cybele* and the *Didon* had come to the United States bringing the French ambassador, General Turreau. Their orders were to carry Jerome back home on their return trip. Once again the young couple packed up and headed north, and this time Betsy's father, in a rare departure from home, went with them. Before they left Baltimore, Jerome asked Pichon for cash to cover the expenses in New York and for the Atlantic crossing. The chargé refused; in the *Didon's* diplomatic pouch he had received an order to provide no more money to Jerome. He suggested that young Bonaparte borrow the money from his father-in-law and leave his furniture, horses, and carriage with Patterson as security on the loan.

By now it was June 12. A New York paper reported the arrival of the young Bonapartes and noted that they attended the theater that night, along with the captains of *Cybele* and *Didon*. The next day Jerome and Betsy, with all their luggage, were rowed out to the warships and put on board the *Didon*. Its captain, Brouard, hoped to weigh anchor in the next couple of days. He chartered a pilot-boat and sent one of his officers out to see whether it was safe for the frigates to leave. The scout found there were two British ships, a corvette and a forty-four-gun frigate lying off Sandy Hook, as well as several heavier craft, farther off the coast. The next day two more ships appeared, one of them the heavily armed *Boston*. Captain Brouard decided it would be madness to risk a fight against such superior force. The French ships moved back into New York harbor and anchored. The young Bonapartes disembarked and returned to their lodgings. During the next three weeks, the newspapers published many rumors. One was a plan to sacrifice *Cybele* in order to get *Didon* through. The conclusion was that that would not work, they would lose both ships.

Apparently Napoleon had made up his mind about the marriage. In the sealed orders that went first to Pichon, then were sent back to the *Didon*, Captain Brouard learned that no French warship was permitted to take Betsy on board. At that, Jerome announced he would not leave without her. William Patterson went home, and the Bonapartes took off for an excursion to see more of America, because, Jerome said, whenever you visit a country you ought to see the sights, and he especially wanted to see the Great Falls of the Niagara.

When they left New York City, they took a boat up the Hudson River, a small sloop carrying some two dozen passengers. The fare was two dollars a person, and included "board and liquors." One of the stops was Albany, New York. Those who wanted to go to Niagara Falls got off there, then from Albany they went by stage to Utica, sixty-five miles away. At Utica the travelers obtained horses for the rest of the journey. Since the Niagara area was almost a complete wilderness, they had to pack provisions, carry them some seventy miles, and sleep on the ground. They were warned that even in warm weather a fire was necessary to keep away horseflies, mosquitoes, and the occasional bear. Later, when Betsy spoke of this, she relished the adventure.

The Bonapartes were quite possibly the first honeymoon couple to visit Niagara Falls. The other travelers who went there in the eighteenth and early nineteenth centuries were explorers, adventurers, travel writers, and wealthy young men endeavoring to see more of the world who often left vivid accounts of the trip. A few took a serious scientific interest and tried to take measurements, but the responses of most viewers ranged from helpless awe to inarticulate terror. One author spoke of having to struggle to free himself from "the spell cast by the falls." [6]

Travelers' accounts reported that the sound of the cataract was so tremendous it could be heard at a great distance, perhaps as much as twenty or even fifty miles away. Astonished travelers approaching the falls told of smothering white fog or huge white clouds like wood smoke. Standing too close to the mist caused the clothing to become drenched, and the spray boiling up was "hellish." Rapids rushed like a turbulent ocean for a distance of a hundred yards. The churning waters, the stunning noise, the mounting clouds were at once thrilling and hypnotic. Terrified, some travelers turned and ran. The French writer and statesman, Chateaubriand, banished from France and wandering in the forests of America, is said to have found God at Niagara Falls.[7]

From Niagara Falls the Bonapartes traveled to Boston, stopping at inns along the way. According to the *Boston Gazette,* on August 13 the Bonapartes accompanied the town's selectmen on the annual formal tour of Deer Island in the outer harbor. A few days later the paper announced that "Jerome and his fair spouse set out from this town on their return southward. During their short residence here, they have received every suitable mark of respect and attention. He will reside in Baltimore." [8]

During the months that followed the young couple tried repeatedly to get to France. In September arrangements were made for Jerome to go on a frigate while Betsy crossed the Atlantic with the new United States Ambassador to France, General Armstrong. Perhaps Armstrong thought better of his agreement to put himself as a new minister into the midst of a Bonaparte family quarrel. At any rate, his ship left several hours before Betsy arrived to board it. Even then he felt his position in Paris had been adversely affected by Jerome's American marriage. Betsy wrote her father with the news:

> *New York, September 5, 1804*
>
> *Dear Sir,*
>
> *We have made a journey here for nothing, as General Armstrong, the Ambassador, after writing to Mr. Bonaparte that he would be delighted at taking me to France with him, changed his mind and went off without me. Tomorrow we are to leave this place for Philadelphia, and from thence we go to Springfield* [the Patterson estate west of Baltimore] *immediately, so that as I shall see you soon, it is unnecessary to say any more.*
>
> *I thought the opportunity of going with an Ambassador too good to be missed, and Mr. Bonaparte was to have gone on the frigate a few days after me.*
>
> E.[9]

There were more attempts to cross the ocean. In October they embarked from Philadelphia in an American merchant vessel, only to be struck by a storm and wrecked as they sailed down Delaware Bay. Betsy, Jerome, Miss Spear, and other passengers had to leap from the deck into a lifeboat. The newspaper accounts say the passengers were nearly naked, and that Madame Bonaparte was the first person who jumped into the boat. They made it to shore and were taken to a nearby home to dry off. Betsy thought the whole thing was a lark. She horrified Miss Spear by wolfing down a big meal of roast goose and apple sauce, when she should have been down on her knees thanking God for their survival. Jerome claimed he'd lost all his money and their clothing in the shipwreck, and Miss Spear never again tried to cross the ocean.[10]

In December they managed to get aboard the *Presidente,* a French warship of forty-four guns moored at Annapolis. By now Pichon and Ambassador Turreau were desperate to get Jerome to go home. They were forced to compromise on the issue of Betsy's travel arrangements, so the couple boarded and the ship immediately weighed anchor and sailed into the Chesapeake. At Hampton Roads they found their way into the Atlantic blocked by British naval vessels, one of which had been disguised as a wreck to lure the French closer. The *Presidente* turned back to the port, and the Bonapartes went home to Baltimore. By then the winter weather was too severe for more attempts at ocean crossings.[11]

They moved into a house. In Betsy's notebooks there are lists of the furniture bought by Jerome. They also had formal invitations printed for the parties they gave, and among her souvenirs are invitations to and from friends such as Robert Gilmor. Nevertheless Jerome was becoming increasingly restless, especially in late February 1805, when news came of Napoleon's spectacular December 2 coronation as emperor, in the Cathedral of Notre Dame. Even more disconcerting was the news of his obedient brothers and sisters receiving titles and other honors. Jerome may have begun to feel he was missing too much; he wanted to go home.

William Patterson, ever a cautious man, had already begun

to plan for his daughter and son-in-law's possible return to France. In November 1804 he wrote to his agent Jonathan Jones in Bordeaux with instructions to set aside funds in case his daughter Mrs. Bonaparte should need them. He explained that they may be arriving in the south of France and that his son-in-law might find it necessary to go to Paris himself first and leave Betsy with Mr. Jones. He wrote:

> *Mr. Bonaparte has conducted himself with the utmost propriety ever since he became a member of my family, and justly merits my warmest attachment, indeed his general conduct in this country has been such as to gain esteem and friendship of every person with whom he has had the smallest acquaintance, and no stranger who has visited this country has ever been so much noticed and respected. Those qualities must necessarily render him very interesting to his country and more particularly to his own family, so that I hope and pray the latter may receive him with that warmth and friendship he deserves.*[12]

Further, Patterson had always said that when the time was right he would provide a suitable vessel for the journey, and when the weather improved in March of 1805, he did. He chartered an almost-new ship, the *Erin*, Captain Stevenson commanding. It was not spacious, but it was long, slim, and very fast, one of the swift schooners later known as Baltimore clippers. Most importantly, the *Erin* was capable of outrunning the British blockade.

By now, Betsy was six months pregnant. Certainly her parents would have urged her to wait at least until her child was born, but it wasn't her style to let herself be left behind. She did agree with her father's detailed instructions about where to go and what to do if they ran into trouble with the French authorities. He gave them to her in writing. If there was any difficulty at Lisbon, she was to head north to Amsterdam and wait there while her husband made arrangements for her to be recognized by his family. If by chance he did not succeed in this, she was to return to Baltimore immediately. He added:

In the meantime that you may be at no loss for money to bear your expenses at Amsterdam, you have herewith a letter of credit on my correspondents there Messrs. Severeyn & Haisebroeck for two thousand dollars equal to five thousand current guilders of Holland, which you can make use of as you may have occasion, and if more should be required in Holland than we have reason to expect, your brother Robert will furnish you with what may be necessary. [13]

In addition Patterson provisioned the *Erin*, because in those days ocean travel required passengers to provide for their own needs, everything from food to bedding. That meant Patterson had to put on board whatever was needed for Betsy, along with the companion no lady traveled without (in this instance, Mrs. Eliza Anderson), and Betsy's oldest brother, William Jr., as well as Jerome, his secretary Alexandre Le Camus, his physician, Dr. Garnier, and several servants. They boarded at Baltimore on Sunday morning, March 10. Two days later they passed out of the Chesapeake and headed for Europe. [14]

Captain Stevenson's journal describes a cheerful voyage, except for the seasickness suffered by Betsy and Jerome. They were not stopped by British ships looking for Jerome; they saw one cruiser, but easily outran it. The passengers spent their time playing games: Backgammon, Chit Chat, or Scandal. Captain Stevenson wrote, "We found Mr. B. quite an agreeable passenger, requiring very little attention, very familiar and extremely good humored." He also enjoyed the company of Le Camus, "a man of good understanding and agreeable manners. [15]

They made their destination, Lisbon, after just three weeks at sea. Since Portuguese vessels required forty days for the ocean crossing, the local authorities put incoming ships in quarantine for as long as it took to lengthen their journey to forty days. That meant nineteen days before Jerome and Betsy could go ashore, but Jerome wrote to his father-in-law that he was determined to make the local French chargé get around that. [16]

On Board of the Erin, the 2d April 1805.

I have the pleasure of writing you, dear father, from the arbous of Lisbon where we arrive this morning the 21st day of our departure from Cape Henry. We shall be obliged to perform a quarantine but I have already found the way for not doing it, and in three days I shall be ready to proceed on my long, monotonne, and fatiguing journey. My feelings for you, my second mother, and all your good family are very well known to you, and it is easier to feel them than to express them. I have left one of my family and will be soon among the other, but the pleasure and satisfaction of being in my first will never make me forget my second.

My dear wife has fortunately supported the fatigues of our voyage perfectly well. She has been very sick, but you know as well as anybody that sea-sick never killed no body.

I pray you, dear father, to do not forget me near my friends, and particularly General and Mrs. Smith and family, Nancy, Dallas, and Dr. McHenry, and remember that you solemnly promised me to never show my letters, and to burn them after having read it.

B

As was his habit, William Patterson endorsed the outside of the letter before filing it away. "Bonaparte, Lisbon, April 1805—received 15th of May."

By then, Betsy was already in trouble.

Chapter 10

The Emperor's Fury

*I*n February of 1805, Robert Patterson had written to his father that Napoleon had threatened to imprison Jerome.

> *Paris, February 16, 1805*
>
> *General Armstrong informs me that he saw a person yesterday who mentioned to him that the Emperor says that it was his determination to throw Jerome into prison the moment of his arrival, where he should remain till he repudiated his wife and married another which he would designate.*
>
> *The gentleman thinks from the decided manner in which he spoke, that he will certainly put his threats into execution. General Armstrong and myself are now of the opinion Jerome will only be safe by remaining where he is. Be on your guard when you receive advices different from other quarters.*

Robert had used the secret cipher the family employed for sensitive business correspondence, and didn't sign the letter, as if he was concerned about his own safety.[1]

Robert wrote again three weeks later, also in code: "Betsy ought by no means come to France. If she were, I think she would be fortunate in only being sent back. Report says that Lucien was arrested in Milan, and he is now confined in the hole there." He also reported that the arrival of *Le President* without Jerome may have prompted the following news item:

> *Paris 15 Ventose*
>
> *From and after the 11th of the present month, all the civil officers of the Empire are forbidden to suffer the transcription on their reg-*

isters, of the certificate of a pretended marriage which Mr. Jerome Bonaparte may have contracted in a foreign country, without the consent of his mother, and without the banns thereof being previously published in the place of his abode.[2]

Napoleon's Council of State had ordered that decree, but behind it lay the emperor's growing impatience with Jerome. That exasperation had exploded into one of his famous rages. Some historians believe these outbursts were not a loss of control but a contrived event to achieve a calculated response. Whatever the motivation, the victim in this case was the minister of marine, General Denis Decrès. The outburst had been set off when Decrès told Napoleon that Pichon had requested an allowance for Jerome's living expenses in America. As the emperor had ordered him to do, Decrés wrote a full account of his reaction and sent it to Chargé Pichon at Washington, along with a matching letter for Jerome. Hence there is a meticulous account of Napoleon's diatribe.[3]

We can imagine the small man strutting back and forth across his study in the Tuilleries Palace shouting, "No money shall be advanced to Citizen Jerome! He has received orders in his capacity of Lieutenant of the Fleet to come back to France by the first French frigate that was returning here; and the execution of this order can alone regain my affection!"

Decrès in his letter to Pichon reported that response, along with further instructions for him.

I am to order you to prohibit all Captains of French vessels from receiving on board the young person with whom the Citizen Jerome has connected himself, it being the Emperor's intention that she shall by no means come into France, and his will that should she arrive, she be not suffered to land but be sent back immediately to the United States.

Napoleon had raved on for a long time, saying that his youngest brother's marriage was a "camp one." It had no more validity than a pair of lovers swearing their fidelity in a garden under the moon and stars. The minister of marine was charged with transmitting all this information so that Pichon could persuade Jerome to mend his ways. Decrès told him to:

> *Represent to him the glorious career to which his destiny calls him, and that it requires of him a necessary sacrifice, due also to his interest, his personal glory, and the desires of the Hero to whom he has the honor to be related. Explain to him that having been absent for several years, he little knows his brother, whose inflexibility can be compared to nothing but the vastness of his conceptions. Cherishing profound and important meditations, he considers himself as having no family but the French people; everything unconnected with the glory and happiness of France is indifferent to him. In proportion as the Hero delights in exalting and honoring those of his relatives who participate in those sentiments with him, does he feel coldness for those who do not partake them, or who walk a different path from that which his genius has traced out for himself.*

During his rant, Napoleon had berated his family and declared: "Unwearied fabricator of my own glory, I bewail in secret that my example is not followed. I am indignant at the obstacles thrown in my way by what I consider to be their effeminacy." He went on to enumerate the achievements and failures of his brothers, adding:

> *As for Jerome, he has indiscreetly and rashly contracted a marriage contrary to our laws, he has abandoned the labors that the country requested of him, he has yielded to an irrational passion; but his youth shall not be suffered to plead his excuse. Ashamed of his indolence, too long protracted, let him seize the first occasion of returning to share these labors whereof he should have given an example, and he will recover his brother in the head of the state.*

In case there was any doubt in Pichon's mind, Decrès affirmed that Napoleon was in this respect *inflexible*:

> *Jerome is wrong, to fancy that he will find in me affections that will yield to his weakness; the relation in which I stand to him does not admit of parental condescension, for not possessing the authority of a father over him, I cannot feel for him a father's affection.*

Sole Fabricator of my destiny, I owe nothing to my broth-ers. In what I have done for glory, they have found means to reap for themselves an abundant harvest, but they must not on that account abandon the field where there is something to be reaped. They must not leave me deprived of the aid and services which I have a right to expect from them. They cease to be anything to me if they press not around my person, and if they follow a path that is opposite to mine.

He cited the example of Lucien.

If I require so much from those of my brothers, who have already rendered so many services, if I completely abandon him who in maturer years has thought proper to withdraw himself from my direction, what has Jerome to expect? So young, and as yet, only known by forgetfulness of his duties, assuredly if he does nothing for me, I see it decreed by fate that I ought to do nothing for him.

Minister of Marine Decrès ended this long letter with a few more arguments for Pichon to use in his effort to bring the willful young lieutenant into compliance with Napoleon's wishes, and he enclosed the extra copy for Pichon to give to Jerome.

Unfortunately, the letter took a very long time to reach its destination. The ship bringing it across the Atlantic was stopped and boarded by British naval officers. The dispatch was scanned and recognized to be of interest, so it was seized and sent to the Foreign Office in London for study. There they copied it, resealed the original, and eventually sent it on to Pichon. Somehow it fell into the hands of a printer in Halifax, who eventually published it. But even then many people, including Robert Patterson, considered it a forgery, and for a long time, the full truth about Napoleon's reaction to the American marriage remained unknown outside of the foreign services of France and Britain.[4]

The warnings contained in Robert Patterson's February and March letters, along with the notice forbidding notaries to register the marriage, and this letter from Denis Decrès, all arrived too late. Jerome and Betsy had already sailed for Europe.

At the beginning of April when the *Erin* anchored outside Lisbon, there was no immediate sign of trouble. Jerome ordered the French chargé for the port to get the quarantine shortened to five days. It appears the mere mention of the Bonaparte name performed miracles. The young couple and their companions went ashore and did what Jerome considered the necessary sightseeing. Betsy jotted in a small notebook: "7th of April visited the Church of St. Roche—saw a superb altar of 3 pictures done in mosaic. 8th of April, visited the Aqueduct." They also went shopping. Jerome bought household linens for Betsy, $180 worth of topazes, and a garnet necklace with matching earrings and bracelet. He had the clasp engraved with the word *"Fidelité."*[5]

Jerome was then forced to leave. Orders from Napoleon had been left at the various ports the couple might have chosen, and they were very strict. Napoleon was in Italy, and the youngest Bonaparte must present himself before him immediately, by way of a specific route: from Lisbon he must go to Barcelona, Perpignan, Toulouse, Grenoble, Turin, and thence to Napoleon's location southwest of Milan. Jerome was instructed that if he departed from this route, he would be arrested.

Before he left Jerome told Betsy that if she had any problem in Portugal, she was to set sail again, as her father had advised her to do, go north to Amsterdam in Holland and land there. Her brother William would see that she was settled somewhere safe, and her other brother Robert would probably join them. Jerome would find her and be with her again as soon as he could, certainly by early June. The lovers said farewell, and Jerome and Alexandre Le Camus set out. Betsy recorded the event in her notebook: "9th April, Mon mari est parti de Lisbon." Then she settled down to wait.[6]

―◦◦―

On their way through Portugal, the two travelers met old friends, the Permon family's daughter Laure and her husband General Andoche Junot, one of Napoleon's earliest and most faithful supporters. He was tall, fair-haired, battle-scarred, famously cool under fire, and now on his way to Lisbon to become the French ambassador to Portugal. For his service Napoleon had rewarded him with the title of Duc d'Abrantès. Years later, as the Duchesse d'Abrantès, Laure Junot wrote voluminous recollections of her life in Napoleon's court. In those *Memoires*, she recorded this meeting with Jerome at an inn on the way to Lisbon:

> *We asked him to lunch with us, and he did. I was struck with the great change in his manner. He was reserved, almost grave. The expression of his face, ordinarily lively and gay, had changed to one of sad thought-fulness. I almost didn't recognize him. We walked with him in the garden of the inn. Junot spoke to him with almost a paternal air, advising him not to resist the Emperor. But Jerome replied with noble firmness, "even admitting I was wrong to marry without his consent, is now the time I should be punished? And on whose head will it fall? On that of my poor innocent wife! A mortal blow to a creature who is as good as she is beautiful!" And he pulled out of his pocket a large miniature. It was the portrait of Madame Jerome Bonaparte. I saw a ravishing face. "You can imagine then," said Jerome, putting away this charming portrait, "if it is possible to abandon a person such as the one you have just seen, when to so ravishing a face are joined all the qualities which make a woman beloved."* [7]

Mme. Junot was also stuck by Betsy's marked resemblance to Napoleon's favorite sister, Pauline Bonaparte Borghese, often described as the most beautiful woman in Europe. Laure wondered whether the emperor would be able to resist this portrait of Betsy, but Junot, who knew Napoleon well, had no doubt that he would.

Back in Lisbon, the messenger sent by Napoleon to confront Betsy had no difficulty resisting her either. Louis-Barbé-Charles Serurier delivered the emperor's pronouncement that she would not be permitted to set foot on any territory controlled by France. She must return at once to America, and she must never use the emperor's name because she had no right to it. "However," he said, "if you return home and never try to use his name, he will give you an annual pension of 60,000 francs." That was about twelve thousand U.S. dollars, a generous sum in 1805, but Betsy was not impressed.

No doubt she drew herself up to her full (and very pregnant) four feet eleven and looked him in the eye. Her answer was brief: *"Tell your master I shall never relinquish a name he has made so famous."* When Serurier tried to reason with her, calling her *Miss Patterson,* she gave him another message to transmit: *"Tell him that Madame Bonaparte is ambitious and demands her rights as a member of the imperial family."* [8]

The *Erin* weighed anchor and headed north toward the Dutch port of Amsterdam and its outer harbor, the Texel. The trip was much worse than the Atlantic crossing had been; it took longer and the weather was bad. The voyagers arrived weary and almost completely out of provisions, even drinking water. Again Captain Stevenson recorded the events.

> We had a very tedious and uncomfortable passage, and were twenty-six days before we got to the Texel River. Having been off the harbor two or three days and not seeing any pilot, I determined to run the ship in without one, and with no little Risk and Anxiety. About 2 o'clock (on the 10th of May) we got around the point of the river in sight of the Shipping. And shortly a boat pushed off from the town and came alongside. . . .A pilot jumped out of the boat [took our helm] and instantly bore away for the anchoring ground. In a few minutes after, a shot was fired ahead of us by a Line of Battle Ship as a signal to bring us to. I asked the pilot if this was customary. He told me it was not. Yet no one suspected anything uncommon from it. We anchored.
>
> Shortly after we were at anchor a pilot boat passed close to the Ship and asked if we belonged to Baltimore. Yes. Do you come from Lisbon? Yes. Then said he, You must not come to Texel, and left us. Our old pilot now seemed to awaken as from a dream and was excessively frightened.[9]

The pilot, an elderly man, managed to explain that he'd forgotten the notice that had been posted three weeks earlier where the pilots gathered, giving a description of this ship and forbidding—

under the severest penalties—any pilot from going aboard her. Now he was afraid he would be hanged, unless his age excused him; then he would no doubt get a severe flogging and imprisonment.

About 5 o'clock, a boat came near the *Erin* and ordered the pilot to move her close to some French warships. She ended up between a sixty-four-gun ship-of-the-line on one side and a sloop of war on the other. Also, two boats were sent to row around the *Erin* all night. In the morning Captain Stevenson shouted to the pilot boat that they were out of supplies and were reduced to eating two-month-old salt beef and biscuit. The pilot boat paid them no attention. There was a gale blowing; the *Erin* was pitching about and got too close to the sloop of war. Someone on the sloop shouted that if they got close enough to touch the sloop, it would fire into them and take them to the bottom. They had now been in the Texel four days. Captain Stevenson's log continues:

> I must here observe that no one but the principal officers knew on what account we were thus treated and I learned after my return to Holland that it was a matter of great speculation among people what it could be owing to. Some imagined we had a full cargo of yellow fever. Others thought we were filled with combustibles to destroy the Dutch fleet and the alarms of some were so much heightened as to conceive we might have some designs of taking Holland. It never once entered the heads of those poor people that all this stir was only to prevent a man and wife from coming together.

Meanwhile, Robert was making efforts to assist on shore. He had learned of their departure from Lisbon and was awaiting their arrival in Amsterdam. As soon as the *Erin* arrived he tried to get on board, but was refused permission. He wrote a letter telling his brother William to direct the vessel north to the port of Emden, where Napoleon's control may not have been so complete, but the letter was never delivered.

Robert went for help to the U.S. consul for Amsterdam, Sylvanus Bourne, who in turn went to a Mr. Schimmelpennick, whose title was "Grand Pensionary for the Batavian Republic." Bourne drew attention to the existing treaty agreements between their two nations that guaranteed the security of American vessels in that port, but Schimmelpennick claimed he was unable to act in this instance. Bourne pointed out Betsy's "condition" and requested that fresh provisions be permitted on board, but again Schimmelpennick pleaded that he was powerless.

The situation on the *Erin* was becoming unbearable. William Patterson Jr. repeatedly urged Stevenson to lower a boat so that some of them could try to get away and obtain supplies, but the captain resisted, certain such a move would be observed and result in gunfire, or worse. He was right. When William Jr., Dr. Garnier, and four seamen got into a boat, cannon were aimed and the tapers lit. Seeing this, Garnier got back aboard so fast he threw himself over the side of the *Erin* and landed flat on the deck.

Still, there was a positive outcome. The commander of the port sent a boat to inquire as to the cause of the trouble. When Stevenson's description of their situation was reported to the commander, he sent word that their needs would be met. The next day a full supply of provisions was provided, including an assortment of wines and liquors. Then, later that day, Stevenson was given written instructions to leave the Texel as soon as the weather permitted and not to return as long as he had those passengers on board. On May 17, following the orders, Stevenson set sail on the first fair wind.

Chapter 11

The Question of an Heir

*O*rdered to Italy by Napoleon, Jerome departed to see his brother. As he traveled, he wrote to Betsy repeatedly. The first few notes were scribbled in pencil on slips of paper torn from his notebook and sent via mutual friends he met along the way. He urged her to take good care of herself and not to worry. He told her where he was, and even what time he was going to bed. She saved these notes and retraced the penciled words in ink.[1]

Later, in April 1805, he wrote a longer letter from the road, addressed to her simply as "Madame Jerome Bonaparte, Lisbon." Already he was concerned about his brother's attitude.

> *Finally we are on our way, my dear wife. Have no black misgivings. Have confidence in your husband. The worst thing that could happen to us would be to live quietly abroad, but when we are together aren't we certain to be happy? There are several things which I forbid you to do.*
>
> 1. *Don't cry because tears do no good and may do you much harm.*
>
> 2. *Take care not to receive visitors or make visits, and have someone always with you, either Mrs. Anderson, the doctor, or William.*
>
> 3. *See everything there is to see because one appears stupid when one comes out of a country without knowing its curiosities.*
>
> *I embrace you as I love you, and you know that I love you very much., JB* [2]

On April 19, Jerome wrote again, this time from Madrid. He addressed her under the name "Madame d'Albert" and sent the letter to Amsterdam.

> *I arrived here the day before yesterday, my good and much loved Elisa. The Emperor and all my family are at Milan where I have decided to go, but that will only prolong my trip ten days or two weeks, so that surely between the first and the fifteenth of June I will be with you. I hope, my dear wife, that everything will go well. At least I will do everything I should do, and after that will place my trust in God, and we will endure our misfortune if nothing is arranged.*
>
> *We will soon have a fine baby. He will bring us even closer and, whatever may happen, when we are together we will be happy. I must do my best with my brother. He is my Emperor and has always been a tender father to me. But after I have done my duty and have nothing to reproach myself with I will live, if it be necessary, withdrawn with my little family in no matter what corner of the world.*
>
> *I have only the highest praise of General Junot and the Ambassador at Madrid. They have assured me that everything will go well, that your family enjoyed the best reputation in France and that everyone is well disposed toward you and me.*
>
> *Goodbye my dear little wife. Don't exert yourself too much. Take care of our child. Take care of your own pretty self. Don't cry and remember that a miscarriage would be terrible for us.*
>
> *You love me, Elisa, I have complete confidence in you, have the same in me and we will soon be reunited.*[3]

On the third of May Jerome directed another letter to Amsterdam: "My good wife, I send you only a few words. We have just arrived at the foot of Mont Cenis. Tomorrow I will see the Emperor. Always remember that between the first and the fifteenth of June, I will be with you."[4]

Jerome's expectation of a meeting the next day with the emperor was not fulfilled. While he had been traveling, Napoleon had made his intentions clear in a letter to his mother, Letizia Bonaparte. He told her that Jerome had arrived at Lisbon with the woman with whom he was living, and that strict instructions had been given that he was to report to the emperor at once, or be subject to arrest.

> *Miss Patterson, who lives with him, took the precaution of bringing her brother with her. I gave orders that she is to be sent back to America. If she disobeys the orders I have given, and if she should go to Bordeaux or to Paris, she shall be taken to Amsterdam to be shipped back on the first American ship. I shall treat this young man severely if, in the one interview I will give him, he shows himself unworthy of the name he bears and if he persists in wishing to continue this liaison. If he is not disposed to wash away the dishonor with which he has soiled my name in abandoning his colors and his ship for a miserable woman, I shall give him up forever and perhaps I shall make an example of him which will teach young officers how sacred are their duties and the enormity of the crime they commit in deserting their flag for a woman.[5]*

When Jerome arrived at Napoleon's headquarters, he was refused entrance, given a letter from the emperor, and told to submit a written reply. Napoleon's letter was uncompromising.

> *Your union with Miss Patterson is null in the eyes of the Church as it is in the eyes of the law. Write to Miss Patterson to return to America. I will give her a pension of 60,000 francs on condition that she never, under any circumstances, bears my name, to which she has no right because of the nonexistence of her union. You tell her yourself that you have not been able and are not able to change the course of events.[6]*

At the same time Napoleon wrote to Lucien saying that Lucien's wife would never be recognized: "because her son might inherit the throne and the Emperor owes it to the dignity of his crown not to expose his immense inheritance to the offspring of a union made against his will." Lucien replied that he would never dishonor his wife and deprive his children of their legitimacy: "Rather than lower myself to such infamy, I am capable of destroying my son and my daughter with my own hand."[7]

Jerome's response, in contrast to Lucien's, was meek, perhaps because in his heart he knew he had done wrong by lying about his age to Betsy's family and had in fact been absent from the navy without leave. He seems to have written Napoleon an abject apology and a promise to make amends. Again the emperor responded in writing: "I have received your letter of this morning. There are no faults that you have committed which may not be effaced in my eyes by a sincere repentance." But Napoleon reaffirmed his position: "Your marriage is null, both in a religious and legal point of view. I will never acknowledge it. Write to Miss Patterson to return to the United States, and tell her it is not possible to give things another turn." [8]

Only then did Napoleon agree to see him. According to one account, the emperor greeted his youngest brother with: "So, sir, you are the first of the family who shamefully abandoned his post. It will require many splendid actions to wipe off that stain from your reputation. As to your love affair with your little girl, I do not regard it." [9]

Jerome had planned to throw himself at Napoleon's feet and get him to recognize his marriage, but obviously the emperor was adamant. He pointed out Jerome's debts, said he would be excluded from the line of succession, from honors and income, and would be forced to give up the luxuries he loved. There might even be a court-martial with the death penalty. Jerome gave in by letter on May 6, but he believed that a period of good behavior would enable him to change his brother's mind. [10]

Napoleon ordered Jerome to report immediately to the port of Genoa for naval duty. Then he wrote several triumphant notes. The ones to his mother and his sister Elisa instructed them to maintain contact with Jerome and urge him to keep his new promises. To Jerome's boss, Minister of Marine Decrès, he announced that Jerome had admitted his mistake, disavowed his wife, and swore to reform. Most significantly, he wrote to his minister of police, the formidable Joseph Fouché, who was hardworking, thorough, resourceful, and ruthless. His undercover agents spied on everything of interest to Napoleon, not to mention a few items of personal interest to Fouché. Now the emperor told this police chief spymaster that Jerome had become convinced his marriage was not valid and that he had given up his American mistress.[11]

These actions suggest that Jerome (and perhaps Betsy, since Fouché's undercover agents operated at times outside the borders of France) had been under surveillance. They also lend credence to Jerome's paranoid-sounding pleas to the Pattersons to destroy his letters and tell no one that he was writing to them. Consequently, after Jerome reported for duty aboard a ship in Genoa's harbor, he tried to send Betsy word by way of his friend Le Camus and his doctor Garnier rather than directly himself. Meanwhile the emperor's work to clean up Jerome's mess wasn't over. He wrote to Second Consul Cambacères regarding the illegality of Jerome's marriage. Cambacères was an authority on France's new laws, but he failed to support his sovereign's opinion; in his view, the marriage was legal. Undeterred, Napoleon wrote to Pope Pius VII on May 24:

> *I have spoken several times to Your Holiness about a young brother of nineteen, whom I had sent on a frigate to America, and who, after a stay of one month, was married in Baltimore, although a minor, to a Protestant, daughter of a merchant in the United States. He has just returned. He realizes his mistake. According to our laws the marriage is invalid. I have sent Miss Patterson, his so-called wife, back to America. A Spanish priest sufficiently forgot his duties to pronounce the benediction.*
>
> *I should like Your Holiness to issue a bull which would annul this marriage. I send Your Holiness various notes, among them one by Cardinal Caselli, which shed much light on the matter. It would be easy for me to break this marriage in Paris, since the Gallican Church considers these marriages as null. It would appear to me better to have it done at Rome, if only as an example to members of ruling families who might think of marrying Protestants. Will Your Holiness treat this confidentially?*
>
> *As soon as I learn that this will be done I shall have the civil dissolution proclaimed. It is important for France herself, that there should not be a Protestant woman so close to me; it is dangerous*

that a minor of nineteen, a distinguished youth, should be exposed to a seduction so contrary to our laws and social conventions.

At this point, I pray to God, Very Holy Father, that He will continue you for many years in the regulation and government of our Holy Mother Church.

Your devout son,

Napoleon [12]

It is said that the emperor sent with the letter a token of his esteem in the form of a jeweled gold tiara. If that is true, it had no effect, although the pope investigated the situation for several weeks.[13] He replied:

In the midst of the mass of business which overwhelms Us, We have made every effort and have gone to the greatest trouble to explore, Ourself, all the precedents, and, by the most careful research, to see if Our apostolic authority could furnish Us with some way of granting the request of Your Majesty, which, in view of its purpose, it would have been very agreeable to Us to support. But, from whatever way We have considered the matter, the result of Our study is that among all the reasons which have been suggested to Us, and all that We can imagine, there is not one that would permit us to satisfy Your Majesty, as We should wish to do.

The pontiff explained why the various reasons Napoleon had presented did not apply in this instance and were in fact "mutually destructive." He failed to mention that, far from being a forgetful Spanish priest, the man who married the couple was the highest official of the Catholic Church in the United States. He closed by assuring the emperor of his paternal affection for him, cautiously adding: "*Your Majesty is too just and too reasonable not to be aware of the grief which this causes Us, and to harbor any doubt as to Our desire to please, had it been possible to do so.*"[14]

Nevertheless, Napoleon's mind was made up. He would find a way to obliterate the marriage, and he soon began looking for a suitable *royal* wife for Jerome.

Once at sea off the Texel River, those aboard the *Erin* discussed their options. Robert Patterson's letter had never been delivered, so they were not aware that he recommended the port of Emden. They considered sailing to another Dutch or German port but feared they might encounter a reception similar to the one at Amsterdam. Betsy was by now into her eighth month, and she emphatically did not want to give birth at sea. They decided on England, the one place within reach where Napoleon's power was not felt. They anchored off Dover, and William Patterson Jr. went ashore to find them a place to stay. It was May 19, ten weeks since they left Baltimore. Captain Stevenson's log described their reception.

> The concourse of persons assembled to see Madame B. land was immense and it was with the greatest difficulty she could get as far as the carriage which was in waiting to take her to lodgings. Mrs. A. [Anderson] got lost in a choir of Military Gentlemen . . . and it was some time before she could join Mrs. B. A great crowd was collected likewise at the Inn door and even on the Stairs and Entry to get a sight of our fair countrywoman.[15]

A local paper, the *Courier*, reported the news of Betsy's arrival, commenting that "she is a pretty little woman, of a fair complexion, and if we may judge by the smiles on her countenance, was pleased with the crowd which had gathered to see her land." The *Courier* was even more impressed by the *Erin*, calling it "a beautiful little ship, about 200 tons, much like a West Indies packet, long and low, very clean and neat."[16]

The Dover representative of the London *Times* also reported the event.

> The sloop Erin, from Baltimore, came into our Roads last night, and it being understood that Mad. Eliza Bonaparte was on board, the public curiosity was greatly excited, and the pier heads and quays were crowded, anxiously awaiting the ship's entrance into the harbour. About three in the afternoon the Erin came in, and Mad. Bonaparte, accompanied by one of her countrywomen (Mrs Anderson), her brother, Mr. William Patterson, of Baltimore, Dr. Garnier, French physician, who attended her from America,

landed. . . . The Hon. Mr. Skeffington led Madame Bonaparte from the ship to her carriage, but the pressure of the crowd to get a sight of the fair American, was so great, that it was with difficulty he could put her into her carriage. She is about twenty, fair, with hazel eyes, and has a beautiful countenance. She appears far advanced in a situation to increase the number of Imperial relatives.[17]

This crush of spectators struggling for a glimpse of Betsy continued to be so great that Prime Minister Pitt was forced to send soldiers to protect her. Meanwhile, Captain Stevenson sailed his "beautiful little ship" back to Amsterdam to deliver the cargo he'd carried for that port. This time he had no difficulty transacting his business but learned to his sorrow that the elderly pilot who had helped them in the Texel had been jailed in a guard ship. There was nothing Stevenson could do but continue on his scheduled journey to other destinations.

Several years earlier, when Napoleon was originally put in charge of an army, the ruling directors of the time gave him the assignment of masterminding a proposed invasion of Britain. After a survey Napoleon had concluded the time wasn't right; France would first need to strengthen its navy. The invasion had not been abandoned, and as Captain Stevenson sailed on his way, he saw the result of Napoleon's plans: "I had a full view of the French troops encamped near Boulogne and the British on the heights of Dover, and thus situated have been for three years, waiting the order of a despot or two to meet and devour each other."[18]

In Dover, Betsy was exhausted. She and her whole party had been under great physical and emotional stress, and apparently insufficiently nourished, ever since they'd left Lisbon a month and a half earlier. Yet nothing could quench the curiosity her situation aroused in the English people. The day after her arrival in Dover, that "honourable Mr. Skeffington," who was a business associate of Betsy's father, wrote to ask if he might call the next day in order to present to Madame Bonaparte some important people: Lady Augusta Forbes, wife of Lord Forbes, Britain's commander-in-chief, and the Honorable General Hope, acting commander-in-chief during Lord Forbes' absence. He also pointed out that General Hope was "the brother of the Earl of Hopetown." But this businessman, in his highly formal way, was not totally insensitive. The note closed stating "Mr. Skeffington sincerely hopes that Madame Bonaparte experiences advantage from the tranquillity of her present residence. Everything that lies within the compass of Mr. Skeffington's ability may be commanded."[19]

The *Times* continued to cover the story, and didn't hesitate to add editorial comments as well.

> *The beautiful wife of Jerome Bonaparte, after being refused admittance into every port of Europe where the French influence degrades and dishonours humanity, has landed, with a part of her family, at Dover, in a state of pregnancy, under the protection of a great and generous people. This interesting lady, who has been the victim of imposture and ambition, will here receive all the rights of hospitality, and all the kind attentions of that consanguinity which, whatever may be the conduct of America, Great Britain will never forget, nor omit to exercise towards her with a parental hand. The contemptible Jerome was, for form's sake, made a prisoner at Lisbon. His treachery towards this lovely Unfortunate, will procure him an early pardon, and a Highness-ship, from the Imperial Swindler his brother.*[20]

After a brief rest in Dover, Betsy and her party traveled to London and checked into a hotel there. Even in the metropolis of London, her presence attracted attention. For example, Lady Frances Erskine wrote to a friend: "Mme. Jerome is in London. I have a great curiosity to see her and mean to visit her when I find out where she is. She must be very forlorn here without her husband."[21]

We don't know how Betsy dealt with these approaches by titled curiosity seekers, or how badly she may have been feeling during these last weeks of her pregnancy. We do know she avoided public places as much as possible, staying away from King's Theater, where she could have seen *The Merry Wives of Windsor,* or the Royal Theater at Covent Garden, where the celebrated Mrs. Adkins was playing the title role in *Rosine.* Despite Jerome's exhortation for her to see the sights of whatever country she was in, as far as we can tell she did not even take a drive to Kensington Gardens, where in good weather people showed off their best clothing, or to Rotten Row, where young dandies displayed their horsemanship. We do know that eventually she went to the Bank of England and there transacted some business. Her foray prompted a critical newspaper comment that compared her unfavorably with British royalty.

> *Yesterday morning Madame Bonaparte paid a visit to the Bank, accompanied by a Gentleman and a Lady. She was received with marked attention and politeness, and shown through the various offices. The name of the fair visitor becoming known, some hundreds of persons assembled to see her return to her carriage, which waited at the front of the building. The spectators were, however, greatly disappointed at not being permitted to see her face, which she concealed by her veil; and no sooner was she seated in her carriage, than the blinds were let down. With deference to the Lady (or her advisors on the occasion) we think she would not have appeared less amiable in the eyes of the Public had she been less fastidious; in which case she would only have imitated the most illustrious, as well as the most virtuous Family in the Kingdom.*[22]

A week later another column in the *Times* put a different spin on the story: "It would be ungallant to say that Madame Bonaparte kept her face veiled on this occasion because she was ashamed to show it in this country, in consideration of the connection she has formed." The anti-Bonaparte bitterness was understandable. As Captain Stevenson had noted, Napoleon's troops remained massed across the English Channel and were still threatening to invade. Thousands of Englishmen were forced to keep watch on their country's southern shores, burning bonfires at night lest the invasion came in darkness. In general, though, the London press was charitable to what they termed "this victim of Old Boney's tyranny."[23]

Betsy had sensed that attracting attention in Britain would

anger Napoleon, so she tried to be inconspicuous. She and her party moved out of the limelight of their London hotel and into rented lodgings in a suburb called Camberwell, across the river on the south bank of the Thames. There, during the morning of July 7, Betsy gave birth to a baby boy. She made sure there were plenty of witnesses, as if this were a royal birth. The record states:

> *These presents have been drawn up to witness that Mme Jerome Bonaparte, whose signature is hereto affixed, is happily delivered of a child, of the masculine sex, in perfect health, at Camberwell, Surrey, Kingdom of Great Britain, the 7th of July, 1805, at about ten minutes to eight in the morning.*
>
> *In witness of which, all those of us present at the said birth, have signed: Elisabeth Bonaparte, Charles Aveline, Han Horic, Elisa Anderson, Elisabeth Orton, Charlotte Crouch.*

The document was authenticated by Benjamin Lane of London, notary public of the king, present at the time, and his certification was attested to by the ambassador of the emperor of Austria and also by the ambassador of the Prussian king.[24]

The other Patterson brother, Robert, who had been unable to join his family members on the *Erin* at Amsterdam, had tracked them to England and joined them there. It was Robert who wrote their father to announce the baby's birth. He wrote that the baby was a fine, healthy boy and had already been vaccinated. Betsy had recovered quickly and was already feeling well enough to come downstairs. "We are still without any news from the continent. The vigilance of Jerome's friends will, I am very much afraid, completely prevent his hearing from us and we from him."[25]

They hoped news of the birth had reached Jerome, wherever he was. Certainly the London papers were read in Paris, and Betsy probably hoped the reports included the baby's name for Napoleon to see. Dauntless as ever, she had given her son the name she was certain he had a right to as a member of the imperial family. She called him *Jerome Napoleon Bonaparte.*

Chapter 12

A New Bonaparte

We have no record of Napoleon's reaction to the name Betsy chose for her son, but we know he read the British newspapers and found their criticisms irritating. Further, he would have already been angry because, instead of going home as he'd ordered, this stubborn girl was aiding his worst enemies by seeking refuge in England. There may never have been a chance that he would soften his attitude about Jerome's marriage, but in the emperor's view, Betsy's flight to Dover justified his rejection of her.[1]

Napoleon had other more urgent matters on his mind. He had annexed Genoa and crowned himself king of Italy. In addition, he was planning a major military campaign in central Europe and needed troops, so for the time being he wrote off the invasion of Britain and withdrew the last units from the west coast of France. In the autumn he fought a series of battles that culminated in his climactic December victory at Austerlitz. Except for the French defeat by the British navy at Trafalgar, 1805 was a very good year for Napoleon.

Yet, in the midst of all the campaigns, Napoleon never forgot his plans for Jerome. He was rewarding his obedient siblings with crowns, and now as he negotiated the treaties his victories made possible, he kept watching for a suitable principality and a royal bride for his youngest brother. Some accounts say his troops marched into battle singing a little ditty about winning a kingdom for *le petit frère.*

Meanwhile, Jerome was trying hard to comply with Napoleon's instructions. He reported for duty aboard a ship at Genoa and kept his promises by having no contact with his wife. Yet he was desperate for news of Betsy, and he longed for her to understand his predicament. He knew she would have gone from Lisbon to Amsterdam, so he sent his secretary Alexandre Le Camus to Holland to find her and show her the orders Napoleon had given him. Unfortunately, by the time Le Camus had arrived, the emperor's instructions had been carried out: the *Erin* had been turned away from the port of Amsterdam. No one, not even Betsy's brother Robert, knew where it had gone. Le Camus met with Robert but was afraid to let Jerome's letter from Napoleon out of his hands. At last he allowed Robert to read it and make notes before he hurried back to Genoa.[2] Robert read that the Christmas Eve wedding in Baltimore was in Napoleon's view invalid, both in French law and in the eyes of the Catholic Church (at least the French branch), and that the emperor would never acknowledge it. Jerome was to tell Miss Patterson that it was not possible to give the situation a different outcome; she was to go back home and never use the Bonaparte name. Jerome himself was expected to perform many brave deeds in an effort to remove the tarnish from his reputation.[2]

Robert Patterson was skeptical, so skeptical that he didn't bother to report this information to his father for several months.[3] He couldn't believe Jerome would ever agree to such an attack on his marriage. And, in a matter so intimate as the relationship between a husband and wife, why didn't Jerome write a letter himself? Why entrust someone else with so personal a message? The fear that Napoleon inspired could make anyone, even a good friend, into a Bonaparte agent. Consider what had happened to Paul Bentalou in Paris after he helped Robert by acting as an interpreter during that March 1804 visit to Lucien Bonaparte. The American war hero was arrested and dragged off to jail. The police even terrorized his French wife, and he was never told why.[4]

After that, Robert in his letters referred to his friend Bentalou as *poor B*_____. But at this moment Robert had a more pressing concern, finding his missing family members. Perhaps his quest was aided by Captain Stevenson's second visit to the Texel, which could have enabled Robert to learn they'd departed for Dover. Robert traveled to England and joined them.

When the family had been reunited and settled in Camberwell, they waited for word from Jerome, but none came. It wasn't owing to a lack of effort on Jerome's part. He knew by now that his wife was in England, and in mid-May he wrote to her himself, in spite of his brother's orders. The letter failed to reach her for more than three years.[5] It is possible the delay was caused by Betsy's determination to be as unobtrusive as possible. She seldom left Camberwell, and a London paper remarked, "Madame Jerome Bonaparte has seen very little company since her arrival in London."[6]

In any case, the only news the Pattersons received about Jerome came from those London papers. In June the *Times* said he had arrived in Genoa to report for duty on the frigate *Pomona* as its commander. A few days later a formal reception was held on board, at which Jerome's sister Princess Elisa and "other distinguished persons" were entertained. They were greeted on their arrival and departure by a double salute of artillery. The paper went on to say that Jerome had been reconciled with the emperor his brother and that Princess Elisa had "exerted herself very much to effect the reconciliation."[7]

Jerome was still trying to contact Betsy. His desperation moved him to approach an English noblewoman then in Genoa, the dowager Marchioness of Donegal. She listened sympathetically to his description of the predicament and promised to help, but apparently could do nothing until she returned to England and found out where Madame Jerome was staying. That didn't happen for another six weeks.

Betsy, while awaiting the birth of her child, tried to contact her husband by any means available. She wrote to Captain Bentalou, though she had no way of knowing whether he'd gotten his freedom. She explained that unhappy circumstances had forced her to go to England and begged him to forward to Jerome the letters she was enclosing for him.[8]

There was no reply, so she tried contacting Elisa Monroe, daughter of James Monroe. James Monroe and his family were in London, where James was now the American ambassador. During the years he had served as envoy to Paris, his daughter Elisa had gone to school with Napoleon's stepdaughter, Hortense Beauharnais, who was now married to another Bonaparte brother, Louis. It was possible Madame could get word to Jerome, so Betsy wrote to Elisa, who was at this time in Paris. Betsy reminded her that they'd met in Richmond and apologized for the intrusion. She explained the combination of circumstances that led her to England, and begged Miss Monroe to write to her with any news she could gather concerning Jerome. She also enclosed a letter with the hope it might be forwarded to him. Miss Monroe did give that letter to Hortense, but again there was no response.[9]

After her son's birth, on July 7, Betsy was even more anxious to get in touch with her husband. She decided to approach the independent Bonaparte brother, Lucien. The French wording of this missive didn't come easily. Her letter book shows she wrote three complete drafts, using various approaches, descriptions of her situation, and pleas for help. In the end, she sent all three, perhaps to different addresses. In contrast, the note she begged Lucien to transmit to Jerome was simple: "Please let me know your intentions concerning myself and your child." Again there was no response.[10]

The only direct communication she got from Genoa came from another unreliable source, Dr. Garnier. Betsy had been suspicious of him ever since, by claiming illness, he (like Chargé Pichon) had avoided attending her wedding.[11] During the voyage on the *Erin* Betsy must have made it clear she didn't want him to deliver her baby, because when Captain Stevenson left the group at Dover, Garnier sailed away with him. Now she and her brothers discounted the contents of the doctor's July 15 letter from Genoa, in which he addressed her at Camberwell as "Mrs. Anderson" and referred to Jerome as "Yoricke."[12]

Yet with the passage of time, what Garnier said turned out to be true:

Upon my arrival in France I learned that Mr. Yoricke was in Genoa, and I went to see him right away in order to tell him of all the strain and unpleasantness that you have suffered in your voyages. The pain and chagrin that this causes him defy expression; he is above all sorry that you should have chosen for your domicile the country where you are at this moment, which is . . . detrimental to the satisfactory resolution of your business, whose prospects you have rendered very poor through this decision. But this can be remedied, and for this reason Mr. Yoricke wishes you to return to your country as soon as your health permits, where you will receive news from him, news that I hope will be very satisfactory. His business on the continent requires that he remain there for a year or eighteen months. . . . He charges you to remain patient and to execute his orders with all the promptness possible.[13]

At the end of July, Alex Le Camus wrote to William Patterson Sr. back in Baltimore. He said that six weeks earlier he had committed to the American consul in Genoa a letter explaining the circumstances of "the separation of your daughter from Mr. Bonaparte." (If this item was actually sent, it never reached Patterson.) Le Camus went on to speak about his meeting with Robert in Amsterdam and said he had explained to him the actions of Mr. Bonaparte, the orders of the emperor, the consequences of an untimely opposition to them, and the plan of conduct to pursue. He said that Robert must have mentioned all these particulars, along with the instructions Jerome had received from his brother. He described how hard Jerome was trying to obey the emperor and how much he was suffering in the effort.

You know him too well, dear Sir, to misrepresent in the slightest degree his intention, and not to be persuaded that he will leave nothing undone to bring the Emperor to a reconciliation to which his happiness is so closely annexed. . . . Nothing is neglected on his part to prove him worthy of your confidence, attachment, and general esteem; but now too much precipitation would be fruitless, and operate nothing else but the ruin of your son-in-law. Your daughter has only to yield to the present, and expect a better time.

Le Camus said Jerome hoped Mr. Patterson would advise her not to reject the benevolence of the emperor—the 60,000 francs pension—because a refusal would offend him and destroy everything. He went on to say that when Madame was well enough to undertake a sea voyage, Jerome desired that she return to America until he succeeded in getting her recalled. She was to live in her own house as if she were expecting her husband at any moment. He would provide everything for that "momentary establishment." Le Camus warned that no one but Mrs. Patterson was to know about any of these arrangements. He added, "Jerome cannot write you at this moment" and that "this privation is very grievous to him. You will soon know the reasons of it."

Le Camus explained that Jerome had under his command a small squadron of five men-of-war and was going on a mission. He added: "If he is successful, he will ask his wife as a reward of his conduct." The letter ended, "Mr. Bonaparte kisses the children tenderly, and sends his love to the family."[14]

It does not appear that Patterson shared this information with his daughter and son in Camberwell. Maybe he, like Robert, was skeptical of a response coming from someone other than Jerome.

Le Camus' statements notwithstanding, Jerome continued trying to reach Betsy. Three weeks after the birth of his son he again defied Napoleon's instructions and wrote her four closely written pages. The letter begins with careful lines and ends in an almost illegible scrawl. He wrote: "You know with what regret I left you at Lisbon and God, who sees into my heart, knows that I live and breathe only for my wife. Undoubtedly, at this very moment I am a father." Jerome mentioned his encounter with Napoleon, and then declared:

> Only I, Elisa, when I shall have the happiness of holding you again in my arms, can give you an account of what occurred. But we must wait for the passage of time to give us what we cannot get by force. My brother is as good and as generous as he is great, and if political reasons force him at present to this conduct, the day will come when that will change.

> *Anyway, darling, you must, and this is the order, or*
> *the desire, of your husband, you must be patient. . . .*
> *all, my darling, be cautious; do not lose your temper, rem*
> *that every word you say against the Emperor, if you say any,*
> *will be carried back to him; I have enemies, but the Emperor*
> *is such a good father to me that we have everything to hope*
> *from his affection and generosity.*

Jerome wanted her to wait two months for a summons to France. If this didn't arrive, she was to return to America and take a house, with "a proper establishment."

> *I shall send you much news which you will have to keep to yourself,*
> *and do not let anyone except your mother know that I write you.*
> *Have confidence in your husband, be convinced that he breathes,*
> *dreams, works, only for you, yes, for you alone and our child. Each*
> *of you is the object of all my cares, of my anxiety and of all my*
> *affection, in sum, you are all I have in the world and for you and*
> *my child I would give my life. . . . I kiss you a thousand times, I*
> *love you more than ever, and I don't take one step, say one word*
> *or do one thing except for my wife.* [15]

Once again, whether due to a flawed postal service, or shipwreck, or possibly even Fouché's efficient secret police, the letter never arrived at Camberwell. Instead, it showed up in Baltimore, eight months later. So Betsy continued to wait through the summer of 1805, not having heard from Jerome since shortly after he left her in Lisbon, three and a half months earlier.

In August the Marchioness of Donegal was able to fulfill Jerome's request from June. She returned to England, but was unable to get to London, so she chose a friend to act for her: Miss Mary Berry, who lived at No. 8 Curzon Street in London. Miss Berry located Betsy in Camberwell and wrote to her there on Saturday, August 10.

> *I am commissioned by my friend the Dowager Marchioness of Donegal now at Tunbridge Wells to convey to you a message from your husband, and likewise to mention that he was quite well at Genoa on the 29th of June and that he was extremely well liked there. . . .*

*I will call upon you at Camberwell any morning next week you
like to appoint, and in the meantime can only assure you that you
may entirely rely upon the honour, the prudence of Lady Donegal,
and upon the sincere good intentions of, Madam, your obedient
servant, M. Berry.*[16]

Ten days later Barbara Donegal wrote to Betsy herself, express-
ing compassion for what she had been suffering. She affirmed her
desire to help in any way possible and promised secrecy, along
with the hope that they might meet when she was able to get up
to London. She assured Betsy that a message to Jerome could be
delivered through her without any risk to him, and that to do so
would give her pleasure.[17]

After Jerome's apparent silence, and the discouraging Garnier
letter, Betsy was deeply grateful for Lady Donegal's encouraging
words, and for Miss Berry's help as an intermediary. Nevertheless,
this news was six weeks old. Where was Jerome now, Betsy wondered, and what was his present situation?

Jerome was at sea with his little fleet. He'd been sent across
the Mediterranean to North Africa to harass British shipping and to
negotiate and pay the ransom for 231 Christian prisoners who'd been
captured and enslaved. He succeeded in doing that and was highly
praised. His next mission would be to join a large fleet charged with
harassing British shipping in the Atlantic from St. Helena to Green-
land. Commanding the fleet would be Admiral Willaumez, the man
Jerome had said "took no orders from anybody." While preparations
were being made for that mission, Jerome was given leave and chose
to spend the time in Paris, where he might obtain support from some
of his other family members. In everything he did, he was trying
to soften the emperor's resolve. He remained convinced that if he
worked hard enough his wife would be restored to him.

Not knowing Jerome's plan, the Pattersons at Camberwell
debated their options. Betsy's companion Eliza Anderson wanted
to go home. Brother William was off tending to the Patterson &
Sons business. Robert thought he ought to return to Paris to get
more information about Jerome's situation, but a lady such as his

sister could not be left alone in a foreign country. Besides, would his going to Paris infuriate Napoleon more? They had to make up their minds soon, before fall came and the weather prevented a journey across the ocean. They decided to keep their choices open by remaining in England until next spring and prevailed on Mrs. Anderson to stay with them.[18]

Meanwhile, in early August, one of Robert's associates, a Mr. O'Meally, noted in a business letter from Paris that Jerome was expected there the following week. A house was being fitted up for him, but he would not remain more than eight or ten days. Betsy's hopes lifted. With Jerome so close, surely he would contact her. But the days went by and no word came.

In fact, Mr. O'Meally's information was incorrect. Jerome didn't return from Algiers until August 31, so his leave didn't begin until sometime in September. However, outfitting that major mission for patrolling the Atlantic took longer than expected, and he remained in Paris through October.

Paul Bentalou had gotten out of the hands of the police and in spite of fear of another arrest, he continued trying to help the Pattersons. As he wrote, "Notwithstanding the persecution I have already experienced, I would brave all danger to act the part of the friend I profess to be." Earlier, on August 2, he had been sent letters from Betsy and Mr. Patterson Sr. to be given to Jerome if there was an opportunity. Now, in Paris on October 7, Bentalou sought out the house where Jerome was staying and knocked on the door. He was not admitted, but he was able to give the letters to Jerome's porter and went away satisfied that they would be placed in Jerome's hands.

Perhaps the letters did reach Jerome, because a woman Bentalou knew mentioned that she had seen Jerome the next evening at the home of a Bonaparte relative, and "He appeared extremely dejected and pensive; everybody took notice of it." Then a few days later a report came from another woman Bentalou described as being "much in our interest." She told him she'd been a guest at the home of one of the Bonaparte sisters. After a concert there, dancing was introduced. Jerome was pressed to take part. He selected Bentalou's friend as his partner and in the course of their conversation he spoke of his wife *"ma bonne,"* always calling her by that endearing name and relating occurrences of a most affecting nature. He commented that he would forever remember the shipwreck they had encountered together. The woman described Jerome's account: "How well on that trying occasion she did behave! How, when danger was over, he pressed her into his arms!" The woman went on to say that "among those who are perpetually in his company all agree in saying, that he is almost always talking about her, delighting in the recollection of her good qualities, and never mentions her name without saying, 'My wife! My dear little wife!'"

Since Bentalou had not heard from the Pattersons since August, he was afraid they might no longer be in England. He addressed this information about Jerome to "Robert Patterson, Esq., or in his absence, William Patterson Senior, Esq., Merchant, Baltimore" and entrusted it to the Paris office of American envoy General Armstrong. It was to be included in the next diplomatic pouch going to the United States.[19]

During Jerome's leave he was relatively free of his brother's supervision, because Napoleon was preoccupied with his military campaign. His army had crossed the Rhine and then the Danube, leading to a series of battles that required his attention.

Jerome took advantage of the emperor's absence to write Betsy several letters. The first of these was dated October 4 and addressed to her as "Madame Bonaparte, London."

> *My darling and beloved wife. . . . Life holds nothing for me without you and my son. We, my dear Elisa, will be separated a short time longer, but eventually our misery will end. Be calm, your husband will never abandon you. Well, darling, even if we do not become princes, we will live peacefully.*

Three days later he wrote again, repeating the information previously given by Le Camus: if she goes home, she is to live in her own place, keep four horses, and live in a suitable manner. He sent affectionate regards to her family and again urged secrecy.

Nevertheless my dear wife, count on me; I am doing what I should do, and I hope I shall achieve my purpose. . . . I am working and suffering only for you and my son. Let people say what they will. Farewell Elisa, I kiss you a thousand times. Best wishes to my brother Robert. Tell him that I wish my wife to be treated with all the kindness imaginable and that I place in his hands my whole life's happiness, my wife and my son.

On October 16 Jerome wrote again, assuring her:

Don't worry, my Elisa, after the war is over you will see your good husband again. . . . I have never had the fatal thought of leaving you, but I am acting as an honorable man, a brave and loyal soldier; I do without my wife, without my son, to fight a war and defend my country and after I have fulfilled the obligations of a brother of the Emperor, I shall fulfill those of a father and a husband.

He lamented that he'd been unable to embrace his son, but he wanted her to tell him, "Your father will always prefer you to distinctions, a fortune, and the glitter of high rank." He closed the letter with: "I kiss you a thousand times, I love you more than ever, and I don't take one step, say one word, or do one thing except for my wife." [20]

Soon Paris gossips were saying Jerome was scouring the shops seeking gifts for his wife. One rumor had it that one of his sisters was in a store and when her companion admired a dress on display, the sister said "that's for Jerome's wife." He had in fact commissioned one of the most sought-after fashion establishments to gather up the latest styles for shipment to her in England; to these he added many items he had chosen himself. By the time he was satisfied, his presents included ten dresses of exquisite fabrics trimmed with laces and embroidery, three hats, a variety of handmade personal linens and handkerchiefs, a box of jewels later called by those who saw them "elegant beyond description," a miniature of himself, and a thousand Louis d'Or (gold pieces worth a total of about fourteen hundred U.S. dollars). [21]

Jerome ordered his secretary to box all this up and send it to Betsy in London. Le Camus entrusted the boxes to Lady Elgin, who was in Paris seeking the release of her husband, a prisoner of war in France. She in turn sent the boxes to the London firm of Glennie and McKenzie.[22]

Betsy knew nothing of this. August passed, and then September. The "eight or ten days" of Jerome's brief stay in Paris, according to Mr. O'Meally's report, were long gone. Betsy felt truly abandoned, longed for her mother, and wanted to go home. Mrs. Anderson was probably delighted, and it is possible Robert had tired of his almost fruitless year-and-a-half mission regarding his sister's marriage. They decided to scrap their plan of spending the winter in England. Business associate James McIlhiny was charged with lining up a ship for the voyage. This would have to be done quickly, as it was almost too late to avoid the bad weather on the Atlantic.

Meanwhile, Jerome's gifts arrived at Glennie and McKenzie. One of the boxes rattled and workers in the office feared breakage, so they opened it to find the noise was caused by the gold coins. The casket of jewels and Jerome's miniature were in perfect condition. The other box, though, had suffered water damage on its trip across the English Channel. They were horrified to find the Paris fashions sopping wet. The wife of one of the partners, Mrs. McKenzie, volunteered to take them home and "put them to rights." She did. She dried the dresses and pressed out the wrinkles. The staff at Glennie and McKenzie were amazed. Now the gifts were ready to deliver to Madame Bonaparte.

It was too late. Mr. McIlhiny had arranged passage on the *Mars*, Captain Murphy commanding. The ship was much less comfortable than the *Erin*, with cramped cabin space, and not as swift, but it was sturdy enough for the coming Atlantic storms. At the end of September the group at Camberwell went down to Gravesend and boarded the *Mars*. A few days later Captain Murphy cleared the Downs, encountered favorable winds with little variation, and sailed for America.[23]

Chapter 13

The King of Westphalia

The Mars docked at Baltimore on November 14, 1805, after a very difficult six-week trip over an Atlantic pummeled by storms.[1] The preceding months in England had been trying as well because of the chronic frustration of not hearing directly from Jerome. Betsy and her brother Robert had become convinced he was virtually a prisoner, not necessarily under guard, but under continuous surveillance. It made sense not to devote any more time to this pointless waiting in England.

It was a joyful homecoming. Robert, having been abroad for more than a year and a half, longed to see again the woman he would marry next spring, Mary Ann Caton. Mrs. Anderson had come into an inheritance through the recent death of her uncle and was eager to attend to her financial matters. As for Betsy, she yearned to embrace Dorcas and place her four-month-old baby into his grandmother's arms.

Jerome, according to his associates Alexandre Le Camus and Dr. Garnier, had instructed her to set up a home appropriate for his arrival, but he had not as yet succeeded in giving her the money to do that. So Betsy and her child were added to an already full Patterson household. The older brothers were still bachelors and, when they were in town, lived under William Patterson's roof. In addition there were two teenage boys and six younger children ranging from one-year-old Mary Ann Jeromia to twelve-year-old Margaret.

After the first happy greetings, it became clear there was a chill in the air, and it was emanating from her father. In his eyes, Betsy was guilty of what he considered an almost unforgivable offense: her stubbornness had resulted in a very expensive invest-ment that had gone bad. He reasoned that he'd been against this marriage from the beginning. When his efforts to prevent the union failed, he had given it his full support, cash on deposit in French, Dutch, and English ports, the personal services of his first and second sons, a fully outfitted chartered ship, and the list went on. He had receipts for everything, down to the $290.91 for food put aboard the *Erin*, including casks of cider and porter for the voyage.

And that wasn't the worst of it. The most egregious offenses had been committed by this willful girl's choice of a husband. Jerome had left town owing money that Patterson felt obligated to pay in order to protect the reputation of his family and of himself as an honorable business man. So he had paid Jerome's shoemaker's bill, his tailor's bill, the rent on a stable for his first-class carriage horses along with a bill for shoeing all four of them, and $373.33 to the maker of a double-barrel gun and a pair of pistols.

Worst of all, back in 1804 when Jerome chartered the ulti-mately wrecked *Philadelphia* for a failed attempt to get to Europe, he'd bought fifty suits of clothes and two hundred pairs of shoes for the ship's crew. Perhaps that was a bribe to overcome the captain's reluctance to cross the ocean in October. At any rate, the captain sailed, wrecked, and eventually charged Jerome for the cost of the entire ship. Patterson's lawyer disposed of that last claim, but payment for the sailors' clothing remained due and required more than five hundred dollars in cash. It took months to clear up the mess, and Patterson stored up his anger along with the pile of receipted bills.[2]

Even with all those charges the Baltimore merchant was lucky. Later, when Jerome left Paris for Westphalia late in 1807, he owed around town some two million francs (about forty thousand dollars) that Napoleon felt obliged to pay for reasons of credibility and family honor.[3]

There was nothing Betsy could do but endure the atmospheric chill in the house on South Street. Patterson's correspondence and later, the will to his estate, show that for him a man's worth was literally measured in money and the way money was handled. So Betsy in her present situation was powerless to change his attitude toward her, and, although she adored her mother, she longed for her father's approval. Her letters to him throughout his life show her continuous attempts to impress him with her thrift and wise management. In addition we know how she felt because she developed a lifelong habit of rereading letters she'd received and writing comments on them. Regarding this period in her life she wrote that Jerome had so far sent her nothing and added, "Money would have been the lever to raise in my domestic circle respect, sympathy, affection; all of which were withheld from, and needed by, the victim of the policy of the Emperor."[4]

When spring came and better weather allowed ships to arrive from Europe, James McIlhiny from London forwarded to her in care of William Patterson & Sons a gracious letter from Lady Elgin and two boxes of gifts. These contained an entire Paris wardrobe, stunning jewels, and a thousand guineas in gold.[5] That last item could have been her freedom to move out and set up the proper establishment her husband had written about, but her father kept half the money. In his mind he had a right to all of it, and more, especially since he was providing a home for Betsy and her child, but he gave her half of the approximately fourteen hundred dollars worth of gold pieces and no doubt felt he was being generous. Eventually Patterson appropriated much of the furniture and china Jerome had bought for Betsy, as well as his horses and carriage. These actions also were recorded in her letter comments: "Jerome remitted to me through England one thousand guineas of which Mr. W. Patterson kept half."[6] Betsy recorded her father's handling of many of Jerome's gifts: "he sold to his own profit horses, carriages, serving to furnish his house at Cold Stream with plate, china, glass, tables, carpets, chairs, beds, etc. etc., all that had been left at Baltimore by his imperial son-in-law."[7]

Throughout the first half of 1806, letters from Jerome arrived in Baltimore. The ones he'd written from Paris six months earlier came to her in April, followed by several written later aboard his ship and sent from various ports. Sometimes he entrusted them to individuals he met along the way, because he continued to feel under surveillance. Jerome's November 21, 1805, letter from Nantes warned that when she wrote to him, she must be sure to send the letters to her father's agents in Europe with instructions to forward them, not addressed to him, but to his steward M. Duchambon at Rue Cerruti in Paris. In that same letter Jerome told her he had sent her another box of Paris clothing by way of a friend of Robert's, a Mr. Wyer, and a watch for her father via the captain of the *Destiny*, bound for New York. Jerome said he was on his way to Brest to take command of a squadron. His flagship was to be the eighty-gun *Veteran*.

> *I hope to succeed in my expedition. You know that the purpose of all my efforts, of all my cares, of all my worries, is to see again my good Elisa, my dear little wife, without whom I cannot live and my fine Napoleon Jerome, as we should call our son. If you could imagine how I worry about something happening to him. Take the best care of him, dear wife; the time is not far off when we will all be reunited, and be well assured that I will refuse to be heir to the Empire were I forced to lose my wife.*[8]

In a letter of May 1806 he wrote that he'd just arrived at Cayenne in French Guiana, and although his ship was four leagues (about twelve miles) from land, he'd gone ashore to find a way to get a message to her. Jerome had looked up the captain of an American schooner in port and was delighted to find the man knew the Pattersons and had seen Betsy and her son three days before he sailed. "Imagine my delight," Jerome wrote, "This is the first moment of happiness since I left you."

The American captain told him that her father had been very disturbed by their separation. Jerome was puzzled. He could not believe that none of his letters had reached her. Any one of them would have removed all doubt about his fidelity to her. "Do you believe, my dear wife, that if I had renounced you I would be in command of one of His Majesty's ships?" He explained that, for an ordinary officer this commission was good, especially at his age, but for Jerome, who by a single word could have been and still could be anything, what kind of a job was it?

> *Be assured, my good Elisa, that if I had wished to separate myself from you and my son who are the objects of all my affection, be assured, I say, that after all I have had to put up with, I should already have done so, and, at the moment that I write you, instead of being a subject I would have been a king.*

In contrast to Jerome's commission, his brother Louis and his wife Hortense Beauharnais had been made the king and queen of Holland, and brother Joseph was made king of Naples. Joseph would later be made king of Spain. Jerome went on with many more affirmations of his devotion: "Let the silly girls and the evil tongues of Baltimore say what they please and rejoice in your happiness, because it is a great happiness to be loved as you are." He assured her that the only reason he would desire a crown would be so that he might give it to her. Again he warned it was essential to keep strict secrecy about his letters. Jerome closed by saying: "Farewell my dear wife; I embrace you and my son with all my heart and I love you both with all my soul."[9]

Betsy made English translations of all his letters and copied them into a small notebook. She read them repeatedly, poring over his words: "If we don't become princes, we will live peacefully. . . . We will be separated for a short time longer, but eventually our misery will end. . . . I have never had the fatal thought of abandoning you. . . . After I have fulfilled the obligations of a brother of the Emperor, I shall fulfill those of a father and husband. . . . After the war is over, you will see your husband again." But the war had been going on for years. When would it end? How could she endure so long?[10]

Encouragement came from another business associate of her father's. In a letter from New York, William Neilson Jr. wrote that he'd made a call upon a ship captain who entered into a conversation about Patterson's son-in-law. The man said he'd dined with Jerome several times, and that "at all times he expressed great affection for your daughter. He spoke publicly of his determination of adhering strictly to his marriage; and that he would not be considered a French-man if his wife was not considered a French-*woman*." [11]

Then an ominous chord sounded in June, when Jerome wrote to her from the West Indies. He confessed his regret that she had left Holland. Back then, he said, Napoleon had relented and she was going to be received at Amsterdam as the wife of the emperor's brother. "Your departure for England was the only cause of our separation. However, my beloved wife, I hope that nevertheless it will not last much longer." Jerome failed to explain what else she could have done when ordered out of the Texel. [12]

After that, his squadron's patrol of the Atlantic took him northward and closer to Betsy. Her brother Robert, then in Boston, wrote home about the rumored nearness of Jerome, adding "He may be with you even as I write." [13] Jerome also wrote a few lines about his nearness to her.

> Just a word, my dear and beloved Elisa. I am well and filled with regret at being only 150 leagues from you without having the happiness of seeing you. I embrace you with all my heart. Kiss Napoleon for me and my compliments to your family. [14]

His previous letters usually opened with some term of affection for his "dear little wife," ended with love to her and often to her family as well, and were signed "Your loving husband" and his first name. In contrast, this one had no salutation and ended simply "J. Bonaparte." And even though some of his letters had been delayed and others were never delivered at all, he had been writing her fairly consistently throughout the sixteen months since he left her at Lisbon. Now the letters stopped. After that, there were only rumors.

That summer was a busy time for Betsy's family. Two weddings took place that must have been very satisfactory to her father. Her brother John married Mary Buchanan Nicholas, called "Polly." Her father, Wilson Cary Nicholas, was the governor of Virginia. Robert married Mary Ann Caton, granddaughter of that first-richest Marylander, Charles Carroll of Carrollton. The ceremony, like Betsy's, was performed by Bishop Carroll.

Betsy tried to remain busy, but outside of the home, nothing much was going on in Baltimore. The cornerstone was laid for the new Catholic Cathedral, which was to be built according to the neoclassical plans of Benjamin Henry Latrobe. Maximilian Godefroy (who would become the second husband of Betsy's friend Eliza Anderson) had designed the new St. Mary's chapel. It would be a small gem, the first Gothic Revival building in the country.

According to the national news, the Lewis and Clark expedition had come to a successful end. After a journey lasting twenty-eight months and covering seven thousand miles, the explorers had appeared at St. Louis. But the only news Betsy was truly interested in was from Europe, and that was slow in arriving. She spent her time caring for her son, helping around the house, and worrying. A traveler named John Melish noted her presence in Baltimore in 1806. He said that on the way to the coffee-house, his friend "pointed out, through a window, a very handsome lady with her child, who he informed me were the wife and child of Jerome Bonaparte." [15]

Desperate for word of her husband, Betsy started visiting Washington, where diplomats received news from Europe and sometimes gossiped about it.

After his stunning victory over the Austrians and their allies at Austerlitz late the previous year, Napoleon set to work redrawing the map of central Europe. In the Treaty of Presburg, in March 1806, Napoleon took large territories from the Austrian empire and distributed them to those who had sided with him. He made Bavaria into a separate country allied with France. He enlarged the lands of

Württemberg, made its elector, Frederick, into a king, and turned that little nation into a French satellite. That action made Frederick's daughter Catherine a royal princess, and a suitable bride for Jerome. She was young, amiable, attractive in a low-key way, and raised to be obedient to her father. She was also related to several of the royal families of Europe. Best of all, she was a cousin of Czar Alexander, who was at that time among France's enemies.

Although now a properly pliant servant of France, Frederick I, new king of Württemberg, had misgivings about the proposed marriage. Everyone knew that Jerome already had a wife. Though Frederick, a Protestant, was not against divorce, others were. Consequently, Napoleon was forced to pause in his war-making long enough to clear up this complication in his plans. Years earlier, he had made a deal with the Vatican called the Concordat of 1801. This restored to Catholicism the status of official religion of France. Although it did not return to the papacy the property seized during the French Revolution, it did promise compensation would be paid. The agreement also gave Napoleon some control over the appointment of bishops and allowed him to have an ecclesiastical court at Paris. Since the pope had declared himself unable to annul Jerome's American marriage, Napoleon turned to that Paris ecclesiastical court for help.

The first step was to present a petition from Napoleon's mother, Madame Mère, requesting the cancellation of her youngest son's marriage on the grounds that he was a minor who had wed without parental consent. The process took several months, but in October 1806 the court announced its nullification of the presumed marriage three years earlier between Jerome Bonaparte and Miss Elizabeth Patterson on the grounds that it was irregularly and improperly celebrated.

When at last Jerome came home from his patrol of the Atlantic, he was greeted as a hero. Napoleon raised him to the rank of rear admiral, made him a prince of the realm, and officially designated him a *royal highness*. Then he was handed a marriage contract to sign.

Jerome balked. He said he couldn't get married. When pressed, he said he needed much more military experience. So Napoleon took him out of the navy, put him into the army, and sent him off to Germany in charge of the Bavarian Division in the fight against Prussia.

~

Back in Baltimore, Betsy was restless to get out of town. For at least part of the year, her Uncle Sam Smith took a house near Capitol Hill, so when she went to Washington she could stay with her Aunt Margaret. Miss Spear was there too, frequenting the gallery of Congress. Miss Spear was not an attractive woman according to the taste of the time; she was much too tall and considered ungainly. But she was clever and witty, so she was a welcome party guest, and she seemed happy to chaperone Betsy around town.

Since President Jefferson was a widower, the wife of his secretary of state acted as his part-time hostess. That was the famous Dolley Madison. She was genuinely democratic, accepting people as individuals, not members of a class, rank, or station. Although it offended some of the foreign diplomatic corps to find themselves sitting at table next to a haberdasher or a file clerk, Dolley was consistent in her principles. She also refused to be swayed by prevailing trends. She wore what pleased her, but because of her good fashion sense, she became a trendsetter in spite of herself.

Dolley's influence was felt in other ways as well. During her early years in Washington she determined to dine at a local place called the Oyster House. Aides tried to talk her out of it. The bar and restaurant was raucous and no place for a lady. Women who went there were described as "prostitutes from Baltimore." But Dolley was insistent, so the owner was warned she would be dining there and he saw to it that the establishment was cleaned up in every way. After that, all the ladies wanted to go to the Oyster House, and the character of the business completely changed.[16]

That was typical of the way Dolley got things done: gently. When Jefferson's second term ended, Madison was elected and

Dolley became the official first lady. When she observed non-public areas of the presidential mansion in need of repair, she was appalled, but she didn't make a fuss. She simply invited a group of senators and congressman to take a tour of the place. When they saw how rundown it was, they got to work and appropriated money for the repairs.

During the legislative session from the fall of 1806 into the spring of 1807, Dolley was very kind to Betsy. Since the latter's aim was to learn news about Europe from foreign diplomats, Dolley's highly prized dinner invitations were a blessing. Their friendship would last for years, during which they consulted each other about symptoms and shared recipes for home remedies, with Dolley addressing Betsy as "my precious friend." In one of those letters she thanked Betsy for information about a remedy for rheumatism by saying, "I flatter myself that there is a degree of sympathy between us, because you offer me the antidote at the very moment of my suffering." Dolley was feeling much better now, but she wasn't sure whether it was because of Betsy's advice or simply her benevolence, "the magic in kindness which sometimes is of more avail than ten Physicians." [17]

Throughout that period, rumors circulated that Napoleon was trying to arrange a second marriage for Jerome. Betsy just could not believe that Jerome would give her up. Then a disturbing newspaper report arrived from Paris, claiming that the American marriage had been annulled. Augustus John Foster, at that time secretary to the British legation, wrote to his mother in England about the effect the news had on Betsy.

> *Madame Jerome Bonaparte is in great distress at Jerome's divorce. She goes no longer out. She said before he had sent her a great many presents and desired her to go to all amusements. She lives in Baltimore some 45 miles from here. The ill-natured Americans don't pity her. They say she deserved it for her vanity, and yet not one but had done the same.* [18]

Additional news was hard to obtain. Most of the talk that

summer was about a possible war. On June 22, 1807, the U.S. Frigate *Chesapeake* had been attacked off Norfolk by the British warship *Leopard*. Three American seamen were killed and eighteen wounded. Then the British boarded and took four seamen into custody on the grounds that they were deserters from the British navy. In time, three of the four were found to be innocent.[19] Belicose challenges between nations at sea were not a recent phenomenon. Although both the French and the British, in their military and economic battles with each other, harassed international shipping, Britain was the worst. In their navy men were poorly paid and treated harshly. Recruitment lagged and replacements were needed, so they took sailors off American warships and impressed them into the British service. Outraged Americans wanted to fight a second American Revolution.

But what of Jerome? The French ambassador, General Turreau, would give no information but persisted in referring to Betsy as "*Mademoiselle Patterson.*" One of the rumors circulating around town said Napoleon had tried to arrange a marriage for his youngest brother with the widowed Queen of Etruria, but she refused, saying she'd rather give up her crown than marry Jerome Bonaparte. For Betsy the divorce itself was disheartening enough, but the thought of Jerome marrying someone else, after all he had said, was beyond comprehension. The only reliable news was that he was off fighting somewhere. No reports about a second marriage were published. She determined to maintain her confidence in his love. Her father disagreed and wrote to his friend (and now an in-law) Wilson Cary Nicholas:

> You may have seen by the last accounts from France, published in the news-papers, that Jerome Bonaparte was restored to favor by his brother; and that a second marriage had, or was about to take place. We have no information on this subject but what appears in the papers, but I am led to believe that it must be well founded; for I do not conceive that the Emperor would be reconciled to Jerome on any other terms. It differs however very widely from his letters to Betsy when he was lately on our coast; and from every other

part of his conduct since he left this country. But the temptation,
in the situation he was placed in, was perhaps too great for him,
or any other young man, to resist. [20]

⟶⟨∽⟩⟵

In July 1807 an unusual meeting took place on a raft in the middle of the Niemen River along the border between Poland and Russia. Napoleon had succeeded in adding Prussia to his list of conquests and had overwhelmed the Russians at Friedland. The purpose of the meeting was to decide how the emperor of France and the czar of Russia could work out their differences and come up with a treaty that would cement their new alliance. The result was the Treaty of Tilsit. Prussia had to admit defeat and pay heavy reparations. The czar and the emperor also set limits on their individual spheres of influence and agreed on new boundaries in Europe. That last item had a direct effect on Jerome.

When Napoleon once again began rearranging nations, he took pieces from Prussia and other sections of Germany and used them to create a new country called Westphalia, east of present-day Belgium and Holland. When Jerome came home from his campaign, which consisted of the siege of Glogau and the invasion of Silesia, his brother promoted him again, this time to the rank of general of division. In addition, Napoleon said his brother was going to have a kingdom. Jerome was proclaimed king of Westphalia on July 7, 1807, two days after his son's second birthday. Along with that new title came another: Princess Fredericka Catherine Sophia Dorothea of Württemberg would now be queen of Westphalia. And of course they would have to be married.

Taking no chances that Jerome would balk again, Napoleon had had a formal betrothal ceremony performed with one of his most faithful generals, Marshall Jean-Baptiste Bessières, standing in as Jerome's proxy. At this point, Princess Catherine was on her way into France. Jerome would travel to Raincy, the Junots' country estate outside Paris, and meet her there for the first time. Laure Permon Junot, in her *Memoires of the Duchesse d'Abrantès,* describes how dismayed she was when she saw this princess for the first time. Laure couldn't help remembering her meeting with Jerome after he'd left his wife at Lisbon, how he had shown her the miniature and said he could never give her up. Laure wrote, "I involuntarily thought of that young victim, who was said to be so beautiful, who was so affectionate and who had a child." Laure also excused from her own entourage at Raincy a woman named Madame Lallemand who had known Betsy and Jerome in America, lest her presence cause him unhappy memories.

According to Laure, the princess was not pretty in the usual sense of the word, although her features were good. Her form might have been graceful "had her neck, and indeed her whole figure, been something less short." Her complexion was quite fair and fresh, her eyes blue, her teeth very white, but she seemed stiff and haughty, and maintained "an expression of dignified pride." But gradually Laure realized that the coldness and hauteur of her manner were caused by fear. This poor woman had been torn from her family and her home to come into a strange country alone because Napoleon had ordered that all her attendants must be stopped at the border and sent back; he would have only French people in her train.

> When the Princess came into the drawing-room half an hour before dinner-time I felt some regret that no one had had the courage to recommend to her a different style of dress. She was about to have a first interview with a man on whom was to depend the happiness of her future life, and whose youthful imagination, poetical as is natural to the natives of the South, could adorn an absent object with additional charms; while Madame Jerome Bonaparte, without the aid of imagination, was really a charming woman. . . . It was certain he regretted his divorced wife, for Miss Patterson really was his wife, and it would have been politic to appear before him with all the advantages dress could bestow, while, on the contrary, hers was in inconceivably bad taste.

Catherine's white moiré dress had gone out of style years earlier. It was very tight, badly embroidered, with a little train "exactly resembling the round tail of the beaver, and tight flat sleeves, compressing the arm above the elbow like a bandage after blood-letting." Around her neck she wore two strands of fine pearls, but suspended from them was a medallion containing Jerome's picture surrounded by diamonds. The medallion was so large that it inflicted heavy blows with every movement.

As the time drew close for Jerome's arrival Laure noticed that Princess Catherine seemed very agitated, and she asked if there was anything she could do for her. The princess confided that she would like a few minutes notice before the prince came so she could compose herself. Laure went out to watch for him, and the moment she saw a cloud of dust rise on the road to Paris, she ran back into the house to alert her guest. When Prince Jerome entered, he was accompanied by members of his household, among them Alexandre Le Camus, who, Laure wrote, "already possessed great influence over him, and who felt it advisable not to lose sight of him on an occasion to which his advice had given rise, and which might prove important to his future career." Laure did not believe Jerome would ever have abandoned his American wife "if he had not been urged to it by counsels which he had not strength of mind enough to resist."

On the prince's entrance Catherine rose, advanced two steps toward him, and greeted him with grace and dignity. Laure says Jerome bowed neither well nor ill, but somewhat mechanically, and he seemed to be there because he had been told "You must go." He approached the princess, who seemed at this moment to have recovered all her presence of mind and all the calm dignity of the woman and the princess. After the exchange of a few words she offered the prince an armchair, which had been placed near her, and a conversation was opened upon the subject of her journey. It was short and closed by Jerome's rising and saying, "My brother is waiting for us; I will no longer deprive him of the pleasure of making acquaintance with the new sister I am about to give him."

Jerome then withdrew to the music room with his attendants. As soon as she lost sight of him, Catherine grew faint and had to be revived with air and eau de cologne. Laure says this fainting fit was certainly caused by "the violent restraint the Princess had for some time put on herself."[21] According to the staunchly pro-Bonaparte historian Frédérick Masson, this first meeting with Jerome left Catherine "in tears."[22]

The party left for Paris. The full wedding, with all the grandeur Napoleon imparted to his major official functions, took place on August 12. Two weeks later Jerome wrote to his brother Lucien, informing him he had made arrangements for his American wife: she would have a small principality of her own, to which her son would be the heir. "You know the feelings of my heart and you know that the well-being and benefit of my family alone forced me to make other ties. Say, Lucien, 'My brother is miserable, but he is not guilty.'"[23]

The new king and queen of Westphalia later took possession of their kingdom. The accounts of this period, though often contradictory in many respects, are unanimous in saying that Catherine was a wonderful wife to Jerome. She grew to love him deeply and endured with grace all his flaws, even his infidelity.

At this point there was no longer any doubt in Betsy's mind. After more than two years Jerome's resolution had finally disintegrated under the force of the emperor's will. Earlier, in 1805, she had written in her notebook: "We landed at Lisbon on the 6th April, where Prince Jerome remained only three days with us. He took leave of us on the 9th." Now she added: "And this leave became eternal."[24]

Somewhere along the way Betsy's grief transformed into a bitter energy. Over the months since her return from England she had begun for the first time to understand the necessity and power of money. It was the pivot that shifted between freedom and powerlessness. She would need money to overcome her status as a charity case in the house of her father and an object of pity in society. She would need it to prove her son's legitimacy and establish his identity as a genuine member of the Bonaparte family. She would need it to escape from Baltimore, which now in her view was a town full of merciless gossips. Most of all, she would need money to get back to Europe, where people appreciated her for what she was and viewed her with interest, sympathy, and kindness.

Her first step was to pursue the pension Napoleon had once offered her, and she was going to get it without giving up the name he had made so famous.

Chapter 14

An Unmarried Woman

*I*t is very difficult to describe Westphalia during the reign of King Jerome without seeming to exaggerate, a problem shared by nearly all the accounts of the period. When the new king and queen took up residence at the capital, Cassel, in December 1807, they found the place very run-down. Nevertheless, Jerome had long looked forward to being a king, and he set to work at once refurbishing the kingdom. Buildings, streets, and parks were renovated, rooms were refurnished with appropriate trappings, and royal garments were ordered for himself, his wife, and his staff.

Jerome had always loved to dress up. When he was a seventeen-year-old naval officer, he'd found his uniform dull, so on occasion he dressed as a cavalry captain, a hussar with a tall shako—a military hat with high crown and plume—and a jacket thrown over one shoulder. Jerome's sartorial style had been disconcerting to his superiors at the naval base in Martinique. Now, though, he was in charge. Soon, Jerome had outfitted his palace staff so that his chamberlains wore mantles of scarlet velvet with cloth-of-gold collars, and wide satin sashes trimmed with tassels and bows, along with lace scarves and plumed toques. Jerome himself had many outfits. His favorite was made of gold-embroidered white satin, which he wore along with a purple cloak and a hat trimmed with diamond clasps and white ostrich feathers. Such finery came at a cost, yet Jerome was shocked when he found the little nation's treasury empty.[1]

The advance group Napoleon had sent to survey the country

had done a poor job of reconnaissance, in part because none of them spoke German. They reported conditions were much better than they actually were, so the impositions for regular tribute and troops that the emperor always levied on new additions to his realm were much too high. Napoleon also reminded the new king that he still owed a very large sum at Paris for the debts he'd made there, and repayment would be expected on time. Jerome's request for a lower assessment on Westphalia and for a delay in the repayment of his personal debt was refused.[2]

Optimistic as usual, King Jerome went on with his governing. He appointed his friends to high offices without considering their fitness for the posts. Jerome was a poor judge of character, and some of his appointees were crooks. Soon they were running the country with the ineptitude of apes threading needles. Still, because he was chronically generous, he rewarded them with abundant pay.

Jerome may have been foolish, but he was also kindhearted. Knowing that in America he had ruined the career of Chargé Pichon, he invited him to Westphalia and assigned him to his Treasury Department. The unfortunate Pichon struggled for a while and finally resigned in despair. When the king's new secretary of the treasury could not find the money to cover his expenses, Jerome arranged for a large loan at eight percent interest from a banker named Israel Jacobson. At the same time, Jacobson secured for the Jews of Westphalia rights and privileges they were denied in other European countries. This action has been historically regarded as the one positive achievement of Jerome's reign.[3]

Napoleon, who received regular reports from the spies he placed in this and other parts of Europe, knew exactly what was going on in Westphalia. He sent a barrage of letters to Jerome, on occasion two or three in a single day, urging him to be thrifty, to manage well, to behave sensibly, and to become a man of honor in regard to his obligations. In one letter the emperor urged Jerome, "Sell your diamonds and your plate.... Sell your furniture, sell your horses, sell your jewelry and pay your debts." Napoleon admonished, "There must be an end to the mad extravagance which already makes you the laughing-stock of Europe. . . . The luxury you indulge in bewilders and shocks your subjects." A few months later Napoleon wrote, "I have seldom seen anyone with so little sense of proportion as yourself. You know nothing, yet you never take advice. You decide nothing by reason, everything by impulse and passion." In a postscript to that letter he added, "My dear fellow, I'm very fond of you, but you're a mere babe."[4]

Jerome occasionally answered by defending the choices he was making but in general paid little attention. He believed that his seeming extravagance was required to maintain his dignity as a monarch. He tried to emulate Parisian high culture by having his own Comédie Française, and kept a theatrical company in residence to perform at his palace. Jerome also gave immense dinner parties, as well as outdoor extravaganzas and sometimes as many as two or three costume balls in a single week. Napoleon's accusations failed to move him. Jerome was sure his brother would relent and forgive everything.

Busy as he was, Jerome did not forget Betsy. In keeping with the plan he'd mentioned to his brother Lucien right after the marriage to Catherine, he began to arrange for his American wife and son to move to Westphalia. Having learned that one of William Patterson's sons was at work for the firm in Tours, he instructed Alexander Le Camus to write to Joseph Patterson there. Le Camus now was no longer simply Jerome's secretary (and procurer of attractive female company for his employer) but rather his minister of foreign affairs, which some critics charged actually meant minister of affairs that were foreign to him. He also had a new title: he was Count Fürstenstein, a German name he had difficulty pronouncing.

So in January 1808, Betsy's younger brother Joseph got a letter by courier from Count Fürstenstein asking him to come to Cassel to discuss "plans of interest to your family." Joseph declined to make the trip until he was given further information about the plans, and evidently heard no more.[5]

During the spring of his first year in Cassel Jerome dictated two more letters to be sent to Baltimore, one for Betsy and one for her father. The letters were in the penmanship of a secretary, but Jerome added in his own hand the place of origin, the date, and the signature. The letters said that he wanted his son and explained all that he could do for him now that he had a kingdom of his own. Upon reflection he apparently decided these items were too dangerous to risk to the mails.

Earlier, Alex Le Camus had invited his whole family to come to Westphalia and take part in the events going on there. At that time, his brother Auguste, on his way from Martinique to Cassel, had stopped in the United States and invited Betsy to give him any messages she wanted to send to Jerome. She agreed and sent Jerome a portrait of their son.[6] It now seemed sensible to send Auguste off with the two new letters for Baltimore and with orders to bring the child back with him to Westphalia. Getting this arrangement under way took until September.

During that summer Betsy heard nothing from Jerome, but she kept busy. During her childhood she'd been given books for every birthday, so early on she'd became a habitual reader. Now she began to read with a sharper focus. She bought two more English-French dictionaries and enlarged her collection of French classics.

In addition she began giving trusted French-speaking friends drafts of the letters she was writing to critique. Among the people who helped was Maximilian Godefroy. Since he was busy designing landmark Baltimore structures such as the Unitarian Church, on occasion he was forced to delay her critique "because he had to go to his building." Another friend was Madame Jeanne de Volunbrun, a refugee from Santo Domingo who ran a tobacco shop in town. Betsy was grateful for the help of these friends and used their advice to polish her style.[7]

She also took care of something neglected during her months at Camberwell: she arranged to have her son baptized, not in her own Presbyterian faith, but as a Catholic, like the Bonapartes. Bishop John

William Patterson

As a young man during the American Revolution, William Patterson became a shipping merchant in the West Indies. By the end of the war he had settled in Baltimore and invested in shipping, trade, and real estate, businesses that would make him a millionaire.

William Patterson

Patterson was successful and wealthy, but he remained critical of the amount of money Betsy and her husband cost him. His letters to his daughter were filled with rebukes and condemnation.

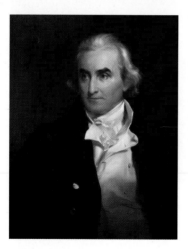

When Patterson died, in 1835, he was celebrated in the press as one of the pioneers of Baltimore's business success, as a shareholder in many local concerns, and a founder of the B & O Railroad.

Dorcas Spear Patterson

From a large interconnected Scots-Irish family, Dorcas married Patterson soon after he came to Baltimore. She is holding Betsy, the fourth of her twelve children.

Edward Patterson

Edward was one of Betsy's six brothers; he sided with Betsy during family quarrels. He married a cousin, one of the daughters of Sam Smith, and was active in the various Patterson businesses.

Joshua Barney

Commodore Joshua Barney served in the navy during the Revolution, rose to captain, and was captured by the British several times. After the war he entered the French navy where he became a friend of Jerome Bonaparte.

Brigadier General Sam Smith

In 1794, Samuel Smith was appointed brigadier general of the Maryland militia. He managed the defense of Baltimore in 1814, was a successful businessman, a U.S. senator, and from 1835-1838, mayor of Baltimore. His wife and Betsy's mother were sisters.

Betsy Bonaparte

For years Betsy avoided her home town and enjoyed her life and the friends she made in Paris, Florence, and Geneva. During that time this portrait by Firmin Massot was painted on wood, on an old and well-aged carriage door.

Betsy Bonaparte

During Betsy's early years in Europe, several artists painted her and sold engravings of her portrait to the public. However, she felt that none of them, except that by Gilbert Stuart, really looked like her. This one is by Flemish painter Francois-Joseph Kinson.

Betsy Bonaparte

Betsy Bonaparte. During their honeymoon, Betsy and her husband Jerome posed for the painter Gilbert Stuart. Unable to decide which side of the bride's face pleased him more, he produced a study of three aspects of her face. This portrait, by George d'Almaine, was painted in a style similar to that of Stuart.

Jerome Bonaparte

Through his brother Napoleon's wife, Josephine, Jerome was exposed at an early age to aristocratic manners and courtly attire. He loved to dress up, powder his hair, and spend time with pretty women.

Jerome Bonaparte

At an early age, Jerome was placed into the navy by Napoleon with orders to work hard and learn enough seamanship to defeat the British, but the uniform bored him. He preferred to dress like a mounted hussar.

Napoleon Bonaparte

Napoleon went from military school into the army, rapidly rose through the ranks to general, skillfully took charge of the French government, and then named himself emperor.

Jerome Napoleon Bonaparte

Betsy's son Jerome Napoleon, or "Bo," made several trips to Europe, but settled in Baltimore. He spent his time raising horses and managing his wife's fortune.

Two views, Bonaparte house, circa 1910

The Bonaparte museum in Bo's house, located at Park Avenue and Centre Street. The top photo shows, from left to right: a bust of Napoleon, the Massot and Kinson paintings of Betsy, and a large framed picture of Charles Joseph Bonaparte as attorney general. Visible in the bottom photo are busts of Madame Mère, Napoleon, and the emperor's father, Carlo Bonaparte.

Susan May Williams

Susan May was Betsy's daughter-in-law, and had come from a wealthy family. During the American Civil War she was so devoted to the Union cause that she spied on neighbors and reported Confederate sympathizers.

Jerome Napoleon Bonaparte Jr.

Jerome Napoleon, Bo's first son, graduated from West Point and served in the army on the Texas border during the war with Mexico.

Jerome Napoleon Bonaparte Jr.

Jerome Napoleon was granted a leave from West Point and traveled to Paris with his father, Bo, upon the invitation of Napoleon III. There the new emperor urged him to join the French army. The young man did so, and won two dozen medals for bravery in the Crimea. Jerome Napoleon remained in the French army and eventually became a colonel. When Napoleon's empire crumbled, the colonel escorted Empress Eugénie to safety in England.

Charles Joseph Bonaparte

Charles Joseph Bonaparte was Bo's younger son. He was a great comfort and help to Betsy in her later years. A Harvard-educated lawyer, he became active in national politics.

Charles Joseph and Ellen Bonaparte

Charles Joseph and his wife, the former Ellen Channing Day.
After Charles died, Ellen Bonaparte gave the memorabilia left
by Betsy to the Maryland Historical Society.

Carroll, in a note to her regarding the time for the baptism, referred to the child as "the perhaps future prince." [8]

A few months earlier, she had received a letter that might have encouraged her to share the bishop's hopes for the child, although the bitterness she'd begun to feel made her skeptical. The letter concerned Jerome and was written by a woman named Anna Kuhn, who wrote from New York to say she had been in France, "where I have had frequent occasions for seeing and dining at the table of your husband, the present King of Westphalia and you, Madam, were no less frequently the topic of our conversation. He speaks of you as the only woman he ever loved or ever shall love, says he married much against his inclination, which the Emperor his brother cruelly imposed on him; saying you and you only Madam were his lawful wife." There is no reply in Betsy's letter book, but to Anna Kuhn's note she added the comment: "The kindness of my Ex-Husband the King was ever of the unremitting kind as no money ever accompanied it."[9]

Several of the letters Betsy received that summer were from her companion on the trip to Europe, Eliza Anderson. She was living in New Jersey, with occasional trips to Pennsylvania, while she tried to track down her ex-husband so she could get a divorce and marry Maximilian Godefroy. Most of these long letters consisted of gossip about mutual acquaintances, but her letter of July 2 contained significant news. Eliza wrote that she'd had a conversation in Philadelphia with the French consul general there, Felix Beaujour, who assured her that Jerome's former wife was going to be given a title and a substantial income.[10]

During the summer months, social activity in Washington slowed, and the city essentially closed down. This was also true in Baltimore, as everyone who could afford a country home went there to avoid the fevers that raged in the cities at this time of year. Mrs. Anderson's letter, however, prompted Betsy to get started on her plan to obtain the pension Napoleon had promised her, and she decided not to wait for the beginning of the fall season at Washington. Betsy wrote to the French minister plenipotentiary to the United States, General Louis-Marie Turreau de Garambouville, and delivered the letter to him herself on July 9. In that letter (carefully composed in her letter book, first in English and then in French) Betsy admitted she had once entertained very lofty expectations for her future, but now she understood that the rights of societies are of greater magnitude than the rights of individuals. Still, she added:

> confidence and hope have not yet left my soul: it is only marked by sadness. Would that you, mon Général, expose to His Majesty the situation of a child so worthy of interest, and that of a mother, who by true and affectionate sentiments, merits all the evidence of esteem and attachment of which a woman may be honored and who owes her misfortunes only to circumstances she cannot master.[11]

She not only was able to give her letter to General Turreau in person, but to have a meeting with him, perhaps because they were already acquainted. For several years Turreau had rented a summer home owned by William Patterson. After Betsy and Jerome left for Lisbon, Turreau tried to buy Jerome's carriage horses, but Patterson had been instructed by Jerome not to sell them until he asked him to do so. Recently Betsy and her father had dined with Turreau at the French embassy, and not long after that Betsy and Miss Spear were guests there as well.[12] Turreau, with his black moustache, presented a formidable appearance. During the French Revolution's Reign of Terror, in which thousands of citizens were executed, Turreau was a Republican commander, notorious for his brutality. Turreau used killing to put down the revolt, calling it "a true crusade."[13]

In her meeting with Turreau, Betsy explained that her son was healthy, happy, and well cared for, but she was concerned about his future. After all, he was the nephew of Napoleon and deserved an appropriate training for whatever his future might hold, preferably a European education. In addition, the crowded conditions in her father's household made it almost impossible for her to begin educating her son properly, but she didn't have the means to set up her own establishment. Further, being told she was not to use the name of Madame Bonaparte made her position in this country untenable; it made her what Americans consider an unmarried woman, a *Miss Patterson*, with a three-year-old child. If she could not use her married name, perhaps she should have a title.

In reply Turreau asked her several questions, which she copied into her letter book, along with her notes on the meeting. Turreau asked her:

> First, will you, on condition that the Emperor gives you a title and a pension, promise never to marry without the consent of the French government?
>
> Second, will you renounce forever the idea of going to England?
>
> Third, will you renounce the United States and go to Europe?
>
> Fourth, do you consent not to leave the town chosen for your residence without informing the Prefect of the place?
>
> Fifth, do you demand that your son should remain with you until the age of seven? [14]

Betsy had no trouble with the first four queries, but the fifth gave her pause. The possibility of a permanent separation from her child was unthinkable. But she might have time to get around that provision, because Turreau told her he doubted he had the authority to set up such an agreement on his own. He was forced to forward her letter to his superiors in Paris and wait for instructions. Napoleon was as usual very busy, so those instructions were a long time coming.

In September, Auguste Le Camus wrote her from New York and enclosed Jerome's two letters originally written on May 16. Jerome's letter to Betsy said the events that had occurred since their separation had not been able to put her out of his mind. He had always kept his tenderness for her and he had not ceased to concern himself with her happiness and that of their child.

It is thus to assure his place in the world that I have sent M. Le Camus to get him. I know in advance, my well-beloved Elisa, what it will cost you to be separated from him, but you will never be so blind to his true interest, and your own, as not to consent to his departure. A brilliant destiny is reserved for him. Our son should enjoy all the advantages which his birth and his name give him the right to claim, and you cannot permit him to lose these advantages without ceasing to love him, and without making yourself responsible for his fate. In this situation, I hope you will be willing to sacrifice everything so that our son may have a suitable position and that you will not listen to the timid counsels which you may be given. Do not give in to grief, my good Elisa; always be hopeful, and count on a happier future. Nothing will ever make me forget the ties which unite me to you and the tender attachment that I have vowed you for life.

Now that he was a king he had added his brother's name to his own, so he closed as "Your affectionate and devoted friend, Jerome Napoleon" and sent best wishes to her mother, father, and all the family. His letter to her father was substantially the same, but he added that this request had been authorized by the emperor. He also said bringing up his son under his eyes "will help to console me for the sorrow I feel at being far from his mother." He was counting on Patterson to persuade her and ended by saying that he hoped to embrace his son by the end of the month.[15]

Betsy was horrified. Did Jerome have the power to take her son away from her? Worse, could the emperor have approved such a scheme? She told Le Camus she would need proof that Napoleon permitted this. Further, she could not allow him to take her boy across the ocean without her. So Auguste sailed away, and Betsy tried to figure out what to do. If Jerome's offer was valid, and if Napoleon was involved in it, how could she protect her child?

There was still no reply to Turreau from his superiors in Paris, but soon Jerome wrote to her again. He thanked her for the portrait of his son that she'd sent with Auguste Le Camus the year before. However, he was very angry, because he had learned from Paris about her request for help from the emperor. Didn't she understand that he was a king now, in charge of his own country? How could Napoleon do any more for her than Jerome could?

> *Were these steps to secure a fortune for my son and his mother? Why should it be necessary to approach the Emperor for that? Am I not a sufficiently good father and friend, and powerful enough to give my son and his mother all the titles and fortune they may desire? . . . I was expecting my son, yes, Elisa, and you too, and a noble existence, and one worthy of the objects of my most tender affection, was planned for you and still awaits you. Then, at least, I shall see my son from time to time, and I promise to his mother, to Elisa, to my most loving friend, to leave her son with her until his twelfth year in the principality which I have chosen for him, and that the only sacrifice I ask of her is to let me enjoy a visit from my son once or twice a month.*

He planned to give to her and their son the titles of Prince and Princess of Smalcalden, a place thirty leagues from Cassel, and he enclosed a map of the area. She would have a beautiful home there, one worthy of her in every way, and he would give her an income of 200,000 francs a year. He advised Betsy to send her reply to her brother Joseph at Tours and tell him to bring it to Cassel. "Your consent will make me very happy, Elisa, and if I can succeed in assuaging your sorrows, I shall at last know the value of power." [16]

Betsy's letter book gives a sense of her desperation. There she wrote a long reply in which she mentioned being in tears and referred to the child as her only happiness. She addressed Jerome in formal terms, calling him " sire" and "your majesty," to such an extent that what at first seemed subservient sounded in the end more like sarcasm. She poured out her heart—and then tore out the pages. Fragments are all that remain: *"My reply to the King. . . . I had delusively flattered . . . I had imagined that . . . maternal tenderness . . . the idea of separation . . . every desire, ambition. . . ."* [17]

In addition, Betsy jotted notes on Jerome's letter. Where he appeared to think he had rights over her, she added that he'd given her "the right to be despised and hated." She said he had left her "poor, unfriended, and alone." And in another place she wrote: "At this awful time, Smalcalden [was] spurned—Westphalia not large enough for two queens." She justified her choice of appealing to Napoleon rather than asking for help from Jerome by noting: "I would rather be sheltered under the wings of an eagle than dangle from the beak of a goose."

Nevertheless she had to ask herself if she was being selfish at the expense of her child, whom she now began calling by the rest of his name, Napoleon Bonaparte, "Bo" for short. Would Jerome's plan be good for Bo? Or was it some kind of plot to enable Jerome or even the childless Napoleon to get hold of an heir? There was a rumor that Catherine might be infertile, and everybody knew that Empress Josephine could not bear children. Although he apparently loved his wife, Napoleon eventually divorced her so that he could remarry and have an heir. Certainly a ruler with Napoleon's power was capable of any crime if he thought it would benefit his nation.

Or was Betsy giving in to wild imaginings? There was no one she trusted to advise her and be discreet about it. Then she remembered that Ambassador James Monroe, formerly at the Paris Legation and later at the London Embassy, was now back in America. She wrote to him at Richmond, beginning with an apology for the intrusion and explaining that she needed his experience to help her understand what had happened. She told him Jerome had formally demanded that his son be sent to Westphalia, where he would be made a prince and take up the rank and position he was born to hold. She explained that she'd been evasive: she refused to let her child leave without her and would do nothing without the unequivocal permission of the emperor. "My maternal duties," she wrote, "certainly prescribe a total dereliction of all self-interest motives and I possess sufficient energy to submit to any privation however painful, which the interest of my son dictates. I wish only to ascertain whether an acquiescence with his father's demand will ensure the prosperity and personal safety of the child." [18]

Monroe answered three weeks later, apologizing for not reply-
ing at once because he'd been away in the country when her
letter arrived. His letter was long and very gracious. He said the
confidence she placed in him by asking his advice on so delicate
and interesting a topic would not be abused.

> With my family, I have always felt great sensibility to the hard
> history which has attended you, and I would have been happy
> to have had it in my power to alleviate it. To the present period
> your conduct has been distinguished by the utmost degree of
> prudence and delicacy. Your return to your father's house, under
> the circumstances which suggested it, was a measure the best
> calculated to preserve your own honor and reflect credit on your
> son that could have been devised.

He said he could understand her anxiety but had no doubt
about Jerome's motive. He also believed Napoleon's interest was
sincere. Monroe thought it inconceivable that either of them would
be capable of deliberately aggravating her misfortunes. Monroe
elaborated:

> The Emperor must also have some sensibility to the hard fortune
> which he has imposed on the wife of his brother, as well as to the
> claims of their infant child. He must be aware too that the atten-
> tion of the world has been drawn to him by his conduct in that
> transaction, as it would be by the surrender of the child by the
> mother to his protection and by his demand. Should any calamity
> befall the infant it would fix a stigma on his fame which could
> never be effaced. It is not therefore from either of them that I
> should apprehend any danger to the child. If his situation should
> expose him to any I should expect it from another quarter. The
> wife of Jerome, or some of her connections might not see this infant
> received under the protection of his father with pleasure. She may
> have children, and he might be thought in their way. Such things
> often happen in courts.

Then Monroe raised additional questions for her to consider.
Would this arrangement contribute more to the boy's happiness
than being educated within his mother's family, where he would

learn the principles of this country? Finally, Betsy had to ask herself whether she could part with Bo forever—"for such, from many causes, may be the consequence." [19]

That wise counsel gave her reassurance and food for thought, but she still had to wait for word from Paris. Fortunately, there were other matters to fill her days.

Chapter 15

The Hopeful Suitors

*W*hile enduring the tedious wait for information to travel back and forth from Europe, Betsy lived at her family's various homes, in Baltimore on South Street, north of town at Coldstream, and for much of the summer thirty miles west at the Springfield estate. She also visited Washington from time to time during the winter, as did many other Baltimoreans. During that 1808–1809 legislative session in the capital, social life was even more active than usual. One woman wrote, "We have been very gay lately — last night made the 7th or 8th ball this winter, besides a great many card parties. . . . The Miss Carrolls, Miss Chases, Miss Cooks and I don't know how many more misses have come from Baltimore. There are parties every night, and the galleries are crowded in the morning." [1]

It was about this time in Betsy's life that she began to make a series of romantic conquests. In this case, the young man was an Englishman, Samuel Colleton Graves, son of Admiral Graves of the Royal Navy. Samuel fell desperately in love with Betsy, visiting her, writing her letters, and giving her books. Although his father was temporarily based in Philadelphia, Samuel's job as the admiral's secretary required him to travel from time to time. On a trip to New England he made a point of spending the night at an inn where Betsy and Jerome had stayed when they traveled from Niagara Falls to Boston. While there young Graves wrote a passionate poem about sleeping in the bed Betsy had used. [2]

After that, Betsy felt compelled to warn him that his sentiment could only result in disappointment. She wrote, "My time and attachment must be devoted exclusively to my son, from whose destiny whether inauspicious, or the reverse I can never divide myself. The resolution of consecrating to him every sentiment and action of my life is irrevocable."

Although her intense desire to obtain every benefit for her son was sincere and remained a consistent aim for a long time to come, using that excuse kept her from having to reveal more personal feelings. She had been crushed and humiliated by Jerome's betrayal and tried to replace that pain with a determination to fight back. Consequently, while being found enchanting by other men was comforting, nothing could be allowed to distract her from her plan.

Young Graves, like the other suitors who were to follow him, refused to be discouraged. Even after he had to return to England, he wrote to her again from his family home, Hembury Fort, near Honiton in Devonshire. He admitted that he should not have addressed her again, but he couldn't help himself. He assured her, "My love will be as lasting as my recollection, and to my recollection there will be no end."

While at Hembury Fort Samuel enlisted the aid of his mother, who wrote Betsy a long letter politely critical of her decision to devote her life to her son. Mrs. Graves urged her not to keep her son unknown and perhaps alienated from his paternal relatives, who would be able to "provide for him, at least nobly and perhaps royally," so that if Betsy permitted, "he will doubtlessly be created everything a mother's heart can wish, reared under a father's eye and perhaps succeed to his throne." She added that she and her husband would accompany their son to meet Betsy anywhere to celebrate the nuptials and to welcome her into their home.

Betsy's reply was firm: she would not change her mind. Samuel went off traveling to try to forget her, but failed. A year later he wrote her again, this time from Gottenburgh to say he still loved her, and as late as a year after that he was still sending her presents.

Her copy of Lord Byron's *English Bards and Scotch Reviewers: A Satire* is inscribed: "To Madame Bonaparte from her sincere friend S. Colleton Graves."[3]

Later, Betsy captivated a young man named Jan Willink, whose father, an Amsterdam banker, handled finances for the United States in Europe. Willink pursued her for several years, but this time she made certain her position was clear from the beginning. As far as she was concerned, they were simply friends, but he, too, wrote her love letters and poetry.[4]

More serious were the attentions of another Englishman, Sir Charles Oakley, secretary to the British ambassador. This suitor caused a great deal of comment, perhaps because he kept leaving his post at the capital to visit Betsy in Baltimore. A local letter writer described the situation on South Street:

> *Madame Bonaparte makes our streets quite gay. Oakley the secretary of the legation to his British Majesty is devoted to her, every evening that he is here, and, he is very little at Washington, he takes tea and is with her until ten at night. Bets are made whether he will offer; if so, whether she will accept or decline. Betsy is dressed with care every visit he pays, and will make a conquest if she can, how far beyond, no one knows.* [5]

Even Bishop Carroll remarked on this courtship in a letter to his sister. "You have heard without doubt of Mr. Oakley having transferred his attentions to Mad'm Bonaparte and of their being well received, as is generally supposed. Some go so far as to declare that they will be married." [6]

Oakley's obsession worried the ambassador, Sir George Jackson. Because of the British attack on the American ship *Chesapeake* and the possibility of war, there was a great deal of sensitive correspondence and information that Jackson wanted the legation secretary to carry personally to London, but Oakley refused to leave. The ambassador confided to his brother: "I am not yet quite sure that I shall get Oakley to go, for he has fallen desperately in love with, and they say plans to marry, the cast-off wife of Jerome Bonaparte."

Sir George added: "I think if he really commits this folly, it will be an obstacle to his obtaining further employment." It took two months for Oakley to be persuaded that his suit was hopeless, but he finally went home with the dispatches.[7]

These romantic incidents did more than help Betsy pass the time while waiting for word from Napoleon. In view of the emperor's well-known extreme sensitivity to anything associated with Britain, the possibility that Mademoiselle Patterson might marry an Englishman disturbed General Turreau so much that he increased his efforts to have the emperor act on Betsy's requests.

The negotiations had already dragged on for almost a year. It was during the summer of 1808 that he had forwarded her July letter to Paris, where the minister of foreign affairs, Champagny, sent it on to the emperor, but Napoleon was off campaigning. In November Napoleon replied to his minister from Spain. It wasn't until the following spring that the answer reached Turreau in Washington.

> *I received the letter from Mme. Patterson. Tell Turreau that he is to inform her that I will receive with pleasure her son and will be responsible for him if she wishes to send him to France; that, as for her, whatever she may desire will be granted; that she may count on my esteem and my wish to be agreeable to her; that, when I refused to recognize her, I was led by considerations of high policy; that I am resolved to assure for her son a future that she desires. Moreover, this affair must be quietly and secretly managed.*[8]

As soon as Turreau received this information, he invited Betsy to come to the French embassy to discuss Napoleon's reply. Betsy was delighted with the news and asked Turreau to relay her thanks to the emperor. In addition Turreau asked her to specify what she wanted for herself. At that meeting and in a subsequent letter she asked the general to add to her thanks to the emperor the fact that since her son was not yet four years old, she must herself bring him to France.

She went on to explain that living in her own country was very unpleasant for her; everyone in America knew her story and either blamed or pitied her. She wanted to live anyplace in Europe that His

Majesty would choose, provided she could educate her son there, but her preference was for Paris. She reminded Turreau of something she'd told him before, that having to use her maiden name put her in a difficult position. "It is easy to imagine that re-assuming the surname of my family in Europe would cause me the very difficulties that I seek to avoid in leaving my country." If she was not to be called "Madame Bonaparte," perhaps she could have a title, but if so she wanted one that did not require to her to marry anyone. She added, "I will wait for you to transmit in writing the authorization for me to go to France with my son." She closed with more expressions of gratitude to the emperor, and to the general for his care in this business. She signed her name *"Eliza née Patterson."*[9]

Turreau forwarded her response to Paris, but he remained worried about the rumors suggesting she might marry an Englishman. He knew that was the last thing Napoleon would want, because it would give the newspapers of the emperor's bitterest enemy the advantage of once again announcing the rescue of this "poor victim of Boney's tyranny."

Betsy's next letter to him multiplied his fears. She wrote to say that in view of Napoleon's recent favorable response to her petitions, she would now like Turreau to pay into her account the first installment of her pension.[10] That must have startled Turreau, who had not yet been given the funds for that purpose. He again informed Paris of the situation and urged quick action. Meanwhile Betsy herself had begun to worry that her rumored romances might prejudice Napoleon against her, so she wrote a flurry of letters to contacts in Paris, Philadelphia, and Washington insisting she had no intention of marrying any Englishman *ever*.[11]

Turreau wasn't sure he believed her. He'd heard that her father was pressuring her to marry one of these Englishmen, and not knowing William Patterson's prejudice against having someone in his family marry into anything but a solid, middle-class, business-oriented American family, he believed it might be true. What if his inability to provide money prompted her to jump into one of these marriages?

He wrote her two very conciliatory and reassuring letters. In one of them he said he was busy working to achieve her wishes, because he was sure her "arrangements can only be agreeable to the French government." He went on, "I number among my duties, Madame, the care of your tranquility and your independence." In the other he told her that as soon as he received a favorable response, he would immediately communicate it to her. "I will then congratulate myself, Madame, on having been the mouthpiece of your wishes; on having found an accord with the sentiments of my duty and that person that has inspired in me the noble quantities that distinguish you." [12]

By December of 1809 Turreau still had not received from Paris the money he'd requested and took it upon himself to use legation funds to start her pension on his own authority. He established a credit of twenty thousand dollars for Betsy to draw upon. She began by taking six thousand as a first installment. It took a few months to get a regular payment plan worked out, but before long she was receiving sixty thousand francs a year in monthly installments of five thousand. Depending on the fluctuating exchange rate, that worked out to be about $950 a month. [13]

Turreau assigned an older man, Louis Tousard, to serve as Betsy's aide. Tousard had served in the French army and also in the American Revolutionary forces, where he lost an arm at the battle of Rhode Island and earned the rank of lieutenant colonel. He'd been working as a vice consul in New Orleans, but now in Betsy's service his job was described as her son's tutor. Actually Turreau intended for him to be a spy and a protector as well, because he feared the British might try to kidnap the boy. [14]

When word of Turreau's actions reached Paris, the judgment was that he'd exceeded his authority but in general had done the right thing. However, Napoleon had indeed found out about those marriage proposals, and he was angry. Again the response came from Minister Champagny:

> *The Emperor was greatly displeased that Mademoiselle P. should have considered marrying an Englishman and that this conduct*

conflicts with the generous and noble sentiments that this lady had
previously manifested, sentiments whose expression had pleased
his Majesty. The Emperor approves what M. Turreau has done,
and authorizes him to furnish Mlle P. the money necessary to
her, while waiting until his Majesty will have decided her fate,
but that if Mlle P were to marry an Englishman this benevolence
would cease.[15]

Although the above refers to a coming decision to "decide her fate," Napoleon had not yet done so. Nevertheless, everyone expected that Betsy would be given or had already been given a title—even her mother. Lady Jackson, wife of the British ambassador, made a visit to Baltimore and received a number of calls from the local women, including Dorcas Patterson. She reported: "Amongst my visitors was Madame Patterson, mother of Madame Jerome. I questioned her politely, and she confirmed that her grandson was made a prince and that his mother was only not yet a duchess because she could not make up her mind to it." [16]

Madame Breuil, one of Betsy's friends who was connected to the French Legation at Philadelphia, wrote about the news from Paris on this topic.

It is said that you will be a grand duchess of Westphalia and your
son a grand duke and that as the queen will never have children
he will succeed his father. It is even said that a superb palace in
Italy is being prepared for you, and that your husband still loves
you very much. . . . It is said here that the gentleman whom we all
await every day is to announce this great event to you because we
suppose that such an important thing will be brought by someone
sent for that purpose.[17]

At any rate, for the next two years Colonel Tousard did much more than tutor Bo. He acted like a titled person's *major-domo.* He collected Betsy's pension payments, made her travel plans, alerted people at her destination to ensure that accommodations would be ready, arranged to have a carriage call for her when needed, wrote letters in French for her, forwarded her mail when she traveled, and sometimes put her little boy to bed in the evening if she was out at a dinner or a ball. Betsy's friend Augustus John Foster described a reception held in Philadelphia during a visit of Madame Bonaparte and her son: "The Colonel would receive visitors in the ante-room, and present both ladies and gentlemen, the boy being styled Prince, and his mother doing the honors." [18]

Colonel Tousard's service with Betsy was difficult for him, because he had to live separately from his own family. When she and Bo were at South Street there was no room for him, so he boarded with Mme. Volunbrun at Betsy's expense. Nevertheless he and his wife were fond of Betsy, and years after Mme. Tousard was widowed, she traveled with Betsy as a companion. Now, though, when a change in the embassy at Washington resulted in Tousard's return to New Orleans, he was probably relieved.

Madame Breuil's letter had mentioned the imminent arrival of an important person with an announcement from Paris. That gossip may actually have referred to a change in personnel at the Washington embassy. General Turreau had somehow lost the approval of his superiors. For Washingtonians, it was about time. Betsy herself must have stopped trusting him as well, because her most recent letter to Napoleon had not been sent from Washington, but rather via Beaujour, the consul general in Philadelphia. [19]

Turreau's legendary cruelty in war seems to have extended into his marriage, for he was repeatedly accused of savagely beating his wife. Several times she fled to neighbors to get away from him, yet when his butler was questioned, he said she "deserved it." Neighbors even accused Turreau of maintaining on staff a musician whose sole job was to play the cello loudly during the domestic quarrels in order to drown out the wife's screams. [20] Betsy herself had been appalled to find that Turreau had planned to get a divorce and marry her, so that when she became a duchess, he would return to Paris as a duke. She recorded this information in her letter book and added that she had refused his offer with the scorn it deserved. That charge was also made by Mme. Volunbrun, who knew Turreau well, and by Augustus John Foster, who wrote:

Napoleon wished to induce Madame Bonaparte to take another husband, no less a person than General Turreau, his minister, who used all his elquence to persuade her, proposing it as an affaire de convenance and urging that it was a shame she should vegetate in such a country whereas at Paris she would shine in the first circles and he would be created a baron of the Empire. But she must give up her son.[21]

Turreau was replaced by Louis-Barbé-Charles Sérurier, the nephew of one of Napoleon's marshals and an experienced chargé d'affaires. He was also the man who had turned Betsy away at Lisbon. Shortly after his arrival in Washington he reported to his superiors in Paris that Mademoiselle Patterson had taken a house in the capital "for her son's education and to be near family," and he wanted instructions as to what his attitude toward her should be.

There is no doubt that her taking up an establishment here will embarrass me greatly; for I cannot act toward her in the way the great title which she has had for a moment would require, and on the other hand I cannot refuse her the respectful attention which her conduct, her position and her misfortune deserve and which also attach her to France.[22]

When Betsy saw that he was dignified and sensitive, she was probably happy to put aside the memory of Lisbon, especially since her pension payments continued without interruption. For Washington society, the change at the French legation was a relief. Serurier and his wife were charming and soon became frequent and welcome guests at the season's parties.

Miss Anne Spear moved in with Betsy and Bo near the Capitol. No doubt the congressional gallery still fascinated "Aunt Nancy." Her interest may have been even stronger now, since among the sights there was an eccentric legislator by the name of John Randolph who entered the legislative chamber followed by his dogs. He refused all requests, motions, and even orders to leave the animals at home. When drawn into an argument, Randolph was known to challenge his opponent to cross the river to Virginia and fight a duel on the far shore—which was legal in Virginia but not in Washington City. Facing off a challenger with a pistol, however, was legal. Randolph made this challenge to Henry Clay, who was at various times senator, congressman, and Speaker of the House. Clay thought the invitation over and decided to decline.[23]

Clay also commented on Washington social life. In the spring of 1810 he wrote from the Senate Chamber a letter to a friend and told him, *"Mrs. Madison has her parties every Wednesday evening. They are gay and agreeable."* Then Clay mentioned Napoleon's recent divorce from Josephine and his subsequent marriage to the young Austrian Archduchess Marie-Louise, who was only nineteen and had what were described as "child-bearing hips."

> *Bonaparte has repudiated the Empress. I suspect he is afraid of being denominated a fumbler, and wishes to operate on a subject more prolific than the Empress. His brother's wife Miss Patterson alias the Dutchess has been figuring away here some time, with her little son. I would recommend her to imitate her brother-in-law's example and take to herself a good strong back Democrat. She looks as if she wanted very much the services of such a character.[24]*

Betsy was emphatically not interested in that sort of thing, but she did have abundant opportunities. Although Graves and Oakley were gone, Jan Willink was still around and still attentive. Like Graves, he was enchanted by the night he had slept in a bed she'd used, at O'Neal's boarding house. He told her he'd dreamed up "lines which I am afraid of putting on paper, but which your lively imagination will easily suggest." There was also a fresh crop of suitors. A man she described as Senator Gold sent her verses entitled "On Madame Bonaparte's Drawing Room on the evening of the 9th of January 1813." Another suitor wrote her a love letter replete with exclamation marks and enclosing a poem that began: "O turn those lovely eyes away, I cannot bear the melting ray, That beams beneath those brows and bids my scattered senses stray. . . . You could not to despair consign a heart that throbs and beats like mine to live alone for you."[25]

There was also a suitor she came to look upon as a friend. It was Henry Lee Jr., grandson of a Revolutionary War general and son of "Light-Horse Harry" Lee. Decades later, his much younger half-brother, Robert E. Lee, would become one of the most famous military men in American history. Henry Jr. wrote Betsy several letters from Alexandria and other places when he traveled. He seemed to want to take care of Betsy, to become her protector, suggesting that since she already had a Spear, maybe he could be her Shield.[26] Certainly Betsy was lovely and dressed beautifully. She was also intelligent and witty, which made her entertaining. But for some her most appealing quality was her celebrity, thus the attentions she attracted could be flattering or notorious.[27]

Understandably, Betsy was growing tired of these inexperienced and possibly shallow young men, because by 1813 her most frequent visitor and escort in Washington was the vice president, Elbridge Gerry. His wife, an invalid, had remained at home in Massachusetts, but he wrote her all about his friendship with Betsy, and when his son came to Washington for a visit, he took him to meet her. With Gerry, however, there was no danger of passionate poetry about sleeping in her bed: Betsy was not yet thirty and he was almost seventy. They passed their time together in carriage rides, sightseeing, and simply talking. It was a friendship both of them enjoyed very much.[28]

Meanwhile, Napoleon never did "decide her fate." No doubt he was much too busy to give any more thought to Betsy, and despite all those rumors, she never did become a duchess.

⌘

After a silence of three years Jerome wrote to her again. It was a brief and very guarded letter. He said it had been a long time since he'd heard any news of her and his son and told her she would never in the whole world find a better or more loving friend than he. There were many things he'd like to write her, but as he suspected that this letter might be intercepted, all he could do was ask for news of her and his son. "You must have confidence that everything will be arranged sooner or later, for the Emperor is certainly the best as well as the greatest of men." He enclosed a separate note for Bo.

> *My dear son:*
>   *I hope that this letter will be more lucky than the others which I have written you and which I suppose you have not received. I hope that you will not forget me because I could not do without your affection and I hope that you are always a good and loving son to your mother, who, as the most noble of women, will always set you the best example. I embrace you with all my heart.*
>   *Your good and affectionate father, Jerome Napoleon*[29]

Two months later Betsy's brother Joseph encountered Jerome in Paris. Joseph wrote her to say Jerome had heard she'd married an Englishman, and when Joseph assured him that could not be true, he asked if there was a safe route Betsy could follow to get to Europe, one that would evade British capture. As the son of an international businessman, Joseph knew how such travel could be routed and told him how to do it. Jerome said he would talk to his brother at once about bringing her and the boy over, and would see Joseph again in the evening with details. Joseph never heard from him again and learned that Jerome had left town the next morning.[30]

Betsy had little interest in Jerome's harebrained schemes. In fact, she was starting to think seriously about a divorce. As for going to Europe, when the time was right she'd make the trip on her own. In the meantime, she had begun investing part of her pension, making small purchases of shares in a variety of stocks: banking, maritime insurance, turnpike ventures, and individual companies. When she found a stock she liked, she made a small purchase, such as her ten shares in the Union Manufacturing Company; then she held it a long time and occasionally bought more. The yield was small but fairly safe, and that is what she wanted.[31]

Her brother Robert helped her buy a small house and lot in downtown Baltimore, on King George Street, on the east side of Jones Falls. It had been owned by Charles Carroll of Carrollton, grandfather of Robert's wife Mary Ann Caton. Robert paid $9,000 dollars for it and Betsy gave him a down payment of $1,324, with a promise to pay off the rest in a year. Robert also, at her instruction, hired a man to plaster the walls and paint the inside. Robert gave her the bill for that, which she paid. This, too, was an investment, as she could always rent out the place when she went to Europe.[32]

Betsy's financial plans were well timed, because things were not going well for her former brother-in-law and her ex-husband. Napoleon had defeated the major European nations with the exception of Czar Alexander's Russia. At Tilsit the two leaders had worked out some agreements, but now Napoleon wanted a much better deal. He tried to bluff Alexander into making concessions by building up a mass of troops along the czar's border. When Alexander failed to back down, the emperor was forced to invade or lose face. Invasion didn't frighten Napoleon. He'd repeatedly beaten large armies with his speed, superior tactics, and smart use of terrain. So in June of 1812 he moved several hundred thousand men (and women: wives, canteen operators, and camp followers) across the Niemen River and headed east.

Napoleon was eager to confront the Russian army on ground of his own choosing and had made careful plans. He'd move troops in such a way that he would divide the Russian forces and defeat them one element at a time. Unfortunately, the man he'd put in charge of the 80,000 soldiers on his right wing, with orders to move fast and swing around behind the Russians, was the King of Westphalia. Jerome didn't seem to understand the plan, or perhaps simply didn't feel like hurrying. He'd gone to the war with a baggage train heavily laden with necessities to maintain his dignity as a monarch, wagons full of bedding, linens, china, and flatware, along with a wardrobe of beautiful uniforms and crates filled with bottles of eau de cologne. He spent four days relaxing in a town he found comfortable and as a result destroyed his brother's strategic plan. A furious Napoleon fired the king from his command, and Jerome went home to Cassel to sulk.[33]

After that the emperor sought another chance to beat the

Russians in a confrontation, but Alexander wouldn't fight according to Napoleon's rules. Following several battles, the czar's forces kept retreating, drawing Napoleon ever deeper into Russia. Cossacks harried the French rear and flanks, while other Russian forces stripped the countryside of food and fodder all the way to Moscow. Napoleon took the city and found it empty. Not only were the people gone, but so were the supplies Napoleon desperately needed. The emperor kept waiting for the czar to ask for peace terms, but Alexander never did. Then a fire started. Some accounts say the Russians burned their own city to the ground.

There was nothing for Napoleon to do but turn around and march home in the middle of the Russian winter. Soon the temperature dropped, at times falling as low as thirty-five degrees below zero. After months of suffering, ten thousand starving and frostbitten remnants of Napoleon's Grande Armée struggled out of Russia. They left behind more than half a million of their comrades, dead in the snow or prisoners of the czar.[34]

Chapter 16

The Winds of War

In 1810 the Congress of the United States approved an amendment to the Constitution that threatened to invalidate the citizenship of any American who accepted a title of nobility "from any emperor, king, prince, or foreign power." It apparently was a reaction by some of the country's Federalists against those Republicans like Jefferson and Madison who were accused of favoring France over Britain. Even Republican Sam Smith was forced to favor the amendment lest he be charged with working to get his niece made a duchess.

It's difficult to understand the intensity of this pro- or anti-British feeling. In Baltimore, for example, people involved in commerce were dependent upon shipping, so Britain's depredations on seagoing trade made them anti-British. In June 1812, as Napoleon was invading Russia, the United States declared war against Great Britain after diplomatic endeavors failed to produce any guarantees from Britain that there would be no more attacks like the assault of the H.M.S. *Leopard* on the U.S.S. *Chesapeake*. When a local pro-British editor, Alexander Hanson, wrote a protest against the war, a mob armed with guns, axes, and hooks fell upon the office of Hanson's *Federal Republican*, tore the building apart, and wrecked the press. Editor Hanson moved his office into a house on Charles Street and a month later, joined there by fellow Federalists, published another antiwar editorial. That night a mob gathered and began throwing stones at the house. Those inside answered with musket fire, one of the crowd was killed, and the militia was called out. The Federalists agreed to surrender and were safely escorted to the jail, then the militia was dismissed. The mob, however, finding the soldiers gone, broke into the jail and viciously beat and tortured the prisoners. One died and eleven others were seriously wounded. Those who survived lived by playing dead. One of the wounded, Colonel "Light-Horse Harry" Lee, the father of Betsy's friend, never recovered from his injuries. When members of the mob were brought to trial, all of them were acquitted.[1]

In this atmosphere of violent hatreds, the anti-foreign-titles amendment had been passed and sent off to the various states for approval and inclusion in the Constitution. It appeared in the government printing office's published copies of the Constitution for years, until a congressman discovered the ratification process had fallen short by one state. Nevertheless, what eventually became known as "the phantom amendment" continued to appear in American history books for decades.[2]

Believing the amendment had the force of law, Betsy sought advice. Lawyer John Purviance concluded that this amendment not only related to titles but also to income, inducements, or emoluments from a foreign power. If it became law, she would no longer be able to sign the receipts for the payments she'd been receiving from Napoleon "without incurring the complete disenfranchisement of all her rights as an American citizen." The only possible way to avoid the penalty, he advised, would be to set up a trust directing all income to her son. Betsy would not be able to use any of it for the maintenance of her home or any of her other expenses. Purviance also provided her with a formal, legalistic explanation to give to the French authorities, with a request that the manner of payment be changed so that it came to her in trust for her son.[3]

After thinking it over Betsy decided not to make that request.[4] Instead, in the fall of 1812, she filed a petition for divorce in the Maryland legislature.[5] Betsy's motive was unrelated to Napoleon's travails in Russia. Few Americans understood that until later. The timing of the petition was prompted because Betsy was becoming a woman of property, and a married woman was not legally free to manage her own financial affairs. There was even a question as to whether she could execute contracts without her husband's approval. Only a single woman like Miss Spear could have free possession of her own money. So Betsy composed a request for a bill that would end her marriage. Her friend William Barney, son of the commodore, shepherded her petition through the political maze of the Maryland state legislature. Barney kept her informed of the bill's progress, and in January 1813 he reported that it had been passed. Betsy was granted a divorce *a vinculo matrimonii*, reserving her rights and those of her son under the marriage contract of 1803.[6]

The result was that as of January 1813, Betsy was free to possess and manage her own money. However, she had not settled the matter of Bo's education. Napoleon still had not given her his permission to come to Paris. Betsy wanted her son to be educated there and had delayed making a decision because she'd been assured she would be given leave to go. Now, though, it was getting late. In July of 1813 Bo was going to be eight years old. Betsy no longer had the help of Bo's so-called tutor, Colonel Tousard, and she'd been unable to find the high-quality teaching she was looking for either in Baltimore or Washington.

Socially, her son seemed to thrive traveling to and from the capital, Philadelphia, and the Patterson homes. He met many people and impressed them with his maturity. He was so used to being around important people, he wrote his mother to ask, "How are Mr. and Mrs. Madison?"

On occasion Betsy's male friends spent time with Bo. Once, when both Betsy and Miss Spear were in Washington sick with colds, Bo was sent home to South Street in the care of Jan Willink, who was on his way to spend time with the Gilmors. On another occasion, while Bo was at the Pattersons' residence, he met Elbridge Gerry. Gerry wrote Betsy of the meeting with Bo, saying he "had a pleasant interview with him. He is in fine health, vigorous in body and mind, and is impatient to see his dear mamma, his first inquiry having been, when was she to leave Washington?"[7]

Another matter of concern to Betsy was the crowded conditions at South Street. Bo liked being there, and even though Betsy was his "dear mamma," like his young uncles and aunts, he called Dorcas "Mother." There was always a housekeeper and there were slaves in the kitchen, but all that responsibility seemed to be wearing her mother down. Dorcas was ill from time to time, and to continue using her mother's home when Betsy had need of it was unfair. So now, while planning their eventual return to Europe, she determined to find a good local boarding school for Bo.

The choice turned out to be one recommended by Bishop Carroll: Mount St. Mary's College in Emmitsburg, Maryland. The teachers were priests who provided full-time supervision and were apparently quite strict with the boys, so Betsy reasoned that perhaps they could fill in whatever gaps there were in Bo's early education before she made the final move to a European school.

Bo resisted at first. For one thing, he objected to the curriculum. He considered the study of Latin completely unnecessary, because his "Grandpappa never studied it and he's a millionaire." Betsy, however, put down her little foot, and soon Bo was writing her letters from "Colege" to say, "I have improved so rapidly that I have advanced to Mair's Introduction in my Latin class." In another letter he wrote, "Doctor Mann has not whipped me yet. I learn my lessons very well. . . . I have had no battles since you've been away." Later he again admitted after one of her visits to him at school, "I have had no battles since your departure but was near having one," and added that Mr. Powell was going to teach him boxing. Soon he asked her for two French dictionaries, and not long after that he told her, "I do pretty well in French," and wrote his grandfather a whole letter in that language. Once he said, wistfully it seems, "I did not receive your letter until the 14th." Many of his letters open with heartfelt thanks for the one he just got from her. He calls her letters "most agreeable, enchanting," and even "adorable."[8]

The school's schedule apparently allowed the boys time at home during holidays and a summer break, so Bo was still able to spend time with the Pattersons. Even then he had homework, with which his mother's younger siblings helped him. He wrote his mother to tell her how much the presents she sent were being enjoyed by "the boys," apparently meaning his young uncles. It was during these times that he seemed to have missed Betsy most. "I am in very good spirits," he told her, "but be sure you attend to your precious health as what would become of me without you I would be a forlorn creature." In another he repeated his hope that she take care, "for you know I love you better than all the world put together."9

Apparently Bo was well aware of the news from Europe. He wrote, "My dear Father has lost his kingdom two or three hours before it was destroyed," then immediately went on to tell her that at the college they made a horse out of snow. He was also aware of her feelings about the news and told her, "I hope your spirits are not depressed on account of the late calamities which have befallen the French."10

The news gave Betsy reason to hope she might go to Paris soon, because the Bonapartes definitely were in trouble. In 1813 Jerome lost his kingdom to the revitalized coalition of Britain, Austria, Prussia, and Russia. He didn't much care; Westphalia was bankrupt anyway. He went back to France and tried to help his brother while the Allies closed in for the kill and the Duke of Wellington moved through Spain to invade France from the southeast. Napoleon continued fighting; there were more than a half-dozen military engagements throughout 1813. Then, during the first few months of 1814 there were eighteen more encounters, but on March 31 the Allies entered Paris, and on April 6 Napoleon abdicated. Jerome escorted his relatively new sister-in-law, Marie Louise, home to her father in Austria, then he and his Catherine sought refuge with her father in Württemburg. The Allies sent Napoleon off to the Mediterranean island of Elba and mistakenly thought that was the end of him.

Betsy kept her spirits up and remained, oddly, a staunch Bonapartist. She was still a frequent visitor in the home of Sam and Margaret Smith, and Sam remarked that she charmed all around her, "She laughs and talks, defends the Emperor and hopes he will destroy all his enemies."[11] She often said, "I have many faults but ingratitude is not one of them."

The French bureaucracy was slow to react to the changed situation, because her pension payments continued for six months after the emperor's abdication. Between November of 1809, when Turreau set up her account with his embassy, and the last payment in September 1814, she had received well over $50,000 from the French government. She'd invested as much as she could and was trying to live on the dividends she was earning. She kept careful records down to the smallest expenditure and totaled the income and outgo month by month, then added up everything at the end of each year. After one of her annual summations she noted: "I have lost 4 cents!" She made her money last by scrimping on everything. Much of the time she did her own laundry. She kept altering her clothing, removing the trimming from one dress and sewing it onto another so it appeared she had something new to wear. She tried to economize on food and made a point of keeping her dinner table conversation entertaining so she would receive frequent invitations to dine. Unlike the rest of the Pattersons, she never owned a slave. The only employees she had were a single maid from time to time and later a part-time coachman. And Betsy had a reputation for being very kind to those who worked for her. Such kindness apparently extended to Bo's dog. It was denied nothing, and in cold weather the canine slept between silk sheets.[12]

The one major item she consistently refused to economize on was education. Betsy never complained about the cost of her son's tuition, and now that Napoleon no longer had the power to keep her out of Europe, she realized she had no idea how to go about finding a good European school. In Washington she'd heard all sorts of things. One diplomat's wife told her the best schools were in Scotland, and another said that Geneva was the best for good schools. Betsy decided to make a short exploratory visit to gather information. To do so, she would need introductions to people who might be able to answer her questions.

She set to work requesting letters of introduction from everybody she knew who had overseas contacts—because certainly in Europe one could not just show up and ring a famous person's doorbell. She received help from many friends. Her Uncle Sam gave her a letter of introduction to his wartime comrade, the Marquis de Lafayette. Jan Willink provided one to his banker brother in Holland, Wilhelm Willink. Robert Gilmor also gave her a letter for that same Amsterdam banker, and wrote as well a letter recommending Betsy to Madame Schimmelpennick, wife of the grand pensionary for the Batavian Republic at Amsterdam, and Madame Liccama, a society woman who lived near Utrecht. Thomas Jefferson wrote her to say that, regretfully, since he hadn't been in France for twenty-five years, all the French friends he'd known there were gone. But Jefferson did give her a letter for the American ambassador now in Paris, Albert Gallatin, and that proved very helpful. Jonathan Russell, an envoy to the Court at Stockholm, told her he would be happy to transmit any messages she wished to send to Europe, but strongly advised her against taking the trip. He warned that living there was so expensive that she would need to spend at least six thousand dollars a year, and certainly more if she took along her child and the required female companion.[13]

The information confirmed Betsy's decision that this trip ought to be short and exploratory. She would travel without her son, and to minimize expenses, would travel with companions who were going anyway, like Dolley Madison's friends Dr. and Mrs. Eustis. Eustis was on his way to a U.S. government post in Holland, and might have diplomatic immunity against capture.[14]

Bo seemed fully aware of what his mother saw as his destiny. He'd begun to sign his letters *JNB* and, at times, the full name: *Jerome Napoleon Bonaparte*. In addition, he knew she was planning to go abroad without him for a time. Betsy had arranged for Dr. Dubois, at the school, to be his guardian during her absence, and her brother Edward and Robert's wife Mary Ann agreed to act as surrogate parents while she was away. When Dolley Madison had arranged for Betsy to go to Europe with Dr. and Mrs. Eustis, there was a trip to Boston to take a ship from there. However, the British had ceased to honor such quaint customs as diplomatic immunity for upstart Americans, so Eustis had to travel on a U.S. warship, leaving his family behind. Betsy, like Mrs. Eustis, had to go back home and await another opportunity for safe travel. But while his mother was waiting to embark, Bo wrote her in care of the Eustis family.

> *How are you? I am pretty well but my spirits are not very good. Tell me when you intend to go to France. . . . If you should see any-thing handsome in Boston I wish you would send it to me. Please send me one of your rings for to remember you if you should get lost in the sea. Do not stay any longer than one year for my sake. You must come for me to go to France with you and no one will do except you and my own Father. Give my love to Mr. and Mrs Eustis. Please answer this letter. Do not forget the promise which you made me to stay only one year.*
> *I am yours affectionately, Jerome N. Bonaparte*
>
> *P. S. Dear Mama I wish you would keep this letter with you all the time you are in France and read it over every month.*

Bo's closing words were: "Dear Mama I love you very much." [15]

Whatever changes were taking place in France, it was clear Napoleon could no longer keep her from going to Paris, but now there was another obstacle: the war against Great Britain. The Royal Navy was blockading the American coast, and any ship that tried to run the blockade was in danger of capture and perhaps destruction. At the same time, the war expanded beyond coastal blockades and raids to more aggressive attacks. With Bonaparte tucked away on Elba, thousands of battle-hardened troops were freed for the lesson Britain planned to teach the Americans.

The first blow fell on Washington. In August 1814, American militia were badly routed at Bladensburg, just northeast of the capital. Only Commodore Barney and his sailors distinguished themselves, but Barney was wounded and taken prisoner. The militiamen simply fled—so quickly that the battle became known as "the Bladensburg Races." [16]

The redcoats marched into Washington. Dolley Madison, who had planned to welcome her husband and his cabinet with a lavish dinner on their return from Bladensburg, eventually consented to flee at the last possible minute. Her final act was to order the removal of the great Gilbert Stuart painting of the first president. British officers entered the vacated President's House and enjoyed the dinner she had prepared, and left her a thank-you note before setting fire to parts of the house and the major public buildings. They spared the rest of the city, save for the office of a newspaper known for its attacks on Britain.

Their next objective was Baltimore. Rear Admiral Sir Alexander Cochrane, commanding the British forces in the Chesapeake, had remarked that dealing with the Americans was like training a spaniel: one had to beat him before one could teach him anything. He also referred to Baltimore as a "nest of pirates," after the swift privateers the city's shipyards produced that were wreaking havoc with British maritime commerce. Washington's fate was mild compared to what Cochrane contemplated for Baltimore.

City leaders raised $500,000 for arms and supplies and placed the town's defense in the hands of Samuel Smith. Believing that the attack would come from the east, Smith ordered the construction of a line of earthworks northeast of the city that reached all the way to the harbor at Fell's Point. Ships were sunk in the channel leading into Baltimore harbor, and a chain boom stretched across its mouth, where Fort McHenry bristled with guns. Townspeople by the thousands joined the thousands of volunteers streaming into the city from the surrounding area and nearby states, to construct those earthworks. When Cochrane's ships arrived late in the second week of September, the city was ready.

Paul Bentalou, William Patterson's friend who had helped Robert in Paris, kept watch for the attacking fleet from atop the State House in Annapolis. Fast couriers waited below for the first sign of British ships. It was not long in coming. Bentalou gave the warning, then ran down from his perch to carry word to Baltimore himself. By the time the British infantry landed at North Point—

east of the city, as Smith had predicted—12,000 men manned his breastworks. Citizens peered down the channel from their rooftops. Many women and children fled the city for safety, but businessmen remained and kept anxious watch over their property.

As Royal Navy bomb ships anchored just out of range of Fort McHenry's guns and commenced a long-range bombardment on what they knew to be the key to the city's defenses, British infantry ran into American militia a short distance from North Point, but this time the outcome was different: the militiamen inflicted heavy casualties and mortally wounded the British general in command, then retired in good order. Early the next morning the redcoats advanced to within sight of Smith's earthworks, saw they were heavily outnumbered and withdrew. After bombarding Fort McHenry for twenty-five hours without result, the navy followed, picked up the infantry, and sailed south down the bay.

While larger events were playing out in Europe and North America, a series of tragedies had shaken the Patterson household. Deaths of the very young were heartbreaking, but unfortunately common. Dorcas had lost Augusta Sophia at age two and Mary Ann Jeromia at three. Then death began claiming her older children. In late fall of 1808 her firstborn, William Junior, who had traveled to Lisbon with Betsy and Jerome, died at twenty-eight. Next came Margaret, already known as an artist. Max Godefroy had taken an interest in her work and urged that she not be allowed to study oil painting until she had thoroughly learned what was taught in drawing classes. Margaret died at age seventeen in January of 1811.[18]

Soon Dorcas herself was ailing. Letters within the family began to report the good and bad news of her condition, which seemed to change from one letter to the next. On January 1, 1814, Betsy's sister Caroline wrote her to say: "Mother is getting much better, but she has been very sick as you may conceive when she sent for the Doctor. She now keeps to her room to endeavor to keep off the chills and fevers, she has succeeded in the first and has had but a slight fever today." Even Bo was concerned and told Betsy, "Mother doesn't leave her room." At length, on May 21, 1814, Dorcas Patterson died at the age of fifty-two. Not long after that, twelve-year-old Octavius died. A Bible entry says he was injured by falling from a horse. That autumn, Betsy's last sister, sixteen-year-old Caroline, fell ill. A letter of November 7, 1814, from Robert's mother-in-law Mrs. Caton to Betsy, ends: "Present me affectionately to dear Caroline who I hope is better for her visit to Springfield." She was not, and six weeks later, on Christmas Day 1814, Caroline died. Betsy wrote that this sister had the most beautiful hair, complexion, and teeth she had ever seen.[19]

After the Eustis trip fell though, Betsy returned to Baltimore and began looking for another way to get to Europe. Now the atmosphere in the South Street house was drearier than it had ever been. Almost everyone was gone. Robert, who managed the WP & Sons ropewalk and had also been elected one of the commissioners of the City Bank of Baltimore, had his own home. John and his wife were in Virginia. The next brother, Joseph, was active in Europe for the company's overseas dealings. Edward spent most of his time with the Smiths; he was going to marry his first cousin, Sam's daughter Sidney. That left only George, nineteen, and Henry, fourteen, still at home. If Patterson was following his usual plan, they would both be working next door in his counting house.

Robert's mother-in-law Mrs. Caton tried to aid Betsy's escape. She explored the possibility of having Betsy sail with a couple named Donleavy, but it turned out their European destination differed from Betsy's and would have inconvenienced them.[20]

In the spring of 1815, Napoleon escaped from Elba and landed in France. For one hundred days he was the emperor again. As he began traveling toward Paris, he was joined by a burgeoning mass of supporters. By the time he reached the capital, he had another army behind him. In June he led them to a place called Waterloo, where he faced the Duke of Wellington and his allies. Napoleon was decisively defeated. Jerome was at his side, and fought bravely even after the cause was lost and Napoleon was forced to order him to stop.

Before Napoleon abdicated he gave thousands of francs to members of his family, ranging from 700,000 to Joseph down to 100,000 to Jerome. Napoleon thought about fleeing to America. Joseph volunteered to take his place and be captured by the British, but Napoleon couldn't make up his mind, and then it was too late. The conquerors took him aboard the H.M.S. *Bellepheron*, called by sailors the "Billy Ruffian," and took him to Plymouth sound. Napoleon planned to ask for asylum, but instead he would be judged and sentenced.[23]

At last all the obstacles that had kept Betsy on the American side of the Atlantic were gone: Napoleon, the blockade, and the war. One of her neighbors, Lydia Hollingsworth, wrote the news of Betsy's plan to her cousin Ruth Tobin out at Elkton.

> *I change the theme and tell you what may perhaps surprise you, that our fair neighbor Bonaparte is on the eve of her departure for Europe at last. . . . It has been the predominant desire of her life for years. She is unattended to Europe by her family or child. He is at school now at Emmitsburg. I sincerely wish her well, this scheme requires a decided character to go through with it. May it eventually prove for her good.*[24]

Like Lydia Hollingsworth, everyone who knew Betsy was aware of her plan. The only person surprised by her departure was her father.

Chapter 17

The Grand Tour

$\mathscr{B}$etsy's decision to leave her son and father to travel to Europe surprised no one but William Patterson. The severity of his letter to his daughter left no doubt as to his assessment of Betsy's decision.

> *Dear Betsy,*
>
> *I am persuaded you are pursuing a wrong course for happiness; but I hope and pray you may soon perceive your mistake, and that you will look to your mother-country as the only place where you can be really respected, for what will the world think of a woman who had recently followed her mother and her last sister to the grave, had quit her father's house, where duty and necessity called for her attentions as the only female of the family left, and thought proper to abandon all to seek for admiration in foreign countries; surely the most charitable construction that can be given to such conduct is to suppose that it must proceed in some degree from a state of insanity, for it cannot be supposed that any rational being could act a part so very inconsistent, and improper.*
>
> *I am, dear Betsy,*
> *Yours very sincerely*
> *W. P.* [1]

The close of Napoleon's reign as emperor produced Betsy's long-awaited opportunity to return to Europe and travel unhindered. Six weeks after Napoleon's defeat at Waterloo, she put her financial affairs into the hands of Miss Spear and, with the best wishes of her friends, sailed for Liverpool. She arrived July 26, 1815, the day before the H.M.S. *Bellerophon* brought the captured Napoleon into the port of Plymouth. There he would await his judgment and the sentence that would send him thousands of miles into the South Atlantic, where he would die.[2]

Betsy had passed her thirtieth birthday four months earlier, yet she had never taken a long trip alone; a lady simply didn't do that, no more than she could seek employment outside her home when she needed money. Still the ex-emperor's former sister-in-law never wavered in her resolve to set out for Europe on her own. According to Eliza Anderson Godefroy, Betsy was "far gone in morbid melancholy" and needed to get away. Eliza had urged her to overcome her sadness by "using her talents."[3] Lydia Russell, whose husband had warned Betsy about how much it cost to live abroad, gave her letters of introduction, including one to the painter Benjamin West, and wished her happiness in Europe.[4] Her son Bo was surprised that after all the previous plans had fallen through, she'd gotten away at last. Soon after her departure, Mary Caton Patterson wrote her to say the boy was saddened and had wanted so much to go with her.[5]

In contrast, William Patterson was furious, and accused her of leaving without the consent of her friends and without saying goodbye to anyone, including her son. Patterson wrote to her contacts in Europe to warn them of Betsy's arrival. As a result, when she contacted James McIlhiny of the firm McIlhiny & Glennie in London, she was shocked to find that her father had written them to say his daughter had "conceived herself ill." He implied that she was mentally unbalanced and asked them to monitor her behavior and inform him about it.[6]

When McIlhiny reported this to her,[7] Betsy wrote her father insisting she had been following the advice of her physicians. She went on about the information she was obtaining in regard to her son's education, and how people accepted her abroad in a way they never did at home. In Europe she was: "cherished, visited, respected, and admired." She'd gone from London to the resort town of Cheltenham, where she was under the protection of her friends, Sir Arthur and Lady Brooke Falkener. Sir Arthur was a retired physician, and he was advising her about her health, while through Lady Falkener she was being invited to all the high-level social events.[8]

Cheltenham, a fashionable spa where people "took the waters" for therapeutic bathing and medicinal drinking, attracted large numbers of wealthy and titled visitors. The lists of arrivals published by the *Cheltenham Chronicle* reads like a British "Who's Who," and the reports of scheduled entertainments range from grand galas and musical concerts to ventriloquism demonstrations and an exhibition of Polito's Traveling Menagerie "in a spacious field near the Crescent of a zebra, elephant, majestic male lion, royal tiger from Bengal, laughing hyena, horned horse, and male and female kangaroos."[9]

Betsy wrote her father scornfully, stating that "It appears to me that, if I have friends in America, their friendship might have been shown in some more agreeable mode than finding fault with me for being miserable in a country where I never was appreciated, and where I can never be contented." Then she seems to have decided to appeal to him in terms of reputation and social standing, concepts he would understand. She pointed out that for him to circulate rumors about her would be detrimental to her and to her son, who would need to make his own way in the world one day.

> *Everyone who knows me has heard that your wealth is enormous, and consequently they think I shall have a large fortune from you. In Europe a handsome woman who is likely to have a fortune may marry well; but if it gets about that her parents are dissatisfied with her, they will think she will get nothing by them, and if she had the beauty of Venus and the talents of Minerva, no one will marry her. People here are not such fools as to marry poor beauties, however much they may admire them. The reputation of your fortune would be a great advantage to me abroad, and I am sure you cannot object to my having the honor of it, provided you keep the substance.*

She ended with a defensive plea to convince him of her worth: "I get on extremely well, and I assure you that although you have always taken me for a fool, it is not my character here. . . . I am very prudent and wise."[10]

Patterson was not impressed. He wrote back to say that her ideas of wisdom and prudence did not accord with his.[11] In reply she kept giving him evidence of her social success abroad and told him: "I am not half as foolish as you imagine, or I should, perhaps, have been more contented."[12] Eventually she came to a bitter conclusion: "I have experienced the perfect truth of the observation that in mediocrity alone can be found happiness."[13]

Even the straight-laced McIlhiny believed Patterson should contribute to Betsy's support, and told him he ought to give her an allowance for her living expenses. Patterson replied that he would never contribute to her support as long as she chose to live abroad, and put it in such emphatic terms that McIlhiny told Betsy there would be no point in his attempting to press the matter further. He was right. According to Betsy, after the original 1805 trip to Lisbon, her father never gave her another cent for the next thirty years.[14]

Betsy's worries about money were well founded. Even if she had been able to spend none of her French pension and invest it all, fifty thousand dollars at the rare prime rate of six percent interest could yield her no more than three thousand dollars a year, roughly half what it would cost her to live in a major European city. Other wealthy merchants of Patterson's generation were not so miserly. When Charles Carroll of Carrollton—a man every bit as thrifty as Patterson—sent his Caton granddaughters abroad, he told them to enjoy themselves, to stay as long as they chose, and he would provide the means.[15] Patterson and Betsy would continue to quarrel for years, but the true depth of his resentment did not become apparent until two decades later with the publication of his will.

On Betsy's side, her anger was prompted by actions extending far beyond his refusal to give her any support when her plans differed from his, or his perpetual criticism of her motives, or his demands that she behave the way a female should. Betsy was also furious at her father's chronic marital infidelity. She complained, as did some other family members, not only about his treatment of her mother, but also of the poor example he was providing to his younger children. Patterson's dalliances continued for years, even while his wife was dying. Apparently, a number of these trysts took place inside the home, since several of the women were the family's housekeepers. As a consequence, one of the housekeepers was forcibly removed from the house by Betsy's brother Edward.[16]

When housekeeper Providence Sommers got pregnant, Patterson paid a man named John Garvin of Gettysburg, Pennsylvania, to marry her. Later Garvin asked for more money, and Patterson gave him another thousand dollars. The child was named Matilda Sommers, and Patterson paid for her tuition at a good school. After a time he wrote to a relative asking her to check on the girl's progress.

> *I take the liberty of enclosing a Note to Miss Matilda Sommers a student at the female Academy of the Visitation at George Town, a young person whom I have taken under my protection for her Education, particulars respecting which I will explain to you hereafter. My object is to request the favor of your calling at the Seminary when you have leisure to deliver the Note, and to make particular inquiry respecting the progress of the Education of this young person, which will greatly oblige me, and I will thank you not to mention or take any notice of this business before I shall have an opportunity of conversing with you on the subject.[17]*

In his will, William Patterson left money and property to Providence Garvin and to her daughter. The bequest extended during her natural life and to the child or children of her, the said Matilda Sommers, and to her heirs forever. Patterson also made bequests to other housekeepers.[18]

Despite her anger, Betsy appears to have remained desperate for her father's approval. In letter after letter she attempted and failed to win it. But Betsy kept her actual disappointment and bitterness submerged except with the close friends she was about to make in Europe, and in the comments she wrote later on her collection of letters from her father.

Apparently Bo recovered from his disappointment over not being with his mother on this trip. Betsy's brother Edward wrote her, enclosing a letter from her son and reporting that he was in perfect health. He also included a list of items he wanted Betsy to buy abroad for the home he and Sidney Smith were furnishing. Even though it was simply some additions to the list he'd already given her, it was a very long list: soup ladles, silver saltcellars, two dozen dessert forks, three dozen dessert spoons, two tall candlesticks, a bread basket, snuffers with trays, and so on. In addition, he wanted her to have a chest made for the silver with room to add the items he already had. He added: "If you don't think of going to France immediately you had better order it at London, it will be in time if here in the spring or summer. I'll thank you to send Sid 6 or 8 handsome morning wrappers and one or two full dresses if you should see anything that pleases you."[19]

Apparently people trusted Betsy's taste. Dolley Madison had written to thank her for a mantle Betsy had sent her and added that she'd like her to buy something more for her "in case you meet with anything elegant in the form of a turban or an evening wrap of flowered lace in gold or silver thread."[20]

Meanwhile Betsy was still thinking about a school for Bo. McIlhiny had advised her to forget about Scotland: England's Harrow was the place for him. Still, Edinburgh had an excellent reputation for its medical school and although she didn't envision her son as a doctor, she feared he would need a calling that would enable him to support himself. Betsy thought that perhaps he should study law, or something else offered at Edinburgh. At the same time she was afraid she couldn't afford either school.

Confused, Betsy decided not to go home just yet. It was now the winter of 1815–1816. The seasonal stormy weather made this a bad time for crossing the Atlantic. Also, she had commissions for purchases best fulfilled on the Continent. Besides, she couldn't bear the thought of going back home without seeing the French capital. As soon as the news from France indicated that the post-Napoleonic chaos there had settled down, Betsy made plans to leave for France. She wrote to her sister-in-law Mary Caton Patterson from London to say she would depart for Paris in a few days: "The fear of returning to America keeps me from getting well and my income is too limited to allow me to remain in the Circle in which I move. All that is wanting to my happiness is a larger income which would allow me to remain in Europe." She also told Mary that since she'd been in London she'd been painted three times. One of the portraits was scheduled for an exhibition the next May, and copies of another one were being sold by subscription. But she confided that her appearance was very much changed because she'd been continually ill thinking of all the misery that awaited her back home.

> *In my dreams I am transported to the populous desert of Baltimore and awake shuddering. . . . You know not my misery about my poor child and how I am torn by contrary desires. . . . I can never exist there and yet how can I live here on my pittance? If I had only money enough to educate my child here, and if I could only know that I should never return to my wretchedness in the United States, I am sure I should get well.*[21]

When she arrived in Paris she checked into a hotel that catered to foreigners. Thanks to Thomas Jefferson's letter of introduction, she was able to present herself at the American embassy and request a meeting with Ambassador Albert Gallatin, a Swiss-American who had been secretary of the treasury in the Jefferson and Madison administrations. From then on Betsy was a frequent guest of the Gallatins, and noted that Mrs. Hannah Gallatin was very kind to her.[22]

The Gallatins had a son, James, in his twenties and a daughter, Frances, in her teens. The young man kept a diary that was eventually published as *A Great Peacemaker: The Diary of James Gallatin with an Introduction by Lord Bryce*. Historians have questioned the veracity of the diary. Its dates are often wrong and some of the entries seem distorted by the writer's personal prejudices. For example, there is an entry describing a famous dinner guest's gross table manners. The reliability of the story is questionable, as it is not supported by any other eyewitness account of this man.[23]

Fortunately for Betsy, young Gallatin liked her. In fact, he seems to have been fascinated by her, and wrote a number of descriptions of her visits to the embassy. Most of these are supported by Betsy's own records and the accounts of others. For example, at the time of her first visit to Paris, James wrote: "Mrs. Patterson Bonaparte is here. She is really beautiful and has a wonderful charm of manner. She is much sought after; her wit and beauty seem to open all doors to her." After she dined with the Gallatins, James recorded the event and added: "Mme Bonaparte was as usual brilliant, and kept the whole table alive with her witticisms."

Betsy's wit at a dinner table is also supported by other accounts. Perhaps the most famous of these is the story about the pompous Englishman who asked her if she'd read the recent book which claimed all Americans are vulgarians. She had, so he asked what she thought of that claim. She said she "would have doubted it, if Americans were descended from the Indians or Eskimos, but since they are descendants of the English, I'm perfectly certain it is true." That remark and many others became a sort of "Betsy folklore," stories that are difficult to track down but were passed around for decades until they finally wound up in her newspaper obituaries.

Later, Gallatin amended his description of her beauty. He said: "She is very lovely, but hard in expression and manner. I don't think she has much heart."[24] Nevertheless, Betsy continued to appear on his pages and some of his comments may be useful whenever verification can be found in more reliable sources.

Through the Gallatins Betsy also made contact with a man who would be a good friend for decades, David Baillie Warden. Though born in Ireland, he was an American citizen and had been secretary at the Paris legation during the ambassadorship of General Armstrong. Now, however, he was—in modern terms—a freelance writer. Warden published English translations of work from French and Latin classics. He wrote by invitation articles on North and South America for inclusion in encyclopedias. His work earned him membership in the Académy Française and the friendship of some of the most intriguing people in Paris. Another aspect of his nature was an inexhaustible willingness to share his knowledge of Paris with others. He helped Betsy move out of her hotel and into a small and reasonably priced apartment, ran errands for her, and took her around town to introduce her to all sorts of interesting people. She became a sensation at the social events where she appeared, in part because of her resemblance to Napoleon's sister Pauline, for whom she was at times mistaken.[25]

Actually, all the Bonapartes had fled France by this time. As a result, the Duke of Wellington, on behalf of his government, bought the Paris home of Pauline Bonaparte. This was the palace of her husband, Prince Borghese, and would from then on serve as the British Embassy. There the duke gave parties to help create a semblance of stability as the restored Bourbon monarchy began taking over the government of the country. Betsy immediately was invited to the balls at the new British Embassy. During one of them, as she danced with the duke, his spur tore the hem of her dress. He boorishly didn't apologize; all he said was "Oh, me damn spur!" and examined his boot for damage.[26]

The news of Betsy's social success was swift to reach her hometown. Her cousin John Spear Smith wrote to tell her he'd heard from Paris that it didn't seem "possible for any one woman to receive as much homage as you did at the Duke of W's ball."

It is now very generally reported that you set the fashions in Paris! How do you stand this torrent of admiration? But why should I ask such a question of one who from the moment she appeared in the world has received this emotion? What would turn the brain of any other, is but habitual and blasé to you.[27]

A month later he wrote again to tell her, "General Scott has arrived and has blazoned forth your fame throughout the country.

He says your levee is crowded every morning with *la haute noblesse* and the lowest rank admitted is a lieutenant general."[28] Betsy was also invited to the new French court, but declined to attend. She was still grateful to Napoleon and refused her friends' advice that she petition King Louis for a continuance of her pension. The new Bourbon king said to Albert Gallatin: "I hear that Madame Jerome Bonaparte is with you. Pray express to her our regret that she will not come to our Court, but that we know her reasons for not doing so." On hearing this Betsy remarked, "That Corsican blackguard would not have been so gracious."[29]

She enjoyed attending social events and no doubt reveled in her reception there, but Warden was also introducing her to the people she found most fascinating: the literary and scientific community whose books she had not only read, but reread and pored over. Through him she became acquainted with Madame de Staël and the Countess Rochefoucauld. Her most frequent associate became the Marquise de Villette, who had been Voltaire's ward and (it was said) kept his heart at home in a small golden container. Betsy and the marquise began seeing each other almost daily, went for rides about the city, dined together three times a week, and shared the marquise's theater box.[30]

It was also at this time that Betsy met the Irish writer Lady Sydney Morgan, whose novels and travel books were the early-nineteenth-century version of our contemporary best-sellers. She had recently completed a book about France and was planning to write one about Italy. Betsy and Lady Morgan shared with each other comments on the places they were seeing and the books they were reading, and the Irish writer even told Betsy about the work she was doing at the moment and promised to have a first-published copy put aside for her friend. Lady Morgan became the person with whom she shared her deepest feelings. Their correspondence is revealing of Betsy's true concerns, which contrasted with the façade Betsy kept up in public. James Gallatin would not have known those true feelings when he wrote that Betsy had no heart. The correspondence was sometimes interrupted by events in their individual lives, but nevertheless it continued from 1816 through 1849. Sydney was the only European to whom Betsy was able to admit how poor she was during the first year of their acquaintance, or the feelings of loneliness and discouragement she hid from the world.[31]

The correspondence began during a separation in August 1816 when Sydney wrote Betsy to say that she and her husband had to leave Paris and go back home to Dublin because their agent there had gone bankrupt and fled, taking their money with him. From the start, each letter on both sides of this correspondence generally ran to several closely written pages, and both writers slipped into French whenever they felt it gave the truest expression of their thoughts. They rattled on to each other about everything that was on their minds, with Sydney's scrawl climbing up around the margins, while Betsy's writing grew smaller to keep her lines straight. Sydney told her, "You are one of the few women who profess less than they feel." It was here that Betsy was able to admit she had frequent spells of profound, even suicidal, depression. In one 1816 letter Betsy told her friend, in the midst of what was an exciting Parisian social life, that she had been very ill and very sad. She said everything in the world bored her and she didn't know why:

> Tout m'ennui dans ce monde et je ne sais pas pourquoi, *unless it be the recollection of what I have suffered. I think the best thing for me to do is to return to my dear child in the spring; I love him so entirely, that perhaps seeing him may render my feelings less disagreeable.*

At the same time she was convinced the climate of America was bad for her health, yet she said any inconvenience was more supportable than being separated from one's children.[32]

While she struggled with these conflicting emotions, her finances were deteriorating. As she had indicated in her London letter to her sister-in-law Mary Caton Patterson, her income was too limited to allow her to remain in the circle in which she moved. The cost of living in Paris was even higher than that of London. As a result, as she wrote to Lady Morgan much later, she was desperately poor during this 1815–1816 winter in Paris.[33]

⸺

Betsy had never shown much interest in accumulating more than a very few household items, or even in home ownership except as an investment. So before leaving Baltimore she had sold to her brothers much of what was left after her father appropriated the horses, carriage, and furniture Jerome had bought for their planned home together. The sale amounted to over a thousand dollars worth of china and silver, and served as her emergency fund for this trip.[34] It was becoming obvious that the interest income from her invested pension was simply not enough to cover her expenses in Europe, and her financial reserves were shrinking. Consequently, when there was an occasion requiring gift-giving, she gave a piece of her own jewelry or something she had made, and there are among her letters thank-you notes praising her handiwork. She carried her sewing box with her everywhere she went and used spare time to create useful items. One of her titled Paris friends even invited her to spend an afternoon helping her make curtains. And from Ireland Lady Morgan wrote to say: "I wish you would embroider me some little thing that I might have some of your work to boast of."[35]

In February Betsy wrote to her brother Robert's mother-in-law, Mrs. Caton. After chatting about mutual acquaintances and offering to make purchases for her and send them on, she complained about her situation.

> *Dress and living are enormously increased in price since the arrival of the English in Paris. . . . I cannot get rooms under 400 francs per month and mine are very indifferent. A carriage costs five hundred francs a month. In short I am very much surprised at the difference between my calculations and the actual state of things here.*

She added that all she needed was eight thousand dollars a year to be perfectly happy. Though admitting there were those in America she loved and regretted, still she had no wish ever to return.

My child, if I cannot send for him to finish his education in England, I shall return to partake of his situation in America, but it will cost me all the pleasure, all the happiness of my future life. I never shall enjoy one hour of content on my return and I never think of it without shedding tears.[36]

Despite her poverty she couldn't resist buying a few books while in the French capital, where she saw displays of secondhand volumes along the streets outside book shops and even on the banks of the Seine. She bought a three-volume set of L'Abbé Prevost's *Memoires et Aventures d'un Homme de Qualité* and the *Memoires de Madame de Staël,* as well as sets of Voltaire and Moliere. Two of her purchases particularly interested her. One was the memoir of a granddaughter of King Henry IV, Mlle. Montpensier, which Betsy described as "very amusing" and read repeatedly throughout her life. The other was *Les Caracteres de Monsieur de la Bruyere.* Her copy is filled with marks in her hand, and in the front she wrote: "Read, re-read this work. It is full of sense & truth & entire knowledge of human nature." In addition, as her Parisian friends got to know her love of reading, they began giving her presents of books, such as a set of Byron's works.[37]

Back home when Betsy needed advice—whether legal, in regard to that Phantom Amendment, or political, when she wanted a divorce—she sought out the best expert she could find. Now that her finances were increasingly a concern, she turned to a former treasury secretary. Gallatin didn't object. He took time to meet with her and give her his advice. It may have been at that time the ambassador convinced her to have her son educated where he himself had been, in Geneva. So in spite of the interesting time she was having in Paris, she pulled herself together and set off for the arduous days-long coach journey to Switzerland for a firsthand look at the Geneva schools.

In Geneva she moved into a boarding house and found among her fellow guests an American whose fortune amounted to several times that of her father. The German John Jacob Astor, son of a butcher, had immigrated to the United States and entered the fur trade, eventually becoming the dominant figure in the American fur trade. He was a successful financier, and perhaps most lucrative of all, wound up owning many acres of extraordinarily valuable New York City real estate. He said he was in Switzerland now for the same reason as Betsy, the exploration of educational opportunities for his children. He eventually bought a home at Genthod, not far from Geneva, and visited there between trips to Germany, France, and Italy. With Betsy he was not only generous with financial advice but also, later on, carried messages between her and the Bonapartes living at Rome.[38]

Also in Geneva there was a group of French-speaking titled Russian and Polish expatriates who migrated more or less continuously back and forth between summers in Geneva and winters in Italy, especially Florence. They embraced Betsy at once, inviting her to their homes repeatedly for dinner, tea, rides in the country, picnics, and parties. One of them, Princess Caroline Galitzin, urged her to move in with her, and when Betsy was reluctant to do that, promised to keep a room ready for her at each of her homes. These individuals also became Betsy's friends, and the friendships also lasted for decades. But now she had to go home.

James Gallatin's diary, August 11, 1816:

> *Madame Patterson Bonaparte arrived this morning from Geneva. Her baggage nearly filled the antechamber. . . . Her son seems to be her one thought. She had a very long talk with father about his future (her son's); she is most ambitious for him. She even has a list of different princesses who will be available for him to marry: as he is only ten years old, it is looking far ahead.*

And four days later, Gallatin noted:

> *Madame Bonaparte left to-day for Havre to embark for America. She is such an interesting person, we will miss her. She gave*

*mamma a ruby-velvet frock to cut up for Frances. To father she
gave a really beautiful turquoise and diamond brooch. He will
never wear it, so I will have it.*[39]

That description is vivid and certainly sounds like Betsy. And
one of the earliest writers to write a book about her and who was
her contemporary, Eugene L. Didier, recorded in *The Life and
Letters of Madame Bonaparte,* that she came back to Baltimore
in the summer of 1816. But apparently she did not.

In April of that year Betsy wrote to David Baillie Warden from
the port of Le Havre. She asked him to put the enclosed letters
into the Paris post office. She didn't have time to do this because
she had to wait until 8 P.M. for her agent, Callaghan, to settle her
account with him. Betsy wrote: "The vessel will not sail for two
or three days. I am tired, triste, discontented. Write to me. Yours
affectionately, E. Patterson."[40]

Then, in a letter later discovered at Bo's school, Mount St.
Mary's, Betsy wrote Fr. DuBois from Paris in June:

*My health is very much improved. The climate and society of
France are equally agreeable to me. I shall remain here another
year. Continue, my dear sir, your attentions to my dear child, and
do me the justice to believe that I shall never forget your kindness.
I remain with the highest sentiments of regard and esteem, your
obliged servant.* [41]

In Paris for the rest of that summer, she received notes from
her friends and the usual flurry of letters from Baltimore regarding items she was to purchase for family members. On August 22
(a week after Gallatin says she left for Le Havre), she wrote a very
long letter from Paris to her cousin John Spear Smith. She wrote
that for some weeks she had been "immersed in Balls, Soirees,
and Dinners which have not left me a single moment to dispose
of." Betsy added that Mrs. Gallatin continued to be very kind to
her, and that she went to the Gallatins' every day. She added that
the Countess D'Orsay gave a ball every week and that very evening
Betsy was going to Mde. De La Rouchefoucauld's. Betsy confirmed

to Smith that she had checked on the china he ordered and gave him further information. She told him about her friend Sydney Morgan and their day trips to Versailles, St. Cloud, and other places in the vicinity. Betsy added: "Pecuniary difficulties, or the impossibility of sending for my dear child may compel me to leave France. Certainly nothing else will induce me to do it." Betsy contrasted her life in America with her life in Europe:

> The waste of life which takes place with us shut up in our melancholy country houses where we vegetate for months alone is happily not endured here. Those long wearisome winter evenings varied only by the entrance of the tea equipage, minding the fire, and handing around apples and nuts do not form any part of the 12 months in happy, wise France.[42]

What happened while she waited for that ship at Le Havre? Was the sailing canceled? Did she become ill? The only reference to a physical problem is a report to the Morgans the next month that she had been suffering from a toothache for two weeks.[43] By mid-winter, however, she seemed to be feeling fine. In January the Duke of Wellington invited her, not to a ball, but to spend the evening at the British Embassy.[44] Then there were a flurry of letters from Baltimore with requests for her to purchase items for family members.

Psychologists say suppressed anger can result in depression. Is it possible that Betsy's unspoken rage at her father can account for her seeming inability to go home? Her comments about Baltimore and even America sound at times irrational. Did she transfer her feelings about the senior Patterson onto her hometown? These are questions only a psychiatrist could answer. But it is clear she began feeling better once she decided to stay in Paris.

By the next spring she was ill. A doctor in Paris said her lungs were congested and her liver was affected. Sydney's husband, Sir Charles Morgan, was a doctor, and when she wrote in May to

Dublin about her diagnosis, he expressed concern; he thought she ought to get another opinion from a British doctor. Failing that, he wondered if she'd had these symptoms before, and had her visit to take the waters at Cheltenham made them any better? Sydney said they were concerned by her "tone of tristesse and suffering." She wished they had a harlequin wand to rouse her out of her illness and laugh her out of her ennui. The Morgans urged her to join them in Dublin so they could take care of her. She didn't accept their offer. In August she acknowledged: "I have lost my health," and told the Morgans she was going to go home to her son.[45]

She began getting things in order so she could return to Baltimore with the items she had purchased in Paris. It took her until September to do it, but by the twelfth of that month she was back at Le Havre. This departure is fully documented.

McIlhiny in London confirms it, as does Betsy herself. She wrote inside a book she was reading, *Lettres Chinoises*: "I left Havre the 12 of Sept 1817 to sail for N.Y. in the Maria Theresa (Capt. Skiddy). Mrs. Tousard with me. EP à la mer Octobre 1817."[46]

<hr/>

It was late in the season for a crossing; the seas were stormy and the voyage took seven weeks. In November she wrote back to Paris and told David Baillie Warden it was "a terrible crossing" but that when she got to New York she had taken care of the errands he wanted her to perform. Then she commissioned Robert White to ship all her packages from New York to Baltimore by water and set off by coach for home.

Since her own small houses were rented and her funds exhausted, Betsy was forced to move into one of her father's homes, where she was reunited with her son and thrilled to find how well he'd done at Mount St. Mary's. He was in the highest French class and had placed first of the seventeen students in the highest English class. When Robert White's shipment arrived from New York she distributed her purchases and gifts; then she sat down with Miss Spear to go over the financial records.

The time was right for a complete reevaluation. Some of her bonds had matured and that money would have to be moved to other investments. In addition, she had gotten a great deal of financial advice abroad and set to work putting those suggestions into effect. Betsy knew now that as things stood, her income was insufficient for living abroad, and certainly not sufficient for Bo's Geneva tuition.

There were bits of good news. Miss Spear had not used the tuition money left for Bo. William Patterson paid it himself and made it clear he didn't want to be reimbursed. He had become very fond of Bo. Once, when he feared the boy was ill, according to Miss Spear, "He carried him to the doctor himself." Her brother Edward told her not to worry about saving up for Bo's future, because their father was providing for him generously in his will.

It took months to reorganize her finances. By the time she had made some progress, outside events began affecting her arrangements. The national economy was sliding into a severe recession that would last several years. The situation was worsened by problems among the banks. Some of them suffered from malfeasance among officers who loaned themselves bank funds to make failed personal investments. About a hundred Baltimore businessmen went bankrupt. Among the struggling businessmen was Betsy's uncle, Sam Smith, who had left his company, Smith & Buchanan, in the hands of his partner while he served in Congress. The partner, Buchanan, also served as president of the local branch of the national bank, where he used bank funds to buy hundreds of thousands of dollars worth of stock. When the stock went down instead of up, his fraud was detected. Sam, as his partner, was drawn into the mess. His wife Margaret gave him her father's legacy, and William Patterson and others also contributed money, but Sam was forced to sell his home, Montebello. His son, John Spear Smith, bought the place back and saved it for the family, but Sam—recently the hero of the Battle of Baltimore—spent years in a suicidal depression.[47]

Betsy must have felt very far away from her two advisors, Gallatin and Astor. She did succeed in getting her finances into proper shape, but it took months, and during that time her European friends kept writing, urging her to come back to them. She stayed in her room as much as possible, reading and working on embroidery.[48]

At last Betsy decided to take Bo to Geneva and enroll him in a school there. She would have to be very thrifty, but she could manage, and she determined to teach her son to be thrifty as well. She provided him with a notebook so he could write down every expense, however small, they incurred on the trip. She also began to teach him the fine points of polite behavior, along with the correct manner of addressing various ranks of nobility. In other words, she began to prepare him for the rank she was certain he deserved.[49]

Chapter 18

The Betrothal

*W*hen Betsy and Bo arrived in Amsterdam in June 1819, the French consul there told them Bo would not be given a passport to travel through France. Betsy argued that she and her son were traveling under the name of Patterson, she as *Mrs. Patterson* and—since one of her brothers had obtained Bo's passport—Bo was listed as *Edward Patterson*. The consul remained adamant. He said the boy's resemblance to Napoleon was so striking that it would cause trouble in France. Consequently they were forced to travel through Germany to reach Switzerland.[1]

At Geneva they moved into a boarding house and Betsy enrolled Bo in the best school in the city. Eventually Betsy gave up on the boarding house; she wasn't getting enough meat and vegetables, and she remarked that apparently the hosts of Geneva expected their guests to be too spiritual to eat. Instead, they were supposed to subsist on the mountain scenery, the view of the lake, and the spectacular sunsets. She moved into a small apartment in town within walking distance of everything, since she couldn't afford a carriage. The place had four rooms, one for her, one for her son on the weekends, and one for the maid she was able to hire. The fourth served as a sitting room.[2]

Bo apparently settled well in his new school. He would be studying mathematics, chemistry, physics, history, geography, languages—Greek, Latin, English, and French—as well as drawing, dancing, fencing, and equitation. The last subject was his favorite, and soon he was asking Betsy to buy him a horse of his own. When she said that was too expensive, he proposed asking his millionaire grandfather for the money. She refused, saying she'd pay for him to have extra riding classes at the school, but they were not going to buy a horse. He did get a dog, though, and gave it the French name for wolf, *le loup*. Betsy grew very fond of Le Loup, remarking that he was much more intelligent than half the people one meets. She arranged for the dog's bed to be fitted with sheets as well as blankets, and he slept with his head on a pillow. She took him on her walks around Geneva, where, she claimed, people complemented her on how handsome and friendly he was.

Before long Betsy became reacquainted with the Russian and Polish friends she'd made during her earlier trip to Geneva, and spent time with the Galitzens, Countess Opalinska, Princess Potemkin, Prince Demidoff, and others. Bo was invited to events that took place on the weekend, and the name of Le Loup was put on an invitation now and then. The boy wrote his grandfather: "Mamma goes out nearly every night to a party or a ball. She says she looks full ten years younger than she is, and if she had not so large a son she could pass for five and twenty years old."[3]

Betsy met John Jacob Astor again and spent some time with him. She liked him, this man who was one of the richest in the world, but she felt a bit sorry for him, saying, "He seems, poor man, afflicted with possession of a fortune which he had greater pleasure in amassing than he can ever find in spending."[4] In the autumn of 1819 Astor went to Rome, where he encountered some of the Bonapartes who'd found refuge in the Italian capital. Napoleon's mother was there, along with her relative Cardinal Fesch and several other members of her family. Her daughter Pauline was also living in Rome at the Borghese Palace, her husband's home. There, it was said, she continued her usual custom of having frequent lovers and invited her admirers to come in to watch her have her pedicures done. The sculptor Canova posed Pauline almost completely nude while he made his famous reclining statue of her. When people asked, "Weren't you *uncomfortable* posing that way?" she laughed: "Certainly not. There was a fire in the room."

Pauline Borghese told Astor that the Bonapartes were interested in her brother's former wife and their son, and that she was especially eager to have the boy visit her. Astor returned to Geneva with an invitation for Betsy and her son to visit Rome. He warned her that the Bonapartes were not trustworthy, especially Pauline. She was said to change her will frequently on a whim, and there were rumors that she had quarreled with her brother Jerome and may have wanted to embarrass him. As for Astor, he was convinced the whole Bonaparte clan was too unreliable to be trusted.

Sydney Morgan and her husband also had come to Geneva from Rome, on their way back to Ireland. They had been researching her new book on Italy, and had encountered some of the Bonapartes there. Sydney's opinion of Pauline matched Mr. Astor's completely.

Betsy was undecided. Her son had never seen his father and he longed to get to know him. But ex-king Jerome was not in Rome. He was living some distance away on a small income from his second wife's family. Considering his spending habits, Betsy was sure he couldn't help with her son's education or the cost of a trip to visit his European family. On the other hand, didn't she owe it to Bo to let him get to know his relatives? Perhaps, but she decided not to interrupt his education on a questionable venture.

Two years later she changed her mind. The overtures from the Bonapartes had continued. The oldest brother Joseph, who now called himself the Count of Surveilliers, was living in the United States, where he had a town home in Philadelphia and a large mansion called "Point Breeze" near Bordentown. Joseph had written Betsy to offer the use of his furnished but unoccupied chalet some distance outside of Geneva. She was forced to decline because she still couldn't afford a carriage, but she also preferred being surrounded by close friends to living alone in the country. Nevertheless, she appreciated the offer, and it made her think perhaps it was time to take Bo to Rome to meet his relations.[5]

In truth, Betsy was proud of Bo and enjoyed taking him places. He seemed to be very bright and was turning out to be a handsome young man. His manners were perfect and he spoke French every bit as well as he spoke English. So at length she decided to interrupt the boy's education for a few weeks and make up for it by arranging for him to continue with his Latin study and learn Italian as well while they were in the Italian capital.

In late fall 1821 she booked carriage seats for herself, Bo, and her maid to travel over the Alps and down into Italy. They also took Le Loup along. It was a chilling journey. Betsy caught a bad cold that left her coughing all winter, but she refused to let that disrupt her plan. Bo, now sixteen, was a great help; as he wrote to his grandfather, he was the one who went looking for rooms for them to rent and made bargains. Soon he was so busy with visits to his relatives he had almost no time to see the sights of the city.[6]

As soon as Pauline learned where they were staying, she sent one of her servants to bring them to her, and soon they were also presented to her mother and the other relatives. The Bonapartes seemed genuinely delighted to meet Bo. They called him *Jerome*, a name the Patterson family had seldom used. The grandmother, Letizia Bonaparte, who had been given the title *Madame Mère* during Napoleon's empire, gave him money and a variety of gifts. Even Madame Mère's half-brother, the churchman Cardinal Fesch, eventually put Bo in his will. Pauline gave him a clothing allowance and promised him the equivalent of $8,000 when he married. To Betsy she gave jewelry and a ball gown, since she and Betsy were both petite and had the same size and shape. A short time later Pauline changed her mind and asked to have the gown back, but then she shifted again and gave it to her once more.

Bo's father was not in Rome, but the rest of the family formed a plan. Joseph, back in America, had a daughter of marriageable age, so Madame Mère wrote to him that he ought to tell this young Jerome to come back to the United States and marry his Charlotte. She said, "I am amazed at him; it is hardly possible to find so much aplomb and good sense in one of his age."[7]

Bo had confided to his grandfather that he really never liked Europe as well as he liked America. He confessed: "Since I have been in Europe I have dined with princes and princesses and all the great people of Europe, but I have never tasted a dish as much to my taste as the roast beef and beef-steaks I ate on South Street." [8] So when it came to this proposed marriage, he said, "I hope it may take place, for then I would return immediately to America to pass the rest of my life among my relatives and friends." [9]

The word was that Joseph was not opposed to the idea, so Betsy helped Bo get his things together, and to return with Le Loup to the United States. One of Bo's Bonaparte uncles, Louis, sent an assistant along to help the young voyager off on a ship scheduled to leave from the port of Leghorn (Livorno). When Bo landed in New York, he sent a message to his grandfather saying he would go to Philadelphia to see his Uncle Joseph first before he came home to Baltimore. That visit seemed to go well. Bo and his cousin Charlotte apparently had a pleasant enough time, but nothing was said about a marriage.

Bo had missed his Baltimore grandfather, uncles, aunts, and cousins. There must have been a series of homecoming events, but there is no record of anything being said about the wedding. On his next visit to his uncle, Joseph was not at home, and Bo was told the count was traveling.

In those days, among wealthy families, dowries were still expected, so Betsy began writing long letters to her father about the marriage contract. Joseph Bonaparte was said to be the only one who came out of the empire with a fortune, and Betsy wrote about how much money she hoped would be settled on her son, and the fact that it must go to Bo's heirs and not revert to the bride's family. Nevertheless, she didn't want to make demands that would endanger plans for the wedding, so William Patterson wrote to his daughter's friend in Philadelphia, Madame Toussard. He apologized by saying this really wasn't the way these things were done in America, but this was a case of young people becoming interested in each other first. Still, he needed information for his daughter, and would Mrs. Toussard be able to find out just what the count had in mind? She tried, but couldn't do it.

Possibly suspecting that things might go awry, Betsy issued instructions: if the marriage was not going to be arranged quickly, Bo was to go to Harvard College. She had spoken in Paris with a Harvard professor who was traveling there. When she answered the man's questions about Bo's studies, he said the young man was lacking in certain key requirements, such as not enough Greek. His advice was to find a qualified tutor who knew what Harvard required and could provide the instruction her son needed. When pressed, he suggested a retired clergyman who lived in Lancaster, Massachusetts.

Meanwhile Mrs. Toussard had managed to obtain some information. Joseph and his wife had been separated, with the wife staying in Europe. The daughter had only recently come to the United States to be with her father. Mrs. Toussard now knew her and had information to share with Mr. Patterson and Betsy: "I meet Joseph Bonaparte and his daughter very frequently in company; she is in size a dwarf and excessively ugly. Jerome is quite too handsome for her; it would be a great sacrifice." [10]

Patterson told his grandson he'd best be off to New England and study hard. Bo went. After eight months of tutoring in the clergyman's house, he took the Harvard entrance examination, passed, and was admitted in February 1823. In March he wrote his grandfather: "I have received another letter from my cousin Charlotte; she invites me, in the name of her father, to pass the coming vacation at their country seat. I have been obliged to decline doing so because the vacation lasts only two weeks." He preferred to spend the time with his American family.

In Europe, Betsy had been hearing rumors that Joseph Bonaparte had been extravagant, that his properties were mortgaged, and his fortune was much depleted. She was willing to write off the Charlotte Bonaparte plan, but she still lived in hope of a brilliant marriage for Bo and pestered her father with warnings about keeping her son from making some foolish choice.

To Betsy—like others of her time, including military men and office holders—rank was crucial. When passed over for promotions, men like Joshua Barney and Sam Smith felt honor-bound to retire or resign in protest. Even a widowed free-thinker like salon hostess Mme. de Staël insisted she could not remarry beneath her standing because it would damage the marriage chances of her daughter. Similarly, the Corsican Madame Mère had refused to acknowledge one of the daughters of her son Lucien after she married an Irish commoner. Now Betsy pointed out to her father that the rank Bo held from his birth was far higher than her own rank from her marriage. That meant no matter what happened regarding Joseph's daughter, it was essential that Bo not marry beneath his rank. Rather than have her boy demean himself that way, she'd rather he never marry at all.

For the time being Betsy was glad Bo was at Harvard. After all, he was not yet eighteen. But she was concerned about Le Loup when she learned Bo wasn't allowed to take him to school. The dog was left behind in William Patterson's care, so she warned him the animal was not used to the Baltimore climate and had to be kept warm at night lest he get sick. She wrote: "If I had known, I should have insisted on keeping him with me as a reward for the poor beast's fidelity."[11]

Earlier, after Bo had sailed away from Leghorn, Betsy had spent her time in cheerful places like Florence, where the Court of Tuscany was always festive. Nobility, high-ranking officials, and foreign diplomats gave balls frequently, and Betsy's wealthy friend Prince Nicolas Demidoff hosted lavish dinners at his palace. He also kept a theatrical company in residence to perform plays and operettas in which guests (including Betsy) often took part.

Betsy was devoted to Demidoff. He had descended from a blacksmith in Russia, whose skill in metalwork led to his creating weapons for Peter the Great. In gratitude, the czar had given him three million acres of land and made him and his descendants noblemen. In time the Demidoffs became extraordinarily rich. Future generations were scholars, promoters of science, art patrons, philanthropists. When he died several years later, Betsy wrote her father: "We have lost poor Demidoff, who died most unexpectedly. He was a great friend of mine. I spent three evenings a week at his house." She said his loss would be felt by every class of persons, because his charity was greater than that of anyone living. "With him gone, Florence is no longer the same place and many people are leaving." [12]

From Florence she went back to Geneva and then to Paris. She missed her son, and her Baltimore investments periodically needed attention, so she decided to go home. She went to Le Havre and sailed to New York. It turned out to be bad timing for Bo.

At Harvard Bo had gone to a meeting of an organization that was perfectly legitimate and for years had been approved for its on-campus events. Unfortunately, on this occasion, after the business of the meeting was done, the boys had celebrated with a glass of punch. That was against the rules. Even though no one got drunk and there was no loudness or disturbance, the students were barred from the campus for ninety days. Further, during that period they were not permitted to go home. Bo decided to spend the time in study at the clergyman's house in Lancaster, Massachusetts. He wrote his grandfather a long letter explaining exactly what had happened and thought the worst was over. [13]

When Betsy found out what had happened she went to the little town where Bo was staying, furious at her son and at the school. Her temper eventually cooled, and they began to enjoy themselves. They traveled a bit, saw some sights, and wound up in Boston. When Bo was able to return to school Betsy was still with him. She was looking for lodgings in the vicinity of Harvard when an official of the college drew her attention to the fact that having mothers hover near the students was frowned upon by the administration. [14]

Betsy then went to Baltimore, where William Patterson assumed she had come home for good. When he learned she had no intention of taking over and moving into one of her rental houses, he made it clear he couldn't have her living with him. Patterson said when she'd done that in the past it had resulted in what he referred to as "confusion." Betsy was angered by her father's words.

All of her brothers were married except George, who lived out at Springfield and managed the place, and Henry, who was twenty-three and studying law. It was clear to her there was nobody in his house to be bothered by "confusion" except her father and his housekeeper. She told him he was mistaken, she had no intention of staying in Baltimore. During this period she summed up her opinion of Baltimore in a letter to Sydney Morgan, calling it "this region of ennui" where her only distractions were embroidery and reading.

> *The men are all merchants; and commerce, although it may fill the purse, clogs the brain. Beyond their counting-houses they possess not a single idea; they never visit except when they wish to marry. The women are all occupied in les details de ménage and nursing children; these are useful occupations, but do not render people agreeable to their neighbors.*[15]

She also told Sydney her net income at present was only $5,000 a year, and now she attended to her property, not so much in an effort to try to increase it, but to assure its safety:

> *I have no confidence in the banks, insurance companies, road stocks, or, in short, in any stock in Baltimore. The people of business there all live beyond their means, all speculate to support the extravagant wants of their families, and from folly are driven to dishonesty.*[16]

At this time Betsy reinvested her money in municipal, state, and local bonds. Then, in June 1825, she left once more for Europe.

She would remain in Europe for nine years. She spent much of that time in Florence, sometimes staying for a year-round visit. It remained her favorite place, although the climate was at times even more damp, cold, and rainy than Baltimore. And Geneva, although it wasn't as enjoyable socially, seemed the best place for her health. Some years she completed a circuit that her friends also followed: winter in Florence, summer in Geneva, and a spring and fall stop on the way between the two, at Aix les Bains in France. People she knew claimed its therapeutic baths cured their rheumatism.

Whenever she tired of these places, she would make a trip to Paris. Betsy had to return there periodically, as Paris was where she kept her European money.

David Baillie Warden was still her friend and fixer of problems, even when she was not in Paris. When Bo's heavy studying gave him trouble with his eyes, Betsy wrote to Warden from Geneva with detailed instructions for a specific type of reading lamp she couldn't find in Switzerland. She wanted him to buy two of them and gave shipping instructions for getting them to Harvard.[17]

Her most disconcerting experience in Florence was an encounter in the gallery at the Pitti Palace. As she moved along to look at the artworks, she espied her ex-husband walking toward her with his obese wife. He saw Betsy, but didn't greet her. As they passed she heard him whisper, "That is my American wife." Jerome and Catherine left town the next morning, and after that Betsy made it a point not to be in Florence whenever Jerome was. Still, there must have been some feeling left, because later she told her friends that she'd opened her cloak to show him that her own figure remained perfect.

∞

Bo eventually finished college and planned to study law, but his Bonaparte relatives had been writing to him, urging him to come back for another visit. Even his father, who had surprised everyone by making two contributions to his education expenses, wrote to him. Bo had never seen him, and he really wanted to. He brought the matter up, both with his mother and his grandfather. Patterson felt no pleasure trip to Europe was ever warranted, but Betsy was in favor of it. She wrote to her father to say she thought it was perhaps a duty to let the boy know his father, "that he may never reproach himself at any future period." She also felt that before he began his study of the law, he ought to travel, to spend a year in Europe. "If you could give him a letter of credit on a banker in Leghorn for twelve hundred dollars, I should commission Miss Spear to pay you."[18]

It was May 1826 when Bo set out for Europe, not knowing his

father had a letter on its way to him warning about the dangers of a visit. The ex-king, who had not been among the Bonapartes urging Bo to visit, said he was in a difficult position. He didn't know how to reconcile the rights of his second family with Bo's "peculiar position."

> *Although my wife, whose noble and generous heart is so well known, would consent to many things on your account, we might find that the courts of Würtemberg and Russia would protest against any act which would have the appearance of invalidating the marriage of their princess.*
>
> *My dear child, you are now a man, and I desire to place you in a natural position, without, however, prejudicing in any way the condition of the queen and the princes, our children.*
>
> *You will find at the American consul's a letter, which will inform you whether you are to wait for me at Leghorn, or where you are to go to find me.*

It was signed: "Your affectionate father, Jerome."[19]

Unaware of the letter, Bo arrived at Amsterdam in May and the next month met his mother in Switzerland. They stopped at Aix on their way to Florence, and Bo wrote his grandfather a description of the baths. He said he planned to stay in Europe until April of the following year, and added: "I have seen a great many things since my departure from home, but the more I see, the more firmly I am persuaded of the superiority of my own country, the more I desire to return to it and remain in it." Nevertheless, he concluded that this journey had been absolutely essential. There were things he needed to do here, but "when it is all over I shall settle myself quietly in America."[20]

After three weeks in Florence, Bo left his mother there for the winter and went on alone to Rome for another one of his family reunions. He renewed acquaintances with his many cousins, the children of Napoleon's brothers and sisters. Soon he felt he had gotten to know just about all the Bonapartes now living. Among them was Louis Napoleon Bonaparte, son of Napoleon's brother Louis and Hortense Beauharnais, Empress Josephine's daughter from her first marriage. For Bo, this cousin became a friend, and an important one. Bo also learned in Rome that his Aunt Pauline had died and left him a legacy, as she had promised, although it was about half as much as she'd said. He wrote William Patterson with a report of all this. He said his grandmother, Letizia, had no specific illness, but she was very thin and weak, yet she was always very kind to him.

He also got word from his father about their meeting. Bo was to come at the end of October to an out-of-the-way place called the Chateau of Lanciano, near Camerino. There Bo found he had two younger half-brothers, Jerome and Napoleon, and a half-sister named Mathilde. His stepmother, the former Queen Catherine, made him welcome and was most friendly to him. He spent two months in the country with this family. Apparently there was no complaint from Catherine's royal relatives, so later they all moved into Rome. Bo described for his grandfather what it was like:

> I am excessively tired of the way of living at my father's. We break-fast between twelve and one o'clock, dine between six and seven, take tea between eleven and twelve at night, so that I seldom get to bed before half-past one o'clock in the morning. My father does not see much company at present, but during much the greater part of the twenty-four hours the whole of his family is assembled together in the parlor, principally for the purpose of killing time. No one about the house does anything, and I find it impossible to read or study. [21]

The other thing that bothered him was the extravagance. He told his grandfather that the ex-king lived on a small income provided by the king of Württemberg and the czar of Russia, but spent three times as much, with the rest provided by Madame Mère. That was true, according to Betsy, who got her information from a friend working in the Paris office of Rothschild's banking concern. The old woman's money, saved so carefully during the empire, was slowly being drained by her favorite son, the one to whom she could never say "no." For this, Napoleon's other siblings resented Jerome.

As for Bo, his tone was beginning to sound mercenary. In

another letter to his grandfather he said regarding his father, "I see no possibility of his doing anything for me." Again, mentioning his grandmother he said he feared she would not do anything for him either. Further he worried that being here would accustom him to living in a style he could not afford, one he would be forced to abandon when he got home. "Moreover, I am now of an age in which I must think of doing something for myself, and America is the only country where I can have an opportunity of getting forward. [22]

In March 1827, Bo joined his mother in Florence, planning to return home in April. He wanted her to go home with him, and she said she would but kept postponing the departure. Betsy was enjoying herself too much. Bo began to enjoy the city with her. He was going to a ball every night and in the daytime rode a horse borrowed from one of his Bonaparte cousins. After a couple of months he decided he'd better go home alone. He still was not permitted to travel through France, so he took a roundabout route, by sea to Holland and England and then finally home.

For the next two years Bo lived in Baltimore and tried to study law. His grandfather complained to Betsy that the young man was not working hard enough but wasting his time, and Patterson had no patience with laziness.

The problem was that Bo simply disliked the law. It bored him. What he enjoyed was galloping about on a horse at one of his grandfather's country places, or attending parties with his Baltimore friends. He liked something else, too—girls. One, Susan May Williams, lived with her widowed mother on North Charles Street in Baltimore. That was fine with William Patterson. It would be a good connection, and surely assuming some responsibility, such as a wife, would inspire Bo to become serious about work.

Patterson paid a call on Susan May's mother, who wasn't much interested in a Patterson-Williams marriage. The family already had more than enough money, and the girl was young; she had ample time to think about marriage. Mrs. Williams's visitor sweetened the deal, promising to give Bo a wedding present so substantial that Susan May would never want for anything in her life. He proposed to give Bo a number of eventually very valuable downtown Baltimore properties and $50,000 in cash (in modern currency, half a million). In return, Mrs. Williams would arrange for Bo to have, not the Williams fortune, but the management of it and the annual income. That amounted to about $8,000 a year, close to twice Betsy's current income, with no one to fuss about how much Bo was spending to buy horses or whatever else he desired.[23]

The young couple became engaged. The date was set for months away so preparations could be made for a big wedding with all of Bo's best friends as groomsmen. He happily informed his Bonaparte relatives of the coming event and congratulations came back, not only from Joseph in Philadelphia, but the whole family in Rome, from Madame Mère to ex-king Jerome, and even from cousin Charlotte and her mother. Later there were more letters from the Bonapartes with invitations to bring the bride for a visit. In these letters Bo's father addressed him as "my dear child" and the others called him "dear nephew" or "dear cousin." Like his mother, Bo was a saver, and one day these expressions of familial affection from the whole range of Bonapartes would prove very useful.[24]

Now, however, since both Bo and William Patterson knew exactly what the reaction of Bo's mother would be, careful steps were taken to keep her from finding out about the marriage plan until it was too late for her to interfere. Betsy was in Florence when, on November 3, 1829, she read and prepared to respond to her father's letter about a possible engagement. In Baltimore that same day, Bo and Susan were being married.

Chapter 19

Farewell to the Patriarch

After Bo had gone home alone, Betsy tried to sail on several occasions. Each time she was ready to leave, something interfered. She was ill, or it was the wrong season, or there wasn't time to go back to Paris to get money for the trip or, in one instance, the scheduled ship was one on which she would never travel again owing to a bad prior experience. Hence, she continued her visits to the places she enjoyed in Europe, keeping Florence as her first choice.

She was considering a possible diplomatic career for Bo. Her friends in Florence thought her son would be good at that. The Swedish minister to the Court of Tuscany told her there might be a chance for him in Sweden, where the king would be very kind to him because of a Bonaparte connection. Instead she suggested to her father that he and Sam Smith should persuade President Andrew Jackson to make Bo the secretary of legation at the American embassy in London. She would have to come up with the money to maintain him there in a suitable style, but she was willing to make any sacrifice in order to do that. Always in the back of her mind, as she spent time with her titled Russian friends, was the hope that Bo might marry one of the young princesses in the Galitzin, Potemkin, Narischkin, or Poniatowski families.

Then her father's letter arrived informing her of Bo's possible engagement in Baltimore. She controlled her anger sufficiently to write back repeating all the old arguments. Her son had too high a rank ever to marry an American. An imprudent marriage was "almost the only misfortune from which a person of sense cannot recover." If Bo was unable to follow her advice in the matter of his marriage, he should not marry at all: "The next best thing to making a good match is not to make a bad one." She would rather support him in Siberia or Africa than see him marry someone and bring a pack of children into the world that neither he nor his mother could support. "Love in a cottage," she told her father, "is even out of favor in novels."

When Betsy learned the marriage had already taken place, she went to pieces. Her grief was so great she thought she was going to lose her mind. The devastation over the destruction of her ambition for Bo was intensified by the realization of the betrayal her father and son had practiced on her by concealing their plans. Her women friends tried to comfort her, but she couldn't talk about the situation without sobbing. She never heard from Bo at all.

The only comforting words she heard from Baltimore were in the letters of her brother Edward, who thought the way the thing was done was "a mean, dirty business." While the plans were being made, he had suggested the wedding be postponed long enough for Bo to go to Europe and get Betsy's consent, but Bo said if he did that the marriage would be broken off. Then he went so far as to write a note to the girl's mother, suggesting that in a business of such importance, the sentiments of the young man's mother should be known. He told Betsy, "This also proved unavailing, and the marriage takes place on the 3 November." Edward had written this letter on October 24 but Betsy didn't receive it until November 18.[1]

Writing to her again several months later, Edward said: "It was a mercenary transaction altogether and carried through in a purely mercantile spirit." He continued: "A total want of ambition in Jerome and an inordinate desire of wealth on his part and that of his grandfather afford the only explanation of the business." Edward also informed Betsy that Jerome had gotten from the Williams family between $180,000 and $200,000, along with property and $50,000 from William Patterson.[2]

The day after the wedding, Betsy's father wrote to tell her

that her objections came too late to stop Bo's intended marriage. Patterson reminded his daughter that she was not in a position to criticize the marriage:

> *Nor ought you to blame him when you look back on your own conduct in relinquishing your family and country for an imaginary consequence amongst strangers who can care little for you, indeed, in place of being displeased with your son's late conduct you ought rather to commend him for his prudence and forethought in providing so well for his future prospects. . . . Jerome although of fine capacity is by nature rather indolent and without much ambition; therefore not calculated for the kind of life you would wish him to figure in Europe.*[3]

When Betsy did not respond, her father contacted her again, encouraging a reconciliation. She felt she'd been treated "as if I had been a maniac or a wretch convicted of an infamous crime," but after a time she pulled herself together and was able to answer. She wrote that while she could never agree with what had been done, she sincerely hoped that Bo's and her father's judgments were better than hers and that everything would turn out well. After more reflection she wrote regarding Bo:

> *I have considered now that it is unreasonable to expect him to place his happiness in the only things which can make me happy. . . . He has neither my pride, my ambition, nor my love of good company; therefore I no longer oppose his marriage. . . . If he can be satisfied with living in such a place as Baltimore—and he is the best judge of this—I have nothing more to urge against it.*[4]

She was still angry, but as she had done after the first Jerome abandoned her, she formed a plan. She would stop pinching pennies. She would spend her money any way she chose, and she would enjoy it. While she would continue making every effort to collect and remit Bo's inheritances from Princess Pauline and Cardinal Fesche, as well as any money her ex-husband sent her for their son, she would discontinue Bo's monthly allowance.

Nevertheless, she kept one of her principles in place. She

believed it was immoral to disinherit an offspring, so she would never cut a child out of his inheritance, even if he had tried to murder her with an axe. In Paris she made a will and filed it with the American embassy there. Her estate would go to her son, and after him, to any children he might have. If he should die first, her bequest would then go to her nearest relatives, her father, and then her brothers. She said, "I have gained my fortune by strictest economy, by privations of every kind; therefore, strangers must not profit by my sacrifices." She told her father all this, adding that she did not dislike the woman her son had chosen. It wasn't Bo's fault he didn't think the way his mother did:

> A parent cannot make a silk purse out of a sow's ear; and you found that you could never make a sow's ear out of a silk purse. It was impossible to bend my talents and my ambition to the obscure destiny of a Baltimore house-keeper, and it was absurd to attempt it after I had married the brother of an emperor.[5]

Betsy also instructed Miss Spear, Edward, and her father to pack up the things she'd left in Baltimore and send them to her. She wanted all her jewelry and whatever clothing she'd left behind.

She implemented her new spending plan. She'd already been buying clothes for Miss Spear whenever she went to Paris. So now, the next time she was in Geneva, she had a superb watch made by a craftsman who spent three months on the task, and sent it as a thank-you gift to John White, the Baltimore financier who assisted Miss Spear in the management of Betsy's money. For herself, she designed a tiara and had some of her jewels set into it. Other stones she planned to place into an elaborate ornament for her waist. She tried not to be a spendthrift: she bought white topazes and pretended they were diamonds.

Once, years earlier, her friend Eliza Anderson Godefroy had told her to overcome her depression by using her talents, and now she attempted to do that. The Princess Galitzin, with whom Betsy traveled and much of the time lived, asked her to design a home she was going to build near Geneva, as well as the decor. Betsy's sketches and watercolor pictures show the exterior done not only with trees, but with the exterior beams covered in bark and the roof of the house and its sheltered walkways made of thatch. The interior floor plan called for large rooms, with lots of windows. In contrast to the rustic exterior, the inside was to be painted in beautiful colors. The furnishings were delicate, with slim legs and fragile-looking decorations, the upholstery in flowered cotton, the bedcovers of silk, and for the windows, center-opening double curtains made of green cotton over white muslin.[6]

Betsy continued her round of seasonal travels for what turned out to be the most interesting years of her life. She kept all her old friends, but added new ones, people she'd never expected to encounter. One was Teresa Guiccioli, a woman who went down in history as "Byron's last mistress." She was from the north of Italy, so unlike southern Italians, she was stunningly fair. Betsy was amazed by her beauty, her luminous pale complexion, bright blue eyes, beautiful white teeth, lovely hands, and the lightest silvery-gold hair she'd ever seen.

In Paris she became acquainted with Laure Permon Junot, who had known the Bonapartes ever since her earliest childhood. She had married Napoleon's General Junot and wound up as the Duchesse d'Abrantès. After the retreat from Moscow, Junot had suffered a mental breakdown and committed suicide. Now Laure had lost all her money and was in need. She became close to the novelist Honoré de Balzac, who liked older women. He urged her to write her *Memoires*. She did, and when they were published they ran to a dozen volumes.

In her book Laure was very complimentary to Jerome's first wife. When Betsy and Laure got to know each other, the memoirist asked for anecdotes about that short marriage. Although Betsy liked Laure very much, she refused to talk about that part of her life. She felt Laure had already praised Betsy too much and had criticized Jerome too fiercely. Did she have any interesting stories about Jerome, his extravagance or his taste in clothing? Betsy still refused; she had standards about things like that getting into print.

In this, Betsy's instincts were right. Although Laure wrote vivid, interesting, and useful accounts of her firsthand experiences, some of them were inaccurate, and people accused her of fabrication. Further, Laure knew Napoleon too well to be in awe of him, and she included in her memoir a number of unflattering stories about him.

Many in France still idolized Napoleon and longed for a return to what they saw as the glory of the empire. In a way, Betsy herself was a beneficiary of the growing Bonaparte legend. As someone whose life had become involved with Napoleon, she was a curiosity and she was usually welcomed everywhere, either as heroine or victim. For her to become publicly associated with this somewhat anti-Bonapartist writer could have made her controversial. The truth is, Betsy had always admired Napoleon. Years later Marshal Bertrand, who'd been with Napoleon during his last years on St. Helena, came to see Betsy in Baltimore. He told her the ex-emperor had admired her and regretted what he'd been forced to do to her. When he heard that she still praised him, he remarked, "Those I have wronged have forgiven me; those I loaded with kindness have forsaken me."[7]

Although throughout Europe she seems to have enjoyed continuous social success, she had found that when she was in the company of intellectual men, such as those to whom David Baillie Warden had introduced her at gatherings in Paris, they were very complimentary to her, even flirtatious, but they were not at all interested in including her in their discussions of serious topics. She sensed that what they really wanted her to do was keep quiet and look pretty.

In Florence in 1829, Betsy met a man who looked upon her in an entirely different way. He liked her mind, and enjoyed having discussions with her on many different topics. Prince Alexandre Mikhailovitch Gortchakoff was the chargé d'affaires at the Russian Legation in Florence. He was an extraordinary man, from an extraordinary family. Nearly all the Gortchakoff men were soldiers, going back to the first one of note, who'd been killed by the

Mongols in 1246. Generation after generation, the family provided Russia with outstanding leaders. By the era of the European wars of the nineteenth century, there were usually at any given time in the Russian Army two or three Generals Gortchakoff. Prince Alexandre, however, had departed from the pattern to become a diplomat. He had been unusually well educated and was a classical scholar, in addition to speaking and writing elegant French. One of his classmates, the poet Pushkin, wrote a poem calling Alexandre "fortune's favored son" and foretold his great success.

Because Betsy was a voracious reader of many kinds of books, they had much to talk about, and Prince Alexandre was perfectly willing to discuss whatever piqued her interest. He said she had the finesse to be a successful diplomat. They wrote long pieces for each other that they called "word portraits," then shared and discussed them. When she was in Paris or Geneva or he was in Rome, they wrote to one another letters as long as a dozen pages. At times they discussed the world at large, and after Andrew Jackson became president of the United States, Betsy explained to Alexandre why she thought Jackson's policies were going to be bad for America.

The prince seems to have presented another, more whimsical aspect to the other women in the Russian colony at Florence: a teasing, flirtatious side for Princess Galitzen or Countess Schouvaloff. With Betsy he was generally more serious, and she told him in one letter that she had the gift of second sight in knowing his worth. "A duller person could not have seen through the mist with which your caprice and impertinence envelope you." She felt she was the only one who knew his true nature. When she was away, she wrote: "Who did you speak to, my spiritual prince? I left no one to understand you."

Yet there was a deep vein of unrest in their relationship. Often their friendly discussions became conflicts. At first it was fun; Betsy said he was the only man she would ever consent to argue with. But on at least one occasion, "that memorable evening at the Martins," their discussion became a quarrel that "amused so many imbeciles at our expense." Nevertheless she still insisted that he was "more worthy than all other men despite the fact that we are unable to live peacefully together."

We don't know what they quarreled about. It is true she admired the emperor that Alexandre's family had fought against for years, but it seems unlikely their conflict was political. There is a clue in some of Betsy's correspondence with her other European friends. They—sometimes lovingly and sometimes critically—accused her of being a "prude." One went so far as to say "You are a severely virtuous woman." Betsy explained herself by telling them this was her only weapon against the Bonapartes, who excused Napoleon's treatment of her by casting her in the role of a loose woman who had ensnared Jerome. Even in 1821, when she took Bo to Rome to meet his relatives for the first time, she felt that although they welcomed her son, they still looked on her as a tramp. A life of complete chastity was her defense and her revenge.

Another possibility for the tension between them could have been an awareness of Prince Alexandre's destiny: the future foretold by Pushkin. From the beginning Betsy knew there was something special about him that no amount of clowning could conceal, and he himself would surely have been aware of the ancestral history he carried, perhaps as a burden he sought to lighten with frivolity.

Whatever the cause, their relationship ended. Seven years after their first meeting in 1829, the exchange of letters stopped. Four years later Gortchakoff married a Russian princess, Maria Alexandrovna Ouroussov, and went on to become one of the most influential diplomats in Europe, a close friend of Bismarck, and a crucial participant in virtually every international congress, agreement, or treaty made in Europe for the next four decades. He was an ambassador, the Russian counselor of state, the minister of foreign affairs, and finally, chancellor of the Russian empire. Eventually his grateful czar decreed that henceforth Prince Alexandre Gortchakoff would be known as "His Serene Highness."

Did Betsy forget him? No; she said his memory was with her everywhere she went. Did he forget her? Apparently not. Sometime during his career he is quoted as saying that if she had been near

Napoleon's throne, the allies would have had a great deal more trouble defeating him. Two dozen years after their last meeting, he contacted her again, regarding an event in Paris that she'd been involved in. She wrote a long reply, starting with her gratitude at "having preserved a place in the reminiscences of Prince Gortcha-koff, whose brilliant talents I had appreciated, and of whom I have ever been an admirer; and what is more rare for any person, a sincere and faithful friend." She went on to tell him about her life in the twenty-four years that had passed since they last met. It was a sad and bitter story, full of disappointments, and so the letter turned out to be a very dreary account. She decided not to send it. In the end, not knowing what to say, she didn't reply at all.[8]

No matter what went on in her life, Betsy kept track of her financial situation, which at the moment was worsening. Her Paris investments were yielding less and less. People were leaving the cities due to a cholera epidemic, and there was a prospect of war with Spain. In the United States, the economy was in disarray. In March of 1834 William Patterson wrote Betsy a letter about it. After chiding her with: "How could you have neglected the duty of writing for so long a time?" he said:

> We are in great confusion and distress in this country, on account of President Jackson's arbitrary conduct in respect to the Bank of the United States. There is no saying how it may end, or that it may not ultimately bring about a revolution. Your presence here is absolutely necessary to look after your affairs and property, and the sooner the better. We will endeavor to make your situation as comfortable as we can.[9]

At that time there was no Federal Reserve Bank or other form of centralized banking control but many banks, each one privately owned but individually chartered by the government. The largest was in Philadelphia, the Bank of the United States (BUS). This was operated by a board of directors, with some members appointed by the government, but actually managed by the board chairman, Nicholas Biddle. President Jackson, convinced the BUS favored the rich while refusing to lend money to small businesses and individual working people, blocked the renewal of the bank's charter. He also removed from that institution all government funds and spread them around to other banks. Biddle fought back, trying to put pressure on the government: he clamped down on credit, called in existing loans for payment, and began redeeming private bank notes. So large was the BUS that these actions set off an economic slowdown that, once started, couldn't be stopped. The country slid into a long and deep recession.

Betsy decided she'd better return to Baltimore and decide what to do with her money. She seems to have looked upon this trip as final, for she bought enough Paris clothing to last the rest of her life, including fifty fashionable hats so that she'd never have to buy one in America. She was now almost fifty years old and still extraordinarily beautiful. Returning to her father's house in Baltimore, she settled in to attend to her business and seldom went out socially. On the rare occasions when she appeared at the theater or an evening party wearing a black velvet dress with a low neck, short sleeves, and stunning jewelry, she was as always the most conspicuous person there.

Betsy's son and his wife now had a three-and-a-half-year-old son named after Bo, Jerome Napoleon Bonaparte. They had a home in Baltimore but spent most of their time in the country at an estate they called Pleasant View, several miles northwest of town. William Patterson had bought the place just after the American Revolution and had now given it to Bo.[10] Betsy visited there, but rarely. She was enchanted by her grandchild, but Susan never forgave the original opposition to her marriage. It was clear Betsy wasn't welcome.

Betsy found her father had aged to a shocking degree. He was in his eighties and, except for servants, was living alone. The only family member who stayed with him consistently was Henry, but that son's health was poor and he frequently traveled to the South seeking a better climate. Patterson had told Joseph to move in with him and bring his family, but for unspecified reasons, that did not happen.[11] Miss Spear had agreed to stay with him, but she hated being there. He never had company, never talked; he just read the paper and went to bed early.[12]

Now Betsy did spend some time with him and they seemed to be getting along better than they had before. He gave her a collection of rare coins that she planned to have made into a bracelet. He probably didn't want to hear about her European travels, but they could certainly talk about the country's financial troubles. After discussions with her father, Miss Spear, and John White, Betsy decided to leave the bulk of her money in government securities, avoid other kinds of investments, and do whatever she could with her rental properties in the city.

During the winter of 1834–1835, Patterson's health began to fail, and he died that February. The local papers were filled with his achievements as one of the early pillars of the Baltimore business community and described him as "the last gentleman in Baltimore who wore small-clothes and a cue." It was said that he believed and practiced the maxim that "money and merit are the only sure and certain roads to respectability and consequence."

Patterson had been so active in so many different enterprises that his touch seemed to be everywhere. He'd been part of the group who established the city's Merchant Exchange, a complex with facilities to accommodate many companies, and also a meeting place for businessmen to gather and exchange information. He was a founder of the Baltimore and Ohio Railroad, an endeavor he told Betsy was going to make Baltimore the most prosperous city on the East Coast.

Patterson had made his will in 1827 and updated it from time to time until his death. It included his autobiography, and the whole document, at twenty-three pages and well over 14,000 words, took up eight full newspaper columns when the *Baltimore News-American* published it. So great was his wealth that it is almost impossible to calculate the amount of his fortune. In addition to the country properties he owned and his various businesses, there were houses, buildings, and warehouses. These possessions were described as "lots with improvements" that were scattered over all the downtown streets. There were also dozens of different stocks: railroad, manufacturing of all kinds, waterworks, and roads. He gave bequests to women who'd worked for him or who had paid him rent for extended periods. He also ordered that his slaves be freed when each of them reached the age of thirty. To his various sons he gave his country places, along with stocks and other properties sufficient to make them, if not millionaires, at least very wealthy men.

Betsy's inheritance was a small fraction of what he gave her brothers: the South Street house where she was born, now occupied by a cobbler, a couple of houses on Market Street occupied by a chair maker and a cabinetmaker, and five other small houses and shops in the same area. He also explained his reasons:

> *The conduct of my daughter Betsy has through life been so disobedient, that in no instance has she ever consulted my opinion or feelings; indeed she has caused me more anxiety and trouble than all my other children put together, and her folly and misconduct has occasioned me a train of expense that, first and last, has cost me much money. Under such circumstances, it would not be reasonable, just, and proper that she should, at my death, inherit and participate in an equal proportion with my other children in an equal division in my estate. Considering, however, the weakness of human nature and that she is still my daughter, it is my will and pleasure to provide for her as follows. . . .* [13]

Then he listed the downtown houses.

Betsy's disappointment was deep, as was her conviction that her father had been unjust and perhaps even unlawful. Yet that wasn't the worst part for her, because she could always make more money. What bothered her most was that surely he knew the will would be published. He may even have arranged for it to be. And in that, at last, he had succeeded in hurting her. She was profoundly humiliated.

Chapter 20

A Father's Will

$\mathcal{B}$etsy confined herself in her room and cried for a while, then pulled out the 1803 marriage agreement devised by lawyer Dallas and signed by William Patterson, Jerome Bonaparte, and Betsy herself. In the will, Jerome agreed that at his death she would have "a one-third share of his property real and personal." In William Patterson's will, her father directed that at his death she would have "a share of his estate equal to that given to his other children."[1] Next she went looking for lawyers and ended up with three. Two, John Sergeant and Horace Binney, were the heads of a Philadelphia law firm so widely experienced in cases involving wills that people said any opinion prepared by them was almost certain to succeed.[2] She also enlisted the help of Roger B. Taney, who had been the federal attorney general, was now the secretary of the treasury, and was on his way to becoming chief justice of the Supreme Court. In addition she prepared a list of a dozen questions for the lawyers to consider, even going back as far as 1814 to her mother's deathbed verbal will, which had been ignored by her father.[3]

At the time of his death, William Patterson had six living children: Betsy and the five remaining sons. One of them, John, was scarcely mentioned in the will. He had been living in Virginia on property Patterson had given him decades earlier. Now he was left only a share of the household furnishings along with the cellar full of wine that was to be divided among all five sons. The other four—Joseph, Edward, George, and Henry—had been generously provided with city properties and businesses, warehouses and wharves, percentages of the value of ships and brigs, and ample shares of stock in banks and companies. Also included were the various country estates with all their buildings, furniture, slaves, implements for husbandry, and livestock. Joseph was given the Cold Stream estate. Edward got the Bagatel property in addition to a city home at the upper end of Market Street. George got Springfield and Henry, Pleasant View. Joseph, Edward, and George were appointed executors, with Henry in reserve if something happened to one of the others.

Grandchildren had been included as well, the most going to Bo and the son of the deceased William Jr. They were given bank shares valued at $2,000, with the provision that—if there was any difficulty cashing them in—an equal amount of money would be taken from Patterson's other holdings to pay them off. In addition, Bo had been left a number of very valuable downtown Baltimore properties. In one of the later codicils, Patterson had taken the Pleasant View estate from Henry and given it to Bo. Apparently Henry didn't want the country place, so his father increased his share in other ways. A further complication was created when Patterson extended his bequests not only to his named heirs, but after them to their descendants and *their* offspring.

Regardless of his grandfather's generosity, when Bo looked at the enormous inheritances of his uncles, he felt slighted. Since he was the sole heir of his mother and would eventually profit by her share, he became fully involved in her effort to challenge the will. He went to Philadelphia for meetings with the law firm Betsy had chosen and wrote her regular reports about their deliberations. Both for Taney and the law firm, the first concern was the penalty clause Patterson had inserted into his will:

> *Should any of my heirs be so far dissatisfied and unreasonable as to attempt to break and undo this my Will, then in that case I do hereby withdraw, revoke, and annul all and every my bequests and devises, that all and every the share or shares of my property here intended for him, her, or them shall be forfeited and that the same shall be divided equally among such of my other heirs who*

may be ready and willing to abide by and comply with this my
last Will and Testament.[4]

In view of that stipulation, one would expect the other heirs
to cheer on Betsy's and Bo's legal endeavors, because a forfeiture of
their share would increase the shares of the others. However, among
the brothers, Henry was a lawyer and the others were competent
businessmen, so from the start they suspected Betsy's attorneys
would conclude that the penalty clause might not be enforceable.
They were right. Her lawyers said the words *"break and undo"*
were not technical terms and hence had no appropriate, settled
significance that could be applied in any legal sense.

Over a period of several weeks during the spring of 1835, Betsy's
three lawyers wrote thousands of words defining their opinions of
Patterson's will, the 1803 marriage contract, the possible effects of
Napoleon's repudiation of the marriage, Jerome Bonaparte's remarriage, and Betsy's divorce. In addition they explored the meaning
of "shares" in the will, and whether these were calculated before
or after the specified or mandatory bequests were paid. Also they
wondered how to establish the relative shares of a child of Patterson and that child's offspring—indicating, for example, Betsy
and Bo.[5]

At the start of their work Sergeant and Binney questioned Bo
about William Patterson's mental condition. Had his age affected
his intellect? They said they had never read so singular a document.
In their view, the will was the product of a deranged mind.[6] Aside
from that consideration, all three lawyers agreed that the will was
unjust, yet adjudication of claims, even if the penalty clause was not
valid, would be challenging. On the other hand, the 1803 wedding
agreement was a contract and hence enforceable. The eventual dissolution of the marriage in France could not invalidate the agreement, because clearly the parties foresaw that possibility and the
safeguards for Betsy and her offspring were included for that reason.
If anything, the dissolution of the marriage and the ex-husband's
remarriage enhanced the need of Betsy and her offspring for those
safeguards. Neither could her Maryland divorce be construed as

invalidating those safeguards, because she remained in need of the benefits guaranteed her by the contract.[7]

However, Betsy and Bo could not collect on both the wedding contract and the will. They must in legal terms "elect" one, either the contract or the will. No one, however, could force them to make that election without complete knowledge of the consequences. To establish those would require a petition to a Court of Equity requesting aid "to enable them to obtain such knowledge of their rights and interests, as will give them the means of making a fair election, reserving the election itself to be freely made after the information shall be obtained." Since evaluation of the shares required a knowledge of the amount to be shared, the court could require the executors of the will to provide an accounting of the whole estate and its value, along with the advancements that had already been made. The lawyers added: "Such a proceeding cannot possibly be deemed to offend against the prohibition in the will." [8]

In the meantime, neither Betsy nor Bo could take any of the benefits specified in the will. To do so would invalidate their opportunity to choose whether to take from either the will or the marriage contract. The whole thing was hugely complicated, and that was why each lawyer's written opinion was thousands of words and many pages long.

Unfortunately, as Betsy studied all this information more questions arose in her mind. If Bo filed in the Court of Equity and she did not, could she still take the properties William Patterson had left her in his will? If she elected to take property under the will, could Bo sue without the penalty of forfeiture being placed on her? And if her son were to prosecute, could she still take over the properties willed to her before the end of what was sure to be a protracted litigation?

Meanwhile, rancor among the siblings was building against Betsy. When one of the Pattersons found their father's copy of the 1803 marriage agreement, they hoped to conceal it from Betsy, and commissioned Miss Spear to question her tactfully to find out whether she had a copy. Betsy, who not only had a copy but had also made more of them, caught on and refused to give the information. Next the brothers set about rounding up Betsy's letters, hoping to find in them incriminating information. Miss Spear possessed some of these letters, and had told Betsy that her letters were so good Baltimoreans carried them about and shared choice passages with one another. She thought Betsy's letters were worthy of publication, and had been saving them for decades. Now near the end of her own life and suffering financially, she sold the letters to Joseph and Edward.[9]

Robert Gilmor, a friend of all the parties, attempted to bring about a compromise. According to Betsy, Gilmor's attempt was rejected by Joseph, who said they wanted to make an exposé of her in order to produce statements to vindicate their father.[10] Betsy's defense against that was a letter she'd saved from Miss Spear describing the father bringing his illegitimate child Matilda Summers into his South Street home and the brothers' reaction to that. She never made that information public, but she wanted it known that she could.[11]

Regardless of what happened in the attempt to defame Betsy and vindicate her father, the long companionship she'd had with Miss Spear was now ended. Betsy noted that Anne Spear "was my confidant and friend until 1835 when she sold my letters to Joseph Patterson." The repeated expressions of gratitude for Betsy's generosity to her and the accompanying exhortations to Betsy to spend more of her money on herself were forgotten now. They no longer spoke, and the next year Miss Spear died.

Irreparable damage was being done elsewhere as well. Betsy and Edward had always shared a great deal in common and were very close. He supported her desire to have Bo educated abroad and sided with her in the matter of Bo's marriage. Now Betsy noted: "Edward loved me until the bad old man's will killed his affection." Even Joseph had helped her by assisting Anne Spear do the accounting work on Betsy's investments, but in Betsy's mind, he had become a villain. Now, dreading the possibility of a suit that would require a complete accounting and evaluation of every bequest, they were all against her, with one exception. Out at Springfield, her brother George tended his agricultural experiments and remained scrupulously neutral. He gave her his share of their mother's death-bed bequest, then backed away from the controversy. He accepted the documents she sent him to read and politely returned them without comment. She told him she was sorry he had given up his usual contacts with her, "but I presume it proceeded from a prudent unwillingness to be implicated, in any way, in a business which, certainly, it is more agreeable to avoid."[12]

Even Betsy's relationship with her son, slowly mending since she'd returned from Europe, now deteriorated. Bo's interest in money put him on her side in the campaign against the will and kept him earnestly at work with the lawyers, but his correspondence became less affectionate. On one of his reports to her from Philadelphia she noted: "He never says 'Dear Mama' any more. He doesn't end with anything."[13]

An escape to her friends in Europe was impossible now, because the financial situation remained so precarious that she was forced to stay in Baltimore to monitor the many small investments bringing her an income. The economy brought further damage. During the summer of 1835 the Bank of Maryland collapsed. When the bank's trustees failed to give any explanation for the actions of the management or for the investors' losses, frustrated customers formed a mob and attacked the homes of the bank's directors, smashing windows and throwing furniture into the streets. The melee went on for three days. None of the measures taken to stop it had any effect. Dozens were killed, countless others wounded, and many properties, including one of Betsy's, were damaged.

On the fourth day of rioting a committee of concerned citizens called on Sam Smith. The general, now eighty-three, had considered himself retired, but he still carried himself like a soldier. Immediately he put together a group of men to act as a patrol to restore order. With them he began marching through the streets carrying the flag. Soon several thousand people were marching behind him. A local newspaper reported that the moment "the American standard was seen moving in the air, riot and rebellion ceased."[14] The mayor, who'd been completely ineffectual in the crisis, resigned and the city immediately elected General Smith their new mayor. He kept the job for three years before he gave it up. A few months later he came home from a carriage ride, took a nap on a sofa, and died in his sleep. His funeral was the largest ever seen in the history of Baltimore.[15]

The city remained orderly, but bad luck persisted. In 1837 the Jones Falls flooded. Nineteen people drowned when ten feet of water rose in the surrounding streets, on which were several of Betsy's properties. In 1837 there was another financial panic, with ruined businesses, more bank failures, and unemployed men literally fighting each other for jobs. For the state and the nation as a whole, the recovery would take years.

Betsy's financial strategy had always been conservative. In her letters she had repeatedly urged Miss Spear and her advisors to select safety over increased profit; better a safe four or even three percent than a risky five. Recent events intensified those convictions. By the time the lawyers had sifted through the documents surrounding her father's will, consulted with each other, and submitted all their opinions, Betsy concluded that regardless of what Bo chose to do, it wasn't worth the risk for her to bring suit over the will. On the one hand, the properties her father had left her, combined with those she already had, would with careful management be sufficient to keep her solvent for the rest of her life. On the other, without those additional bequests she might be very uncomfortable. Risking forfeiture and loss was unacceptable, and living for months or even years with that risk while the case was tried would be unendurable. Taney informed the other lawyers of her feelings, explaining that the "bare possibility of incurring the forfeiture would make her anxious and unhappy while the proceedings were pending." In time Bo apparently came to the same conclusion.Betsy requested the lawyers' bills and paid them.[16]

Betsy's relationship with Bo and his wife never became close or even comfortable. No matter what Betsy did or said, Susan May could neither forgive nor forget her mother-in-law's original disdain for the marriage. There was further isolation from family members. Betsy may also have been grieving over the loss of Edward's loyalty and friendship. Betsy had never enjoyed living in Baltimore, and the prospect of a life spent there without contact with even one family member—except George, thirty miles away at Springfield—was simply too discouraging.

Although the will left her the house and lot on the east side of South Street "where she was born, now occupied by Mr. Duncan the bootmaker," Betsy chose not to live there. She could have fitted up one of her properties, or even bought herself something new, but she never did. Even when she lived in her favorite place, Florence, she said, "I hate the idea of not being able, by the encumbrance of an establishment, to leave it for Rome, or Paris, or any other place." Instead she moved into a boarding house. It may have been an economy measure, but there's also no doubt she wanted the freedom to put her belongings in storage and travel to Europe whenever she chose.[17]

She'd continued hearing from Lady Sydney Morgan, but had to apologize for not writing back. She had given up all correspondence with her friends in Europe during her "vegetation" in Baltimore: "What could I write about, except the fluctuations in the security and consequent prices of American stocks?" Nevertheless, in the summer of 1839 she decided to go back to Europe. She seemed unable to stay away indefinitely. As she'd said in a letter from Florence:

> I believe no one who has lived long in Europe can ever be happy out of it—but in this vale of tears there is perhaps no happiness to be expected in any place, only there are more ways here of forgetting one's misfortunes than can be found in America.[18]

Her son was already on the continent. Bo, along with his wife, mother-in-law, and eight-year-old son Jerome Junior, were in

Europe so that he could show his family the sights. Bo's intent was to work his way to Italy to see about collecting the legacy left to him in Cardinal Fesche's will.He had a valid passport, one that showed him as a man of forty-eight years, five feet nine and a half inches tall with a small mouth, prominent chin, and dark eyes, hair, and complexion.[19] Yet he was having trouble obtaining visas. The banishment of all Bonapartes from France, enacted after Napoleon's fall, was still in effect, in part because of the activities of Bo's cousin Louis-Napoleon.

That young man's parents, Louis Bonaparte (one of Napoleon's younger brothers), and Hortense de Beauharnais (Empress Josephine's daughter by her first marriage), had separated when the son was very young. Following the separation, the elder Louis Bonaparte settled in Italy and Hortense in Switzerland. Since the boy lived with his mother, he grew up away from the other Bonapartes. Nevertheless he knew he was not only Napoleon's nephew, but also that in his early years he had been treated by the emperor Napoleon like a cherished grandson and possible heir. As a result, young Louis-Napoleon appears to have had from childhood a conviction that one day he was going to be the emperor of France. He prepared himself by studying and writing treatises about politics, government, and even the use of artillery.

His first attempt to overthrow the existing government ended in failure. When he was arrested in 1837, King Louis Philippe (then ruler of France as a result of the Bourbon restoration) decided that a trial would make a martyr of the young revolutionary, so he simply got Louis-Napoleon Bonaparte out of the way by having him put on a boat and sent to America.

Years earlier, Louis and Bo had become acquainted in Rome, so when, in April 1837, the newspapers reported his cousin's arrival in New York, Bo wrote offering him the use of one of the houses he owned. Louis replied that as soon as he commenced his travels into the interior of the country, he would certainly visit his American cousin.That visit did take place, but Louis's stay in Baltimore was brief because he found a way to get a forged passport. He used that to get back to Europe and soon was working on another uprising.[20]

As a result of such actions, the powers of various European countries were wary of any young Bonaparte, no matter how authentic his passport looked. Their caution would begin to affect Bo's travel plans. Officially, he was not welcome anywhere in France, so the American Bonapartes waited at Amsterdam. However, the American ambassador at Paris, Lewis Cass, was only able to obtain for Bo permission for a very brief trip. This permission did not include a carriage and baggage. That required a separate authorization called a *laissez passer*, which included a thorough search of the vehicle and all baggage. This examination would take place while the passengers stood outside in what was now the depth of winter. Traveling with a family made that stipulation out of the question, so they took a roundabout way to Geneva and stayed there while Bo tried to arrange visas for Tuscany and Rome.[21]

Meanwhile, Betsy, known in Europe now as *Madame Patterson*, was visiting her friends in Paris. They had been sending her letters urging her to come back ever since she'd left several years earlier. She told David Baillie Warden she was seeking "by a change of scene forgetfulness of all or part of, the troubles which I have experienced for the last five years in America." She asked him to help her find a small apartment along with a maid and a manservant.[22]

Among many Frenchmen, nostalgia for the old empire was still strong. There was even a movement to bring Napoleon's remains home from St. Helena so they could be interred in Paris. In that atmosphere Betsy began to feel comfortable, and she began looking up her old friends. Although a few had died and some had moved away, she still had many contacts and was going out for daytime visits and evening parties several times a week. [23]

Still she wasn't having a very good time. Laure, the Duchess d'Abrantès, had died in poverty. Lady Morgan and her husband were back in Dublin. Her Russian friends were not in Paris because the czar had forbidden them to go there. She couldn't visit Florence because of the presence of her ex-husband. Her friend Princess Alexandre Galitzin was still living outside Geneva, but Betsy felt she no longer had the energy to travel to Switzerland. She regretted this, because she was very fond of Alexandre, and the affection was returned. In fact, Princess Galitzin may have saved Betsy's life during the 1831 cholera epidemic. From Geneva Betsy wrote an account of that to her friend and banker, John White.

> *My intention was to pass this winter in Paris. My trunks were all packed to go there, my carriage engaged when Princess Galitzin heard that the cholera morbus was in England. She immediately ordered her carriage, drove into Geneva, came to me, and declared she never would leave my room until I gave her a solemn promise not to go to France. She fancied that the cholera would reach Paris, that I would die with it, or perhaps be buried alive out of a hotel if I became ill.*[24]

Almost a decade later, Betsy still remembered, and wished she could see Alexandre again. She wondered, however, could she be happy anywhere? She felt that the troubles she'd experienced "have stupefied and discouraged me, and left me only painful recollections and gloomy anticipations." At fifty-five, she felt too old and too careworn for Europe. Maybe early hours, old friends, and taking care of her finances were more in keeping with her present inclinations. Of course Baltimore was dull, "but all places were wearisome after one has gone through a tempestuous life." Worse, "melancholy and regrets have become a chronic disease from which I can never recover." So she went back home to Mrs. Jenkins' boarding house on Lexington Street.[25]

Soon she found a surprisingly enjoyable summer resort near New York City. Rockaway Beach was becoming a haven for European diplomats and other interesting people who fled there to escape the July and August heat in America's cities. Some of her American friends went there as well, among them the Whites and the Gallatins. Former ambassador Gallatin's son James was now president of the National Bank of New York and was happy to arrange reservations for her, so she began going there almost every summer. Occasionally she traveled to the spas of Virginia, and even paid for a lifetime pass at Berkeley Springs, but she never took advantage of the mineral baths because she felt the water used by so many people was probably unsanitary. On one occasion, when she was not going to Rockaway, James Gallatin wrote at the bottom of a business letter:

> We regret extremely to learn that we shall not have the pleasure of seeing you this summer; but perhaps you may yet be induced to change your mind and that you will come on and pass a week or two at Rockaway; for you know that you have always derived great benefit from the sea air.[26]

In general, she seems to have preferred the beach and went so far as to invite her young grandson, Junior, to spend part of the summer with her at Rockaway, offering to pay all his expenses and see that he continued his school work during the vacation. She was not surprised when his "unamiable mother" refused the offer.[27]

Bo was still getting letters from his Bonaparte relatives filled with family news, such as the marriage of his half-sister (the ex-king Jerome's daughter Mathilde) to the son of Betsy's old friend Prince Nicholas Demidoff. Meanwhile in 1840 his revolution-minded cousin Louis-Napoleon began serving a life sentence in a fortress for his second overthrow attempt. Louis said, "Though fortune has twice betrayed me, yet my destiny will none the less surely be revealed. I wait." While he waited he kept busy studying, seeing visitors, corresponding with journalists, and as it turned out, planning his escape.[28]

Betsy kept up with events in Europe by reading foreign newspapers and making frequent trips to Washington. The widowed Dolley Madison had moved back to the capital and wrote Betsy notes such as, "My sweet friend, take a social cup of tea with me this evening."[29]

Jerome Junior was off at Harvard College, and like his father before him got into a bit of trouble there. This time, it was not a simple glass of punch at a meeting, but the more serious offence of staging a cockfight in his dorm room. Bo, however, was busy working on his Washington contacts to have his son appointed to West Point. He succeeded, and after a year at Harvard, Jerome Junior went to the military academy in 1848.

One of the contacts with whom Bo corresponded was West Point commandant Robert E. Lee. The commandant had been stationed in Baltimore for four years during the construction of Fort Carroll, and while living in town became acquainted with the American Bonapartes. Commandant Lee recognized military talent in this youth with the illustrious name, and in one of the letters he wrote to Bo said, "Jerome has all the qualities to make a good soldier, and when he can perform the most service, it will always be agreeable to him." In another letter Lee told Bo, "I think you can fairly take pleasure in comparing him to his princely relatives. Where worth makes the man and rank is but the stamp, his head can tower as lofty as the best."[30]

So young Jerome did well at West Point, although his famous grandmother caused a mild stir by making a visit to watch him on parade. Though she was now in her sixties, those who saw her claimed she was still amazingly beautiful, and she attracted attention wherever she went. The cadet was also visited at West Point by his parents, who brought with them his baby brother, a second child born two decades after their first. The boy was named Charles Joseph, for Napoleon's father and Jerome's elder brother. Eventually Jerome Junior was appointed an assistant teacher of French at West Point. After graduating, he served in the U.S. mounted artillery on the Texas border during the Mexican War.

Meanwhile, in Europe—and six years into his life sentence— Louis-Napoleon escaped to London. There, he began to use politics rather than force to fulfill his imperial dream. Over the next two years the situation in France changed. By 1848 severe economic troubles along with discontent with King Louis Philippe added to a fierce yearning in the hearts of some Frenchmen for the old days of the empire. That yearning burst forth as bloody violence, and three thousand citizens were killed on the streets of Paris. The carnage led to the formation of a new government known as the Second Republic. Frenchmen wanted expanded male suffrage, fair elections, a moderate constitution, a voice in the government, and no more Bourbon-type kings. As the new order set about undoing the old, the exile of all Bonapartes was repealed, and when an election was held for membership in a new General Assembly, three of Napoleon's descendants won seats. One of them was Louis-Napoleon Bonaparte. He had learned a great deal during his years in prison, mostly about political tactics, and he was not content with membership in the General Assembly. In the next national election he ran for president and won an enormous victory, taking over seventy percent of the votes.[31]

Betsy was thrilled and apparently energized. She wrote Lady Morgan to say that even though "the Emperor hurled me back on what I hated most on earth—my Baltimore obscurity; even that shock could not divest me of the admiration I felt for his genius and glory." In her enthusiasm, she confessed that:

> I do feel enchanted at the homage paid by six millions of voices to his memory in voting an imperial president. . . . I never could endure universal suffrage until it elected the nephew of an emperor for the chief of a republic; and I shall be charmed with universal suffrage once more if it insists upon their president of France becoming a monarch.

Betsy was also delighted with Sydney's news that she and her husband were no longer living in Dublin. They had moved to London, and Betsy wrote that even though "It is not my desire ever to return to France," she would come to England next year and see Lady Morgan in London.[32]

Betsy began writing friends in England for information on the cost of rented lodgings for a stay in the capital. Late in 1849, she went to London. First, she went to see Lady Morgan, who had written her before she left Baltimore to tell her of the death of Dr. Morgan, speaking of her "deep calamity, and all that was dearest on earth to me gone!" Sydney had been ill with bronchitis more or less continuously ever since. Betsy comforted her as well as she could and then went looking for a place to rent nearby.It was a disappointing search. To rent, for a short time, several small rooms with space for a maid and a footman/coach driver, would cost five guineas a week, plus additional money for the furnishings, linens, and the firewood for heating. After one or two failed attempts she ended by renting upstairs from a hat-maker, having had the woman's references checked first.[33]

Once settled, she began spending time with Sydney Morgan. Over the next several weeks some two dozen notes passed between them. One such note read: "My dear Madame Patterson, will you take soup with me tomorrow at 6 o'clock tête à tête. I am so tired. I should like much to drive out with you tomorrow at a quarter past one." It was signed, "Affectionately, Sydney Morgan."[34]

Betsy still had to attend to her finances, especially her business with her Paris bankers. She wanted them to sell her French investments and remit the money to London.In keeping with her usual practice, she looked for someone who knew more about such arrangements than she did and found another extraordinary helper, the well-known American banker and famous philanthropist, George Peabody. He handled her Paris business, paid bills for her, and gave her advice and encouragement throughout her stay in London.[35]

❧

Betsy's hope that universal suffrage would insist upon the imperial president becoming a monarch came true. Louis-Napoleon, now called the "Prince-President," had a great many plans for a Napoleonic-style regime (he had even written a book about what he called "Napoleonic Ideas"), and his reforms were going to take time. Unfortunately for him, the new constitution prohibited a president from running for reelection. In December 1851, before his presidential term expired, Louis-Napoleon took a bold step. With the support of the army, he skillfully arranged a coup d'état that crushed opposition and resulted in 26,000 arrests across the nation.

A few days later he held a plebiscite to "sanction the extension of the Prince-President's authority" and won approval. The next year another plebiscite resulted in the establishment of a hereditary empire. And on December 2, 1852, the anniversary of Napoleon I's great victory at Austerlitz, Louis-Napoleon instituted the Second Empire and gave himself the name Napoleon the Third. [36]

When Bo wrote to congratulate him, the new emperor replied:

> *My Cousin—Notwithstanding distance and a very long separation, I have never doubted the affectionate interest with which you have followed all the chances of my destiny. Therefore, I have received with great pleasure the letter which conveys to me your congratulations and good wishes. I thank you for it. The news which you give of your son's vocation for a military career, and of his admission into a regiment of mounted rifles, has not been less agreeable. When circumstances permit, believe me, I shall be very happy to see you again. I pray God that he will have you in His holy keeping.*
>
> *Written at the palace of the Tuileries, 9th February, 1853.*
>
> *Napoleon*[37]

Bo wanted to go to Paris and he wanted to take his elder son with him, so he sought to procure a leave from the army so Junior could visit his relatives. It took numerous letters and visits to Washington, and the effort was not successful until Bo admitted that they wouldn't just be going to visit relatives, but specifically to see by invitation his cousin, Emperor Napoleon III.[36]

They arrived in Paris in June 1854. The reception there was everything Bo hoped for. Prior to the trip he had gathered and sent ahead the documents that proved his identity: the record of his mother's marriage to Jerome Bonaparte, the certification of his birth a year and a half later, and the verification of his baptism. As a result, on their first visit, the emperor gave Bo an official form stating that the minister of justice, the president of the senate, and the president of the Council of State had studied the matter of Jerome Bonaparte's marriage to Elizabeth Patterson and concluded that

Bo was a legitimate child of France, that he was French by birth, and if he has lost that title, a decree could restore it to him under the terms of the Civil Code.[39]

Louis invited his American cousins to dine with him several times at the palace of Saint-Cloud, for dinner and once even for breakfast. The Empress Eugenie liked the young soldier so much that she gave him free use of her horses, and the emperor was so impressed by Jerome Junior that he suggested that he should consider a career in the French military. Later that summer Junior resigned from the U.S. Army and went into the French military as a second lieutenant in the 7th Regiment of Dragoons. Within a month he was off to the Crimea, where armies from Turkey, Great Britain, and France were arrayed against Russia. He began almost at once to receive citations for bravery and in less than a year he was promoted to first lieutenant.[40]

Former king Jerome had returned to Paris when the Bonapartes were readmitted to France. Louis had given him a highly paid government post as governor of the veterans' hospital, Les Invalides, which required little of him. Louis also allowed him to live at the Palais Royale. Now the former king of Westphalia invited his American son and grandson to dinner. In a private conversation the elder Jerome told Bo he was afraid his presence made bastards of his second family. Bo reassured him that there was nothing he could or would do that would harm the second family, and the discussion ended amicably. At that time he also renewed his acquaintance with his half-sister Princess Mathilde and his half-brother Prince Napoleon. (Their elder sibling, Prince Jerome, had died in 1847.) Princess Mathilde liked Jerome Junior so much that when he went off to war she corresponded with him and passed his letters on to Bo so he could share them with his wife, Susan May, back in Baltimore.[41]

Before long, however, the warmth of the Americans' reception began to cause unrest among certain of the Bonapartes, primarily Prince Napoleon. There was now an imperial succession at stake. Ex-king Jerome was the last living brother of Napoleon, which meant that if Napoleon III died without a male heir, old Jerome and his son were next in line. Prince Napoleon, who was much younger than Bo and very active in French politics, was determined there would be no question about who that next-in-line *son* was. The prince, active in the General Assembly, was often a critic of the emperor and hence was not on very good terms with him, so he put pressure on his father to do something about Bo.

Bo had decided to confirm his status by reestablishing his French citizenship, and in July he made a formal request to the emperor to that effect. Louis forwarded the application to the proper authorities and wrote back to Bo to warn him that his uncle the ex-king had written him to say that he would never consent to having Bo live in France. "I have answered him that, if the laws of France recognize you as a legitimate son, I cannot do otherwise than recognize you as a kinsman, and that if your residence in Paris was embarrassing, you alone were the judge of that." He suggested that Bo should, without irritating his father, continue on the course he'd planned.[42]

In August, Bo received his formal proof of citizenship. His son was automatically included as the child of a French citizen. In addition, French law stipulated that no divorce or annulment could deprive children of their right to an inheritance. So Bo's position seemed secure.

Still, Prince Napoleon kept up the pressure. He was becoming increasingly concerned about Bo's son. The American lieutenant was winning medal after medal at the siege of Sebastopol and the battles at Balaclava, Inkerman, and Tchernia. In contrast, Prince Napoleon, although he'd been given the rank of general, had come home from the Crimean War claiming he was sick. His soldiers had another view: they said he was so frightened and flinched so much at the *plomb plomb* sound of heavy artillery that they nicknamed him after it. Those Parisians who favored him claimed he had gotten the nickname in childhood because he could not pronounce his name. Anyway, the name "Plon Plon" has followed Prince Napoleon down through history, and still appears in some of the texts that mention him.

Soon Napoleon III—treating Bo as a member of the royal family—gave him a pension of 70,000 francs a year "from the civil list beginning the first day of last January." Next the emperor announced that he had decided to make him the Duke of Sartène and his son the Count of Sartène, naming a place on the island of Corsica.[43]

Bo was beginning to wonder whether he was being used as a pawn in Louis's conflict with Prince Napoleon. Was the emperor trying to force Plon Plon to behave by making the American Bonapartes more of a threat in the line of succession? Or had Louis changed and, like his ancestor Napoleon I, chosen political expediency over all other considerations? Was there already a deal, with the emperor backing off his original support for Bo and giving in, so that Bo and his son would no longer threaten Plon Plon by being known as Bonapartes?

Bo refused the title. He was not going to give up his name. But then a further move disturbed him even more. After Lieutenant Bonaparte had been awarded the Order of the Mejiidie by the Sultan of Turkey and the Crimean medal by Queen Victoria, his commander Marshal Pelissier nominated him to be a knight in the French Legion of Honor. When the Crimean War had ended, the American soldier had transferred to the 1st Chasseurs d'Afrique. When that award came to him, it was addressed to Lt. Jerome Bonaparte-Patterson. He refused to accept the letter "addressed to him under a name which was not his own."[44]

The intrigue intensified when the head of the family of the elder Jerome's deceased wife came to town. The King of Württemberg declared his concern about the presence of this American in Paris. It seems that prior to the wedding of Jerome and Princess Catherine of Württemberg, the first Napoleon had made a secret agreement with the rulers of Russia and Württemberg to guarantee that nothing would ever stand in the way of that marriage. Now Prince Napoleon, with the backing of his mother's relative, insisted that Napoleon III convene a Council of the Family.

The council consisted of the chairman (His Majesty, or a

family member chosen by him), a prince of the family, the minister of state, the minister of justice, the presidents of the senate and of the assembly, a member of the council of state, the president of the court of cassation, and a marshal of France or a general of division. Such a meeting was called from time to time to rule on matters of rank, precedence, or obligations in reference to the imperial family. Now they met to discuss whether Jerome Patterson of Baltimore and his descendants should not henceforth be forbidden to bear the name of Bonaparte.

Bo appeared before the council to defend his right to use the name he had borne for half a century and showed them his proofs of identity. After a long deliberation, the council ruled that the marriage of 1803 had officially been made null during the first Napoleon's reign, but that the name Bo had borne and been known by, even among the rest of the Bonapartes, could not be taken from him. However, the council also ruled that its decision gave Mr. Bonaparte no rights under Articles 201 and 202 of the Civil Code—the laws declaring that even if a marriage has been ended, it created civil rights—such as the right to inherit from a parent. Napoleon III added a note to the decree in his own hand: "His Majesty the Emperor by his conduct toward the descendants of Madame Patterson, since the judgment was determined, has thought it right to prove that he did not consider them as belonging to his *famille civile.*"[45]

Bo wrote to the emperor enclosing the letter his son had written him about his refusal to accept the Legion of Honor knighthood under a name not his own. He told Louis that, since no man creates himself, there is no dishonor in being born a bastard and accepting the consequences.

> *Had I been in that category, I would have long ago accepted, with gratitude, the offers which Your Majesty had deigned to make me. But, since my birth is legitimate and has always been so recognized by my family, by the laws of all countries and by the whole world, it would be the height of cowardice and of dishonor to accept a warrant of bastardy.*

Bo concluded by saying that, "faced with such intrigues, calumnies and falsehoods" he requested His Majesty's permission "to go with his son into exile and await there the justice that, I am sure, heaven will reserve for me, sooner or later."[46]

Bo had done all he could do for now, but he wasn't finished fighting. The elder Jerome was not going to be around for long; he was seventy-two and not in very good health. When the end came, Bo wanted to be ready for another round. He contacted a man considered to be one of the best lawyers in France, Pierre Antoine Berryer.Berryer had been elected to the chamber of deputies, was a member of the French Academy, and had participated in a series of high-profile cases, including that of the man now known as Napoleon III. When Louis-Napoleon was charged by King Louis Philippe with high treason for his second overthrow attempt, Berryer had defended him and by winning the sentence of life confinement in a fortress, probably saved him from a death penalty,

Now Bo hired Berryer, gave him the relevant documents, signed over his power of attorney, and went home with a list of items he would need to gather and either send or bring to his lawyer.

Betsy had taken no part in those proceedings in Paris.After Bo's marriage she almost never mentioned him in her correspondence, or in her notebooks or the comments she wrote on the letters she received. In contrast, she was always avidly interested in her elder grandson. She felt strongly that his place was in France. For several years she'd been telling her friends that he ought to be there, and she was glad when he went to Paris with Bo in 1854. From the time he joined the French army she sent him large amounts of money for his horses, his uniforms, and eventually, the apartments he maintained in Paris, and, on occasion, at Versailles.[47]

During this time, Betsy was becoming interested in the French situation on her own behalf. In 1857 she began writing letters to Berryer, sending him a copy of her 1803 marriage contract, asking him whether it would be enforceable in France, and corresponding with him on the topic.[48]

On June 24, 1860, Jerome Bonaparte, former king of Westphalia, died and was honored with a state funeral. Among the royal family's imperial guard, in full uniform with all his decorations on his chest, was an officer by the name of Jerome Napoleon Bonaparte Junior.[49]

All the American Bonapartes were ready for the next round.

Chapter 21

Life's Fitful Fever

*E*arly in 1861, *Harper's Weekly* published in installments the new Dickens novel, *Great Expectations*. On the page that opened Chapter 21 was a large picture of Betsy Bonaparte accompanied by an extensive article about her life. The piece opened by saying:

> All our readers know, of course, that this lady is now prosecuting a suit in the French Courts for the recognition of her marriage with Jerome Bonaparte. The lady herself, though seventy-five years of age, has gone to Paris for the purpose, and is instructing her lawyers in person.[1]

In Betsy's first contact with lawyer Pierre Antoine Berryer in 1857, she told him that ex-king Jerome's "ill-advised conduct towards my son, and towards Lieutenant Bonaparte my grandson, has determined me to ascertain, vindicate, and enforce my rights."[2] During their ensuing correspondence, Berryer assured her that her marriage contract could be enforceable, but warned that at the time of her ex-husband's demise, she must act immediately.[3] So shortly after news came of old Jerome's death, Betsy made arrangements to travel to Paris.

Her son was making preparations as well. He had stayed on in Paris and continued working with his lawyer until Berryer advised him to return to Baltimore and gather more information there in preparation for a suit to be filed at the time of old Jerome's death. Bo did so, and after taking a brief trip with Susan May and little Charles Joseph to the Virginia springs, he began collecting every letter he'd ever received from his Bonaparte relations, including the one from Plon Plon which ended with "I am for life your devoted brother and friend."⁴ He also borrowed the letters Betsy had been saving since 1803, translated the English letters into French, and set about making copies of them all. To help with the copying, he even invested in a couple of new inventions. One made it possible to avoid dipping into an inkwell all the time: it was the innovative "fountain pen" being manufactured in Baltimore. Another was the new machine called a "copier" which he thought was a good idea, except that it took at least half an hour to copy each page. Finally he got the whole collection officially certified as being true copies.⁵

Soon after Betsy checked into a suite at a hotel in Paris, Bo joined her there and together in preparation for turning them over to Berryer, they began going over all the documents they had gathered.

By this time ex-king Jerome's will had caused a stir among the European Bonapartes. Since Jerome's death had a bearing on the Second Empire succession, the offspring of one of Napoleon's brothers, Lucien, felt they had claims to pursue. They requested Family Council to examine that issue.

With reference to money questions, there was little to discuss. Old Jerome had always spent more than he possessed and had been supported by others all his life. Since 1852, Napoleon III's government had paid him over five million francs, but apparently he had spent all that as well. So there were only two mentions of money in his will. One established a pension for his third and last wife, Marquesa Bartolini, who as his mistress and later as his wife had supported him for years. The other confirmed Princess Mathilde's marriage settlement. Since it had been given to her at the time of her wedding to Prince Demidoff, she withdrew herself from further involvement in the will. There was no mention of Jerome's first marriage. That left the surviving son of his second marriage, Prince Napoleon, as the principal inheritor and sole legatee.⁶

There is some evidence Napoleon III, or at least the Empress Eugenie, tried to use Bo's son to head off the confrontation. She sent a mutual friend to explain to Jerome Junior how unreasonable the Americans were being. The intermediary asked whether Bo would desist if he were given a third of the ex-king's estate. Junior expressed his regret over the dissension that had arisen within the family, but explained that he had no power to act in the matter; however he believed that no sum of money would make his father desist in his effort to establish his legitimacy. The intermediary wrote to Bo:

> I am confident that the E. will do all in his power to prevent the suit, as it will produce much scandal, which he of course will desire to avoid. Plon Plon and Mathilde it appears are already at loggerheads, so that you will have a jolly little time. If the E. can arrange affairs so as to satisfy all parties, he will give another proof of his consummate statesmanship. If he should send for me, I shall repeat to him what I have always said – that I deplore the want of harmony in the family circle, but that during your life I am utterly powerless.

Jerome Junior also told his father, "Plon Plon is all powerful at present," and added: "He and the Empress are very intimate, which always happens when he is in favor as she is terribly afraid of him."[7]

❧

The French attorney hired by Bo to represent his case, Pierre Antoine Berryer, had originally wanted to be a priest, but his father convinced him to follow him into the legal profession. Now at age seventy-two Berryer still worked vigorously on cases in which he strongly believed. In preparation for a Bonaparte versus Bonaparte trial, in the summer of 1860, Berryer and his associate Charles Legrand took a series of legal steps that ended with a suit filed on September 6 against Prince Napoleon "demanding that there be an accounting, liquidation and distribution of the assets constituting the estate of His Imperial Highness, Prince Jerome." In his *Exposé des Faits* (or Statement of Facts), Berryer included all the verifications of the marriage, birth, and baptism along with more than sixty communications from various Bonapartes attesting to their recognition of the offspring of Jerome's first marriage as a "dear son," "grandson," "nephew," or "cousin." This *Exposé des Faits* required 139 printed pages and was published so that the court could examine it prior to the trial.[8]

With Betsy and Bo present, the hearings took place the following January. Berryer's courtroom oratory was described as "the living personification of forensic eloquence."[9] He told the whole story of Betsy's marriage and eventual abandonment, then said:

> She comes from her distant home beyond the Atlantic; she appears before this august court asking for the declaration of her rights, and demands the vindication of her honor and the establishment of her child in the position due to his birth.[0]

Prince Napoleon's lawyer, M. Allou, fought back. He insisted that the 1803 marriage was completely invalid, because it was contrary to the laws of France, since Jerome was a minor who had failed to obtain the permission of his parent. Berryer wondered why, if that were true, Napoleon felt obliged to ask the pope to annul it? Allou went on to assert that the Patterson family knew at the time the marriage was illegal, yet went on with it, and he charged further that the young and inexperienced Jerome had been entrapped in Baltimore—a city with a reputation for vice and a "Sodom of impurities." In addition he criticized the character of the young woman and quoted the passage from William Patterson's will that described his daughter as willful, disobedient, and guilty of folly and misconduct. He claimed that Madame Mère's repudiation must be counted from the time she learned of the clandestine marriage and hence it was made within the one-year time limit. The fact that Miss Patterson accepted a pension from the first Napoleon was a tacit admission that she knew the marriage was invalid, and she confirmed and strengthened that nullification with a divorce in her own country. He also contended that the 1856 Family Council had reaffirmed once and for all that the marriage of Jerome Bonaparte and Miss Patterson was null and void, and he insisted that it should not be possible to keep bringing up the same question again and again. On February 15, 1861, the court agreed with him.

Although the decision of the court went against the Americans, there was another lawyer involved in the proceedings, an impartial "friend of the court." This was a M. Duvigne, who represented the French attorney general. He found Berryer's arguments sound and agreed with his conclusions. On the strength of that, Betsy, Bo, and the Berryer team decided to appeal.

Meanwhile the case was getting extraordinary press coverage in Britain, France, and the United States, and the commentary was sympathetic to Betsy's cause. The *Illustrated London News* devoted many columns to the trial, not only to the arguments, but also to the whole history of Betsy's marriage, the life of her son, and even her elder grandson's extraordinary military record. The *Examiner of London* said:

> The Napoleon marriage case, heard only on successive Fridays, has amused Paris more than any other Periodical, and there will be many to regret that the last of its weekly parts was supplied yesterday by the non suit of the Pattersons. . . . Of the various characters in the Imperial Drama, every one has turned out as bad as was expected, or else worse.

The *Examiner* also criticized Allou's attack on Betsy with the use of William Patterson's will, since "such clauses in wills discredit only those who put them there," and added that the desire to speak cruelly against a child from the grave indicated "a temper disposed to exactions." [11]

The Paris correspondent of the *New York Express* reported the decision was considered there to be "in conflict with the law, the evidence, and the elementary principles of justice." This anti-government support in France reflected the opposition of monarchists, who opposed the Bonapartes as usurpers, as well as Catholics, who took exception to the first Napoleon's treatment of the pope, who refused to annul Betsy's marriage. [12]

During the time it took to mount an appeal, the Bonapartes

attempted to counteract some of their bad publicity by publishing an edited version of *The Memoires of Roi Jêrôme*. It was supposed to tell the story in a light more favorable to Jerome, but because of the nature of most of his life, the work failed in its objective. The book review in the *Atheneum* remarked that Jerome was a naughty boy who had been very kindly treated by a law court that had been "very hard upon the beautiful young lady whom he betrayed and abandoned; but opinion in Europe is not yet governed by the Code Napoleon." The review's conclusion was that the memoirs hadn't helped his reputation. As for Jerome, "he was through life a fool and a poltroon. The fine epithets and sentimental phraseology in which the courtly editor of these Memoirs dresses his conduct does not disguise the very ugly look of his actions, both public and private."[13]

Once again, Berryer and Legrand presented their case in great detail before an appeals court. Those hearings lasted through June of 1861. In July the court delivered a judgment covering every point raised and debated in the previous trial. Its conclusion was that the second marriage of Prince Jerome could not be sacrificed for a marriage made contrary to the laws of France by a minor of nineteen years. Consequently the court rejected the appeal, declared the actions of attorney Berryer's clients unfounded and inadmissable, dismissed their claims and arguments, and condemned the appellants to pay a fine plus the expenses of the appeal.

It had been a costly venture. The Berryer bill was four thousand francs, while the court costs and other expenses came to 19,468 francs—almost fifty thousand dollars in today's money. Betsy urged Bo never again to seek justice from the current French administration; she intended not to spend another cent on such endeavors. Bo remained in Paris, perhaps because his elder son was off fighting on another distant battlefield and he felt closer there to news of his son's military exploits and well-being.[14]

As for Betsy, she went home. She landed in New York in early August during what turned out to be the midst of a busy tourist season. Some sort of fair was going on and every hotel room was filled.

She left her luggage at the port and managed to get to the home of the Gallatins. Albert and Hannah immediately took her in and sent their son James off to retrieve her baggage. While staying with the Gallatins, Betsy wrote a final letter to Berryer to tell him of her safe arrival in New York and to express her thanks for his efforts. She asked him to give her power of attorney for her grandson, Captain Bonaparte, and told him that after "the eminent talent which distinguishes yourself had failed before two courts to have our rights recognized," she had been forced to conclude that justice from any court in France was unattainable. Then she gathered up her baggage and made her way back to her Baltimore boarding house.[15]

One good thing had come out of the time spent in Paris. In St. Petersburg her old and very dear friend Prince Alexandre Gortchakoff had been following the trials. Unsure how to get in touch with her, he contacted an acquaintance who was going to be in Paris and asked her to deliver a message. The woman, a Miss Worthington, called on Betsy to give her his regards and his good wishes. Immediately Betsy wrote to him, but this first attempt was a failure. She found herself pouring out in French the long miserable story of all the things that had happened to her, and ended with a several-thousand-word lament. She filed it away with the notation: "After reflection I decided not to send this letter."[16]

Her second attempt was better. She sent Gortchakoff a copy of Berryer's *Exposé des Faits* along with an account of her grandson's military career, a short update about herself, a brief description of her current problems with the Bonaparte family in Paris, and only a couple of nasty remarks about her ex-husband. She closed with a reminder that she had always been a sincere admirer of the talents she had recognized in him, and said the friendship she felt for him would accompany her throughout her life. She sealed up the letter and took it to the Paris office of the Russian embassy for transmission to Gortchakoff. A reply arrived promptly from St. Petersburg.

> *Madame, I am touched by the good memories you have kept of me.*
> *I am doubly touched, even with the many years that have passed,*
> *by the kindness and spirituality you gave me in Florence.*

I have followed with interest this new phase which has come in an existence as eventful as yours, and I said to myself that whatever the issue, it would find you supreme over every outcome. This drop in eternity that we call life has no greater value than the one that teaches us never to forsake our selves. This conviction was always embodied by you in every situation; it never left you at any time.

In the position that circumstances have placed me, I often regret no longer having in my reach the fine and remarkable insights which I enjoyed there on the bank of the Arno, when public life did not yet have any thorns for me. Times are very much changed. This era has wiped away all illusions and most of our hope; and what is most grave, I find myself called upon to pose in front of history at a moment when the contemporary scene offers nothing but a chaos of principles, covetousness, and self-interest, and where man must appear to posterity as very small. It is a good lesson in humility for the salvation of the soul, but will not sharpen the quill of the future Plutarch who may be interested in the history of our times.

Pardon the digression. I only made it to tell you that in recommending resignation to desperately tried souls like yours, I do not hesitate to apply to myself the same conviction.

Madame, please believe that all my best wishes accompany you. If you go back to the retreat which you have chosen, I will be happy as long as you are persuaded that in Europe there exists a corner where an affectionate thought will never stop being devoted to you. . . .[17]

Betsy was not as certain as Prince Alexandre that she had prevailed in this last situation, but she supposed she had not forsaken her own interests. She had to admit she had lost some of her illusions, but not all of her hope. There was always her elder grandson, and somehow she still believed his time would come. The French situation had changed repeatedly. It would do so again. Then the people who still remembered the first Napoleon would seek a Bonaparte who was brave, who did not fear the sound of guns, and who knew how to lead men to glory.

That meant she must get to work. When young Captain Bonaparte's time came, he would need a lot of money, and right now her fortune was shrinking. The country was in the midst of the Civil War.

Maryland was a border state, combining elements of northern and southern culture, commercial and agrarian concerns, free and slave economies. As such, the loyalties of its citizens were divided between pro-union and secessionist sentiments. But, as President Lincoln and Baltimore mayor George William Brown understood, these divided loyalties had to be reckoned with. Baltimore's proximity to Washington meant that it was crucial for the defense of the national capital, and Union troops would have to travel through Baltimore, potentially raising the ire of the city's southern sympathizers. On April 19, 1861, these passions erupted in a riot. When troops from the 6th Massachusetts Regiment of volunteer militia arrived in Baltimore on their way to defend Washington, they were attacked by a mob determined to stop the "Yankee invaders." Angry citizens, some brandishing firearms, pursued the volunteers up Pratt Street, tearing up cobblestones and hurling them at the troops. When they returned fire, the riot escalated, leaving four soldiers and a dozen citizens killed and many more wounded.[18]

Betsy's son Bo, who sided with the North, complained that he could not go out socially anymore because of the prominence of secessionists in Baltimore's wealthier circles. He had been instrumental in founding an organization called the Maryland Club and had served as its first president, but now it was so pro-Confederate that he didn't care to go there any more. He told his son, "The Secessionists and the loyal people here do not meet together, and many do not speak when they meet." The congregation of one of the Episcopal churches in town threw out their minister because his sermons were against secession.[19]

Eventually the city was put under martial law. Artillery placed on Federal Hill was aimed across the inner harbor toward downtown. The guns of Fort McHenry were turned away from seaward and pointed in the direction of the city. So many suspected Confederate sympathizers were arrested that the jail at Fort McHenry was jammed full. Bo's wife, Susan May, sought to aid the North in her own way. She was such a rabid federal supporter that she spied on her acquaintances and reported southern sympathizers to the authorities.[20]

For both Betsy and Bo the chief concern in this war was economic. Even while they were still in Paris for the trial, they'd begun receiving letters from their agents complaining that business in Baltimore was almost at a standstill. Properties were empty and could not be rented. Renters who remained could not pay. One of Betsy's tenants, a woodworker, could no longer sell his furniture and turned to making coffins to stay in business. Others would not pay because they feared they were going to have to flee the city and needed cash to take with them. At the same time, the agents continued, funds set aside for upkeep and repairs were being exhausted. As a result, roofs were leaking, walls were caving in, and the privy of Betsy's rental house on South Street had a plague of frogs.[21]

Yet the federal government needed money to fund the war, so it was offering government securities with a profit rate of six percent. Betsy decided to start rebuilding her fortune with those. She was impartial, though, and also bought some bonds for the state of Virginia. The latter didn't work out very well, but the former made up for it.

Betsy was also beginning to enjoy her younger grandson. Charles Joseph was ten years old now and although she was still not on visiting terms with Susan May, Bo often brought the boy to see her. It was the beginning of a relationship that would sustain and assist her for the rest of her life. As Charley grew up, went to college, and then to law school, he shared what he was learning with her. In return, when she made a purchase of stock or securities for herself, she bought some for him as well. She still tottered around town carrying a carpetbag to look after her investments, but when Charley settled in Baltimore and opened a law office, he took care of business for her. She kept him supplied with updated lists of all her holdings so he would be prepared in the event she could no longer handle her affairs.

Betsy's other grandson Jerome Junior was a different story. He stayed in the French army, eventually becoming a colonel, and served Napoleon III. During this time, while the Second Empire was disintegrating, the emperor got into a series of conflicts ending in French defeats. Jerome Junior remained faithful to Empress Eugénie, personally guarding her during her flight from Paris and into England. After that the colonel came back to the United States and broke his grandmother's heart by marrying an American woman, a divorcée with children. They would live in Washington and Paris. Betsy wrote him to say she never wanted to see him again, but later relented.

It was younger grandson Charley who delivered the news to her that on June 17, 1870, Bo had died. He was only sixty-five at the time of his death, and it came as a shock to Betsy, as Bo had earlier written that he was in good health:

> *My health is better than it has been for the last twenty years, when, unfortunately, it was always under the influence of monkey [whiskey]. I breakfast and dine very heartily, sleep well, take a great deal of outdoor exercise, drink nothing but ale, very rarely taste wine, and have not tasted monkey, in any shape for months.*[22]

Betsy told Charley that she was so distressed she didn't think she could attend the funeral.

Actually, Bo had smoked heavily, especially cigars, and had died of throat cancer. He left a large fortune to Susan May and his two sons. Part of the legacy was a house, Chestnut Hill, in a northern suburb of Baltimore, but Jerome Junior did not want to live there. Betsy paid him for his half of the property so that Charley could own it all.

Betsy had outlived not only her son, but also all of her brothers. She hadn't kept in contact with any of them except George. She'd often visited him at Springfield, in her later years traveling the twenty-two miles there by train. After George died, his wife Prudence Ann and daughter Florence remained close to her. Betsy also retained close connections among the Spears, and some of them helped care for her during her later years.

Betsy resided in a large room on the second floor of a boarding house on Cathedral Street. In the room she kept a desk where she wrote and a comfortable rocking chair given to her by Charley. But most of the space was taken up by her trunks of memorabilia. She reread and continued to annotate her many letters, adding comments like: "A Frenchman's word is as brittle as pie crust." On one of her sadder days she remarked: "When I was young I had everything but money, now that I am old I have nothing but money."

She spent much of her time writing. The journals she had kept for years became a multi-volume memoir titled *The Story of My Life*. Back in 1860, when she listed her possessions, this diary had already expanded to thirteen volumes; but she continued to keep it up, always putting in wry comments about politics and society and the famous people she had known. In 1873 a publisher offered ten thousand dollars for her diary; she refused.[23] She also wrote a work of fiction, *Dialogues between Jerome and My Father in Hell*. It was two volumes long. Betsy never forgave either of them, although she eventually softened her attitudes about Jerome. She concluded that although Jerome had faults, he was never deliberately mean and, unlike her father, had never tried to blame her for the things that had happened.

Her most difficult problems were crank letters, appeals for money, and intrusions from the press. People wrote her to say they were related to her as a sister or, in one case, a bastard child. Mrs. Virginia Mosby, mother of the famous Confederate raider, John Singleton Mosby, wrote to say their grandmothers were sisters and now that the victorious Union army had taken everything she had, could Betsy provide financial assistance? Another woman asked for Betsy's beauty secrets so that she could support her family by marketing them. There were also proposals of marriage. One man wrote to say he had decided to marry her and was coming to town to meet her at noon the following day in front of the church.[24]

Betsy refused to give interviews, and when a reporter managed to locate her boardinghouse room, Betsy answered the door saying, "Madame Bonaparte is not at home." In 1873 the Baltimore correspondent for the *New York Herald* did get to see her and wrote: "Though eighty-eight years of age, Madame Bonaparte retains traces of her once wondrous beauty. Her complexion is still smooth and comparatively fair, while her peculiarly beautiful blue eyes are as yet undimmed." (Other accounts said her eyes were hazel.) He said she had been ill, but upon hearing her physician Dr. Mackenzie say she might die at any moment, "she straightened herself up in bed and said, emphatically, that she intended to live until she was one hundred years old" . . . and then got better.[25]

Betsy did not live to see one hundred. During the winter of her ninety-fourth year, she got a bad case of bronchitis. She remained as mentally sharp as ever but could not get well. Charley told his brother he'd better come home, and both her grandsons were with her when, on April 4, 1879, she slipped away.

Her body was placed in a walnut coffin in Susan May's house at Park and Centre Streets, where she had not been welcome before. The funeral took place there. It was supposed to be a private ceremony, but a mass of people filled the street in the chilly April rain, and then followed the hearse. The cortege proceeded—not to the Patterson family graveyard, but to the Green Mount cemetery and to the plot she'd bought for herself years before, saying: "I have lived alone and when I die I shall lie alone."

Betsy left an immense fortune; today it would be valued at between ten and fifteen million dollars. Most of it was accumulated through careful investing during the years after the Civil War. Even though Jerome Junior had disappointed her, it was against her principles to disown an offspring, so she left her fortune to be divided equally between her two grandsons. In addition, she willed to Charley her silver, china, furniture, and jewelry, as well as all of her souvenirs, the hundreds of letters she'd saved, and her personal writings, including the multi-volume *Story of My Life.*[26]

She was still so famous that major newspapers in the United States and abroad devoted many columns to her obituary. Behind those public aspects of her life, she had been both adored and hated. Everyone agreed that she was lovely, but she was not always lovable.

Betsy was by turns affectionate and bitter, generous and miserly, despondent and driven. Yet as Alexandre Gortchakoff told her, she had never forsaken her *self*, that inner identity that was determined to be, not a collection of female functions, but an independent individual . . . *someone.*

In her 1876 novel, *Daniel Deronda*, George Eliot captured the intensity of Betsy's drive to be independent. Daniel's mother tries to explain that quest to him in terms of her conflict with his grandfather:

> *You may try—but you can never imagine what it is to have a man's force of genius in you, and yet to suffer the slavery of being a girl. To have a pattern cut out . . . "this is what you must be; this is what you are wanted for; a woman's heart must be of such a size and no larger, else it must be pressed small, like Chinese feet; her happiness is to be made as cakes are, by a fixed receipt." That was what my father wanted.[27]*

Unfortunately, the men who chose the wording for Betsy's tomb didn't understand this message. So although the line from *Macbeth* inscribed on her tomb was a nice touch, Betsy's grandsons in their final act deprived her of the identity she'd been feverishly burning for all her life. The engraved monument reads:

SACRED
to the memory of
ELIZABETH
daughter of
WILLIAM PATTERSON
and wife of
JEROME BONAPARTE
born February 6, 1785
died April 4, 1879
After life's fitful fever she sleeps well.

AFTERWORD

*D*uring the summer of 1995 a man called the Maryland Historical Society from Washington, D.C., to make an appointment to come in and trace his roots. When he mentioned his name, a staff member called me because of the work I was doing on this book, and the next day I went in to the society to meet a tall, good-looking young man by the name of Jerome Napoleon Bonaparte. He was the great-great-grandson of the former rulers of Würtemburg, King Jerome and Queen Catherine. The young man's home was in Switzerland, but he'd gone to college in the United States and his English was perfect, with only the faintest trace of a French accent.

The staffers and I took him through the galleries to show him Betsy's porcelain and silver, her jewelry, the little red trunk she traveled with, the mahogany wardrobe her husband bought for her, and the paintings of her and of her relatives. At the portrait of William Patterson we mentioned that he was a millionaire. Our guest was surprised. His family had the impression that Betsy was a penniless gold digger and Napoleon had been forced to pay her off.

Then, in the society's Special Collections Department, Curators Jennifer Bryan and Mary Herbert pulled out Manuscript 143, the collection of the first Jerome Bonaparte's correspondence. They offered the guest a chair at a table in the department office and opened the folder containing the letters Jerome had written to Betsy during the early years of their courtship and marriage. He began reading the French aloud, but then, as he turned the pages he grew quiet. After a few minutes he stopped and looked up at us, seemingly close to tears, but at the same time amazed. He swallowed hard, then said: "He really loved her, didn't he? He really *loved* her."

Yes, he did. But not as much as he loved the idea of becoming a king.

Our guest's relatives were not the only ones who had an inaccurate or an incomplete opinion of Betsy. Many of her fellow Baltimoreans had distorted views of her as well. They thought her father was a pure pillar of the community, while Betsy was an inexcusably selfish and ungrateful daughter. They thought her son, in contrast to her, was a patriotic American who had no interest whatever in France or in being a Bonaparte. They believed his traveling about town in a coach and four with servants in livery and a Bonaparte crest on the door was all Betsy's doing. They didn't know about his trips to Paris after his cousin Louis Napoleon came to power and made himself Emperor Napoleon III. They hadn't seen inside his house on the corner of Park Avenue and Centre Street filled with Bonaparte memorabilia, statuary, and portraits going all the way back past Napoleon to Carlo and Letizia Bonaparte. And, of course, neither Betsy, nor her son, nor her grandsons made any effort to change their neighbors' minds: they didn't give a hoot what anybody thought. After all, they were *Bonapartes*.

The mind of that young visitor from Switzerland was changed by his exposure to source material about Betsy. In the thank-you letter he wrote the day after his visit he said: "Jérôme and Elizabeth were definitely deeply in love and we would have expected that history would have given them another end. But here came the burden of Duty and Power raised by Napoléon I."[1]

The young man is one of a great many Bonaparte descendants alive in Europe and other parts of the world today. The American Bonapartes, however, did not survive so well.

The much-decorated elder grandson, retired Colonel Jerome Napoleon Bonaparte, lived with his family in a Washington, D. C. home on K Street near 16th Street. Locals nicknamed it "the Chateau Bonaparte."[2] In 1893 he died on vacation in Massachusetts, but was brought back to Baltimore for burial near his father. He left his immediate family so well situated that nobody bothered to record his will officially until thirty years had passed. When Jerome Napoleon's family finally got around to reviewing the will, they found that, since some of the property mentioned was in New York, they owed a penalty on that part of the proceeds of ten percent a year times thirty.

Of the colonel's two children, the daughter, Louise Eugenie, married a Danish count, moved to Denmark, and raised her five children there. The colonel's son was named Jerome Napoleon Bonaparte, like his father and grandfather. Interestingly, he was once approached by representatives from Albania about becoming their king, but he wasn't interested. Jerome Napoleon Bonaparte lived in a New York City apartment hotel, and when he died childless, in 1941, he was the last of the American Bonapartes.

Betsy's second grandson, Charles Joseph, had a distinguished career. He and his wife, Ellen Channing Day, lived in the Roland Park area of Baltimore in a house called Chestnut Hill. When a trolley line was established in the area, Charley felt the neighborhood was getting too crowded.[3] He bought a large estate called Bella Vista fourteen miles from Baltimore and rode into town every morning in a horse-drawn carriage. He had set up a law practice in Baltimore, but he didn't need money so he devoted himself to causes he cared about.

One case that Charley handled involved a black man who had fought on the Union side during the Civil War. When the soldier returned after the war to Annapolis, Maryland, he was ready to take advantage of the full citizenship soldiers like him had been promised. But when he went to vote for the first time, he was told the government of the city had ruled that no one could vote whose grandfather had been a slave. Charles Joseph Bonaparte took the man's case all the way to the Supreme Court and won.

Charley's chief interest was corruption in government, whether at the local, state, or national level. He was a leader in the creation of the National Civil Service Reform League, and this work put him in contact with a fellow reformer named Theodore Roosevelt. The two became close friends, and after "Teddy" became president, he appointed Charley as his chief investigative counsel to root out government corruption in the U.S. Postal Service. After that, Charley served in the Indian Bureau. Next, Roosevelt made Charley secretary of the navy, and later, attorney general of the United States. In that office Charley was troubled by his agency's inability to investigate the cases they were supposed to be pursuing. So he made recommendations that eventually resulted in the creation of the Federal Bureau of Investigation. When Roosevelt's term in office ended in 1909, Charley left federal service and went back to the local causes that most interested him.

As noted earlier, although Betsy's will gave her two grandsons an equal share of her fortune, she had left all her personal possessions to Charley, including the diaries that had become her memoirs and the work of fiction she called *Dialogues between Jerome and My Father in Hell.* These writings meant a great deal to Betsy. She shared them from time to time with her closest friends, and their positive reactions to this or that part of her memoirs or diary appear among the letters she kept. She told Sydney Morgan and Alexandre Gortchakoff that they appeared in her memoirs.

We know Charles Joseph had these materials in his possession. In the Bonaparte collection, there is a note in his hand saying that in 1872 he had placed with the Safe Deposit Company of Baltimore: "one large black box containing jewelry, four volumes of Memoirs and Dialogues of the Dead, thirteen volumes of Diary, and other valuable papers and letters." [4]

Later, Charley would invite friends to Sunday brunch at Bella Vista and read aloud to them hilarious passages from his grandmother's memoirs. After Charley died—without children—in 1921, his widow presented all of these inherited items to the Maryland Historical Society.

On January 9, 1922, at the regular monthly meeting of the historical society, the organization's president announced Mrs. Ellen Bonaparte's gift of the Betsy materials. He described the collection of portraits and portrait busts formerly displayed at Bo's Baltimore home: "all bearing upon the history of the Bonaparte and Patterson families." Then he went on to say:

> A part of this collection was removed by the late Colonel Jerome Napoleon Bonaparte, but the remainder continued in the pos-

session of our late member, Attorney General Charles Joseph
Bonaparte. Mrs. Bonaparte is led to make to the society a gift
of the whole of this collection by her interest in our Society, her
recognition that these memorials of two families so intimately con-
nected with the history of the City, should not pass into the hands of
any other institution—and especially by her splendid generosity.

When the meeting adjourned, the attendees were invited to view
the newly mounted Bonaparte exhibit on the second floor.[5]

The president of the Maryland Historical Society at that time
was a man named William Hall Harris. His wife Alice was the daughter of Betsy's brother Henry Patterson. There is a loose note dated
January 8, 1922, in one of the folders of Betsy's letters that says: "Do not
open. W.H.H." So it may or may not have been Mr. Harris who took
over management of Betsy's diaries, memoirs, and fiction. Whoever
it was may have limited access to them because they felt these items
were too controversial to be available for public viewing.

The documents were placed in the library of the Maryland
Historical Society with a restriction upon them: those materials
were not to be made available to researchers until 1960. However,
when the time limit was over, that material had disappeared, and
an intensive search of the facility failed to recover any of it. So while
the Maryland Historical Society contains over seven hundred items
that belonged to Betsy along with fifty-two boxes of Bonaparte and
Patterson letters, there is no trace of the personal writings about her
life, her experiences, and her deepest feelings.

It is known that at some point in time, someone stole the letters of Colonel Bonaparte because he wanted to write a book about
him. Apparently the book was never written. After the man died,
the stolen collection wound up in the hands of a New England
manuscript dealer. He realized where the documents came from
and sent them back to the Maryland Historical Society. Perhaps
that is what happened to the other missing materials, but without
the happy ending.

Regardless of the answer to this mystery, it appears that someone finally succeeded in silencing Betsy Bonaparte.

ACKNOWLEDGMENTS

I owe profound gratitude to numerous people. Some of them are the scholars who appear in this book's references. Others are the unsung, often anonymous librarians, archivists, and curators who work selflessly to preserve the past so that it can answer our questions.

For example, consider Mary Herbert of the Maryland Historical Society's Special Collections Department, who, for years, scanned every manuscript she touched to find stray references to Betsy; set her volunteers and interns to work making photocopies for my research; and then, when I planned a trip to Paris, arranged her vacation so she could go with me and help at the Bibliothèque Nationale. Then there is Maryland Historical Society Librarian Francis O'Neill, whose remarkable memory puts the fastest computer to shame. What computer can answer a question by walking over to a shelf and handing you the book you need, opened to the proper page?

There are dozens of stories like those about helpers and encouragers of all kinds, here in Maryland, across the nation, and in England, France, and Portugal. Some have now gone on without us. There are far too many to thank each individual, but here is a list of some of the people to whom I am grateful: Patricia Anderson, Joseph Arnold, Connie Atkinson, Mary Catherine Brown, Louise Brownell, Jennifer Bryan, Nancy Davis, Jeannine Disviscour, Patrice Donoghue, Bill Dunne, Bill Earle, Bob and Elborg Forster, Richard Hook, Emily Hubbard, Lance Humphries, Pam Jeffries, Burt Kummerow, Mark Letzer, Charlene Lewis, Mary Markey, Mary McLanahan, Deborah Mitchell, Jacqueline Pitcher, David Prencipe, Elizabeth Proffen, Kathy Sewell, Donna Shear, Gregory Stiverson, Warner Sumpter, Heather Venters, Anne Verplanck, Byrne Waterman, Barbara Weeks, Ann Williams, and Donna Williams.

Then there are the descendants who helped: Alex Demidoff,

Louise Harris, and the contemporary William Patterson. And I can never forget the French majors from Towson University who struggled to translate the faded old letters in appallingly bad handwriting, that I simply hadn't time to deal with: Carrie Curtis, Nathalie Delpêche, Megan Dignan. Heather Ganzman, Paul Keller, and Gramm Richardson.

Not least though last, there is my family: five incredibly loving adult children, an amazing son-in-law and daughter-in-law, and six spectacular grandchildren, who gave me cheer, helpful books, carry-out dinners, and every other kind of support so that I could keep working. And finally, my thanks to what everybody needs for the nourishment of the soul: a couple of wonderful best friends.

A NOTE ON SOURCES

ABOUT THIRTY-FIVE YEARS AFTER Betsy's father died, his old warehouse on Gay Street was sold, and a dealer in papermakers' material was authorized to clear out the place. That company found, in addition to the wastepaper it usually dealt with, a group of old documents they offered for sale. Among them were packets of English and French letters arranged in order by date and neatly tied together in William Patterson's typical style. These were bought by a man named W. T. R. Saffell, who turned them into the first book written about Betsy Bonaparte. Prior to the book's 1873 publication, as a courtesy, Saffell sent Betsy proof sheets of *The Patterson-Bonaparte Marriage in 1803 and the Secret Correspondence on the Subject Never Before Made Public.* She replied that the publication of the volume was a matter of perfect indifference to her.

Her grandsons, however, objected, and Charley called upon Saffell. Charley declared he did not deny the right to publish, but requested that the volume not be issued. By then the book was in the last stages of preparation, and Saffell felt he needed to go ahead with it. Charley then asked that the following words be placed in the preface: "This work is published in opposition to the formally expressed wishes of Col. Jerome N. Bonaparte and Mr. Charles J. Bonaparte." After the book's publication the documents on which it was based vanished, so Saffell's book became the only source for those letters.

Several years later, in 1879, *The Life and Letters of Madame Bonaparte* was published by Eugene L. Didier. As the letters Saffell used covered the years 1803 through 1806, this second book repeated all of Saffell's material and continued on from there. Didier doesn't say where he got his documents, only that the letters written to Betsy's father during the "period of her social success" had been recently discovered. Much of the material Didier used also disappeared later, so his book, like Saffell's, remains a sole source for certain key materials.

The documents in both books are undoubtedly genuine and their later loss may be a simple matter of authors returning letters to living relatives of the principals, which then wind up in an attic somewhere and once again become wastepaper.

For the next eight decades most of what was written about Betsy consisted of highly creative accounts based on the bare bones of her life. In two films, one from 1928 and one from 1936, fantasy triumphed over fact. One of the films was partially shot in the old Patterson home called Pleasant View in the countryside northwest of Baltimore. It replaced the main family home downtown on South Street with a country plantation house with pillars spanning the verandah and slaves in the adjacent fields singing in three-part harmony. Jerome, played by a crooner named Dick Powell, sang too.

In one of these Hollywood dream factory confections, Betsy was a peroxide blond with penciled eyebrows who showed her rebel nature by climbing trees in a bouffant ball gown. Hollywood portrayed Jerome as an ambassador sent to America by Napoleon (played by a scary Claude Rains) on a goodwill tour to promote the Louisiana Purchase. In the other movie, Jerome was a refugee hired by William Patterson as a French tutor for his daughter. Both movies portrayed happy endings. In one, Jerome and Betsy triumphantly sailed off to France together, and in the other, the young man defied his brother and lived happily ever after with Betsy in America.

Although Betsy's story was told from time to time in books about the Bonapartes, there were no more works devoted to her. At length, in 1958, Sidney Mitchell published a serious book called *A Family Lawsuit: The Story of Elisabeth Patterson and Jérôme Bonaparte*. The author was a banker who had lived for years in France and who said he was "a remote kinsman" of Betsy. He had decided to spend his retirement writing about the Paris trial of 1861. Fortunately, his record of the trial is good and his translations from the French are excellent, so those parts of the book are useful. The rest is based on the books by Saffell and Didier, which include mistakes in names and dates.

Finally, there is Dorothy Mackay Quynn, who spent several decades doing research for a book about Betsy, traveling to Paris, London, Italy, and the West Indies, and going through the mass of Bonaparte material at the Maryland Historical Society.

It is clear Quynn was a gifted and tireless researcher, but unfortunately she was a poor organizer. The manuscript she put together is so chaotic it is almost impossible to use. Her notes outweigh the text by far, so superscript numbers pepper the pages and one is forced to flip constantly back and forth to understand what's being said. She expects the reader to be fluent in French and incorporates great chunks of untranslated material into her narrative and notes. Also, she fully accepted the folklore that Betsy's father was a saint and that her son never had any interest in being a Bonaparte. Quynn appears to have disliked Betsy so much that in the rare instances when she had something good to say about her, it came out as a slam. For example, after admitting that some people were quite fond of her, she adds the patronizing remark that Betsy "possessed that quality not unknown in the case of disagreeable people, that of being exceedingly kind and pleasant to servants and inferiors."

In Quynn's defense it must be said the book was unfinished when she died. Her husband put the final chapters together from her innumerable notes. Then he set out to look for a publisher and met rejections. When the Publications Committee of the Maryland Historical Society turned the book down, he asked if they could place the manuscript in its collection so that all that research might be of use one day. It has been. During the course of her research, Quynn published several good articles that appear in the present book's references.

REFERENCES

Chapter 1

For much of the information in this chapter, I am indebted to the Reverend Paul Thomas, former archivist for the Archdiocese of Baltimore.

1. Archives of First and Franklin Street Presbyterian Church, *History of First Presbyterian Church* (Baltimore, 1962), 189–90; J. Thomas Scharf, *Chronicles of Baltimore, Being a Complete History of "Baltimore Town" and Baltimore City from the Earliest Period to the Present Time* (Baltimore: Turnbull Brothers, 1874), 54–56.

2. Letter from William Patterson to his lawyer, Alexander J. Dallas, November 16, 1803. Microfilm 3504, "Letters and Notes Concerning Elizabeth Patterson Bonaparte," Maryland Historical Society (MdHS), Baltimore, MD.

3. As is the case with many events in Betsy's life, there are several conflicting stories about the location of the wedding. Robert Lynn Mayall, "Elizabeth Spear Patterson Bonaparte and the American Bonapartes," MdHS TS 2788, is a 38-page typescript of information compiled from sources at the Maryland Historical Society and from the recollections of Mayall's great-grandmother. In childhood, she knew Betsy as her "Tante Betsy." Mayall says his great-grandmother told him the ceremony was performed "at St. Patrick's Catholic Church on Broadway," but records show that edifice was built three years after the marriage. Another early account says the vows were exchanged at William Patterson's "Cold Stream" estate north of town, but he didn't buy that property until later. Reverend Paul Thomas, former archivist for the Archdiocese of Baltimore, says there is no record of the ceremony having taken place in any of the Catholic churches in Baltimore on that date. And Brother Thomas Spalding, author of a history of the archdiocese, told Father Thomas that the bishop was known to have performed a marriage in a private home on at least one other occasion. So it seems likely that the South Street home was the location of the wedding. It was the only Patterson residence in the town's center, and was convenient for the bishop and for guests. The location of the house is shown on South Street in Thompson and Walker's *Baltimore Town and Fell's Point Directory of 1796* (repr., Silver Spring, MD: Family Line Publications, 1983), 41.

4. The list of witnesses comes from the Patterson-Bonaparte prenuptial marriage contract, dated December 24, 1803, MdHS MS 142, box 12.

5. The words of the ceremony appear in "Ritus Celebrandi Matrimonii Sacramentum," *(Rituale Romanum, 1775)*, 247–49.

6. The description of the couple's clothing is given by Eugene L. Didier, *The*

259

Life and Letters of Madame Bonaparte (New York: Charles Scribner's Sons, 1879), 8 [hereinafter Didier]; and by Annie Leakin Sioussat, *Old Baltimore* (New York: Macmillan, 1931), 159–60. Sioussat used early records, letters, and the reminiscences of family members for her book, but she did not provide specific references.

7. The vital statistics are from Betsy's French passport, MdHS MS 142, box 12. The responses to Betsy's beauty appear in several contemporary accounts, among them: Miss Phoebe Morris to her sister Rebecca, quoted in John Clagett Proctor, *Washington and Environs* (written for the *Washington Sunday Star* between 1928 and 1994), 59; and a letter from Margaret Bayard Smith to her sister, Jane Kirkpatrick, January 24, 1804, quoted in Gaillard Hunt (ed.), *The First Forty Years of Washington Society* (New York: C. Scribner's Sons, 1906), 46–7.

8. John Gilmary Shea, *The Life and Times of the Most Reverend John Carroll, Bishop and First Archbishop of Baltimore, Embracing the History of the Catholic Church in the United States 1763–1815* (New York: J. G. Shea, 1888), 511.

9. Letter to James Barry, December 26, 1803, in Thomas O'Brien Hanley, S.J., *The John Carroll Papers* (Notre Dame, IN: University of Notre Dame Press, 1976), 2:427–8.

Chapter 2

1. Patterson's wealth was mentioned in several places, most notably in a letter from Thomas Jefferson to Robert Livingston, U.S. Minister to France, October 28, 1803.

2. The description of William Patterson was written by John H. B. Latrobe and quoted in Edward Hungerford, *The Story of the Baltimore and Ohio Railroad 1827–1927*, 2 vols. (New York: Arno Press, 1973), 1:56. The Patterson genealogical information comes from several MdHS sources: Genealogy reel G 5010, Hall Harris record, as well as the Baer and Wroe manuscripts. In addition, William Patterson of Portugal (a direct descendant of Betsy's brother Henry) provided a lengthy genealogical manuscript that is the work of several family members.

3. An account of Patterson's life, along with his opinions on business, morals, and family, was written by him in 1827; this autobiographical essay forms a preamble to his will. There is a copy of the will in Annapolis at the Hall of Records (the Maryland State Archives), Book 15, Folio 254, entered into probate July 12, 1835. The first half of this document is a typescript flawed by errors and omissions; the latter half is a photocopy of the actual will and three codicils of later dates. A more accurate handwritten copy is in the MdHS Special Collections Department, MS 645. It appears to be the work of a counting house employee or a legal clerk. Unless otherwise noted, the biographical information and the passages in Patterson's own words in this chapter are from these documents.

4. John Melish described Philadelphia in *Travels in the United States of America in the Years 1806 and 1807, and 1809, 1810, & 1811*, 2 vols. (Philadelphia: privately printed, 1812), 1:153.

5. Barbara W. Tuchman, *The First Salute: A View of the American Revolution* (New York: Ballantine Books, 1988), 5–7.

6. The comparison of money values is from John J. McCusker, *How Much Is That in Real Money?* (Worcester, MA: American Antiquarian Society, 1992), 312, 325, 332.

7. Any account of early Baltimore must depend upon the work of John Thomas Scharf. From 1884 to 1892 he was commissioner of the Maryland Land Office and wrote five books about the history of the city and the state. This chapter uses his *Chronicles of Baltimore, Being a Complete History of "Baltimore Town" and Baltimore City from the Earliest Period to the Present Time* (Baltimore: Turnbull Brothers, 1874), 52–57.

8. William Dollarhide, *Map Guide to American Migration Routes, 1736–1815* (Bountiful, UT: Heritage Quest, 1997), 3.

9. In 1780 Maryland voted to seize Loyalist and British property in the state. Robert J. Brugger, *Maryland: A Middle Temperament, 1634–1980* (Baltimore: Johns Hopkins University Press, 1988), 134. According to the *Encyclopedia of American History* (New York: Harper & Bros., 1953), 110, Maryland obtained over two million dollars from the sale of Loyalist property.

10. Maritime historian Byrne Waterman provided a description of the Smith and Buchanan house flag. In addition, he created a picture of the William Patterson & Sons flag from the 1802 and 1806 "Private Signal Flag" charts at MdHS.

11. Archives of the First and Franklin Street Presbyterian Church in Baltimore; Robert Barnes, *Maryland Marriages 1801–1820* (Baltimore: Genealogical Publishing Co., 1993), 173.

Chapter 3

1. Some of the genealogy for the interconnected families is in MdHS MS G5010, the Wilson Miles Cary collection, which includes information from a Bible owned by John Spear Smith (son of General Sam Smith). The Galbraith material was compiled by William N. Wilkens in 1958 from various sources, including the records of the Donegal Presbyterian Church in Lancaster County, PA. There is also extensive data in the archives of Baltimore's First and Franklin Street Presbyterian Church.

2. James G. Leyburn, *The Scotch-Irish: A Social History* (Chapel Hill: University of North Carolina Press, 1962), 83–4.

3. Leyburn, 25.

4. Bernard Bailyn, *The Peopling of British North America: An Introduction* (New York: Alfred A. Knopf, 1986), 26.

5. Leyburn, *Scotch-Irish*, 151.

6. David Hackett Fischer, *Albion's Seed: Four British Folkways in America* (New York: Oxford University Press, 1989), 609, says the *Dublin Journal* in 1773 put the total at 400,000 people who left Ireland for America, "mainly from Ulster" between 1733 and 1773. Bernard Bailyn, in *Voyagers to the West* (New

York: Alfred A. Knopf, 1986), 26, puts the number at between 155,000 and 205,000. Leyburn, 180, says the conventional estimate is 200,000, but the true number may be much higher.

7. Leyburn, *Scotch-Irish*, 191–2.

8. Fischer, *Albion's Seed*, 610.

9. Sir Walter Scott, *The Heart of Midlothian*, cited by Leyburn in *The Scotch-Irish*, 194–5.

10. Frank A. Cassell, *Merchant Congressman in the Young Republic: Samuel Smith of Maryland 1752–1829* (Madison, WI: University of Wisconsin Press, 1971), 5.

11. Leyburn, 305, citing for the Hessian Captain: Jonathan Smith, "The Scotch Presbyterians in the American Revolution," in *Granite Monthly*, 41. For Continental Congressman Sergeant, see Theodore Thayer, *Pennsylvania Politics and the Growth of Democracy, 1740–1776* (Harrisburg: Pennsylvania Historical and Museum Commission, 1953), 184–5. And for the New Englander, see Vernon L. Parrington, *Main Currents in American Thought*, 3 vols. (New York: Harcourt, Brace and Company, 1927–30), 1:359.

12. The "birth, marriage, and death" quotation is from Edith Kermit Roosevelt, in Sylvia Jukes Morris, *Edith Kermit Roosevelt: Portrait of a First Lady* (New York: Coward, McCann & Geoghegan, 1980), 525–6.

13. Letter to Mrs. Gallatin, March 5, 1801, in Henry Adams, *Life of Albert Gallatin* (Philadelphia: J. B. Lippincott, 1879), 265.

14. Robert Hunter Jr., *Quebec to North Carolina in 1785–86*, ed. Louis B. Wright and Marion Tinling (San Marino, CA: 1943), 180.

15. Mayall, MdHS TS 2788.

16. John S. Pancake, *Samuel Smith and the Politics of Business: 1752–1839* (University, AL: The University of Alabama Press, 1972), 145.

17. William Patterson's will, MdHS MS 645.

18. Thank you letter from Betsy to her brother George Patterson, August 12, 1835, MdHS MS 142, box 6.

19. Fawn M. Brodie, *Thomas Jefferson: An Intimate History* (New York: Bantam Books [W. W. Norton], 1975), 35–6, citing Edwin M. Betts and James A. Baer, eds., *The Family Letters of Thomas Jefferson* (Columbia, MO: University of Missouri Press, 1966), 51; Mrs. A. J. Graves, *Women in America: Being an Examination into the Moral and Intellectual Condition of American Female Society* (New York: Harper & Brothers, 1842), 195.

20. Will and Ariel Durant. *The Age of Napoleon: A History of European Civilization from 1789 to 1815* (New York: Simon and Schuster, 1975), 255, citing F. M. Kircheison, *Memoirs of Napoleon I, Compiled from His Writings* (London: Hutchinson, 1929), 152.

21. Diary of Virginia Wilson, July 20, 1851, MdHS MS 833.1; Diary of Mary Matthews Dobbins, February 20, 1853, MdHS MS 2385.

Chapter 4

1. This painting by Robert Edge Pine is in the Maryland Historical Society.

2. Brugger, *Maryland: A Middle Temperament,* 140.

3. Scharf, *Chronicles of Baltimore,* 250–51. According to George Washington's diary, six weeks later the little ship sank during a storm.

4. Ibid., 251–52.

5. Hunter, *Quebec to North Carolina in 1785–86,* 180.

6. Henri Herz, *My Travels in America,* trans. Henry Bertram Hill (Madison: State Historical Society of Wisconsin, 1963), 53; and Thomas Hamilton, *Men and Manners in America* (Edinburgh: Blackwood, 1843).

7. Extract from *The Journal of Baron de Closen,* Rochambeau Papers, Library of Congress, repr. as "French Troops in Maryland," *Maryland Historical Magazine* 5 (1910): 231.

8. General information about Sam Smith's life is based on Cassell, *Merchant Congressman in the Young Republic* and Pancake, *Samuel Smith and the Politics of Business.*

9. Cassell, *Merchant Congressman,* 58–9.

10. *Annapolis Maryland Gazette,* September 18, 1794.

11. Pattterson's Will, MdHS MS 645.

12. *Moreau de St. Méry's American Journey 1793–1798,* ed. Kenneth Roberts and Anna M. Roberts (Garden City, NY: Doubleday, 1947), 186; Didier, 5.

13. Rosalie Stier Calvert, letter to her mother, 1803, in Margaret Law Callcott ed. and trans., *Mistress of Riverdale: The Plantation Letters of Rosalie Stier Calvert* (Baltimore: Johns Hopkins University Press, 1991), 62.

14. Elizabeth Smith to Miss Elizabeth Patterson, February 1802, MdHS MS 142, box 1.

15. Scharf, *Chronicles,* 52. T. Stephen Whitman, *The Price of Freedom: Slavery and Manumission in Baltimore and Early National Maryland* (Lexington, KY: University Press of Kentucky, 1997), 11.

16. Dorothy Mackay Quynn, "Maximilian and Elizabeth Godefroy," *Maryland Historical Magazine,* 52 (1957): 11–12, 16–17. Thompson and Walker, *Baltimore Town and Fell's Point Directory of 1796,* 30. The roster of students is from Mayall, MdHS TS 2788. He says he found the school's records, but he does not say where.

17. Mayall, MdHS TS 2788.

18. Mary Buchanan Smith married Lord Mansfield. Mary Caton first married Betsy's brother Robert. After Robert died she married the Duke of Wellington's brother, the Marquis of Wellesley. Louisa Caton first married Lord Hervery-Bathurst, and later married Francis Godolphin D'Arcy Osborne, the 7th Duke of Leeds. Elizabeth Caton married George William Jernington, the 8th Baron Stafford.

Chapter 5

1. *Norfolk Herald,* July 16, 1803.

2. *Norfolk Herald,* July 21, 1803. Miss Susan Wheeler later married Stephen Decatur. Reubell is spelled various ways in the sources: Reubel, Rewbel, and Reubelt. Merounet is also spelled "Meyronnet" in some texts.

3. The account of Jerome's attack on the British vessel is from Dorothy Mackay Quynn, "Jerome Bonaparte aux Antilles, 1801–1803," *Revue de Institute Napoléon,* No. 60, Juillet 1956, 90–91.

4. Villaret-Joyeuse letter to Jerome, May 1803 in MdHS MS 143.

5. Jerome's instructions, MdHS MS 143.

6. On September 30, 1801, Jerome was a midshipman; in January 1802 he was an ensign; and in October of that year he was made a lieutenant and commander of the brig *L'Epervier,* MdHS MS 143. Also Frédéric Masson, *Napoléon et sa famille,* 13 vols. (Paris: Ollendorff, 1897–1914, 1991), cited in Sidney Mitchell, *A Family Lawsuit: The Story of Elizabeth Patterson and Jerome Bonaparte* (New York: Farrar, Straus and Cudahy, 1958), 14.

7. Napoleon's life and the major events in the lives of his family are widely documented in the hundreds of biographies devoted to him. The citations below cover only the less frequently discussed points.

8. Napoleon's extraordinary teenage reading is described in several of his biographies, among them: Robert Asprey, *The Rise of Napoleon Bonaparte* (New York: Basic Books, 2000), 25–31; Emil Ludwig, *Napoleon,* trans. Eden and Cedar Paul (New York: Boni & Liveright, 1926), 10–14; J. M. Thompson, *Napoleon Bonaparte* (Cambridge, MA: 1990), 7–8, 11–12, 15–16.

9. *Memoires of the Duchesse d'Abrantès,* condensed as *At the Court of Napoleon* (New York: Doubleday, 1989), 133. The duchess was born Laure Permon, daughter of the Madame Permon who advised Napoleon to put Jerome into the navy.

10. Ibid., 132.

11. *Napoleon's Letters Selected, Translated, and Edited by J. M. Thompson* (London: Prion, 1934, 1998), 71.

12. Jerome's description distributed throughout the fleet: Quynn, "Jerome aux Antilles," 95.

13 . Pichon to Talleyrand, July 20, 1803, in Mitchell, *A Family Lawsuit,* 29.

14. Ibid., July 22, 1803, 30–31.

15. Mary Barney, *A Biographical Memoir of the Late Commodore Joshua Barney from Autographical Notes and Journals in Possession of His Family, and Other Authentic Sources* (Boston: Gray and Bowen, 1832), 3–6. Mary Barney was the commodore's daughter-in-law.

16. Scharf, *Chronicles of Baltimore,* 204–5. See also the 1928 *Dictionary of American Biography,* vol. 1, 632–35, citing Cooper, *History of the Navy,* 1839. The commemorative painting of the battle is at the U.S. Naval Academy, Annapolis, MD.

17. Hulbert Footner, *Sailor of Fortune: The Life and Adventures of Commodore Joshua Barney, U.S.N.* (New York: Harper & Brothers, 1940), 132.

18. Mary Barney, 240.

19. *The Times* [London], October 24, 1803.

20. For the spending, Pichon to Talleyrand, November 1, 1803, cited in Mitchell, *A Family Lawsuit*, 40–41. In 1804 Victor DuPont endorsed a promissory note to Jerome for 15,750 francs. The note can be found in the Manuscripts and Archives Department of the Hagley Museum and Library in Greenville, Delaware, DEHV4-A46. The Hagley Museum and Library online catalog states: "Victor lost considerable sums in bankrolling Jerome Bonaparte, who did not repay his loans, contributing to Victor's bankruptcy in 1805." Hagley Library, http://www.hagley.org/library.

21. Sioussat, *Old Baltimore*, 157–8.

22. Barney, *A Biographical Memoir*, 240–1.

23. Scharf, *Chronicles*, 305–7.

24. James Gallatin, *A Great Peacemaker: The Diary of James Gallatin* (New York: Scribner's Sons, 1916), 34.

25. Betsy to Prince Alexandre Gortchakoff, n.d., MdHS MS 142, box 5.

26. Baltimore Cathedral Register of Marriages, August 25, 1803; and Robert Barnes, *Maryland Marriages 1801–1820* (Baltimore: Genealogical Publishing Company, 1993), 152.

Chapter 6

1. Charles A. Cerami, *Jefferson's Great Gamble* (Naperville, IL: Source Books, 2003), 6 –8, 35, 37, 40–1, 43.

2. *The Times* [London], January 21, 1804. For the British funding: J. A. Spencer, *The History of the United States from the Earliest Period to the Administration of James Buchanan*, 3 vols. (New York: Johnson, Fry & Co., 1858), 2:39.

3. William Patterson to Alexander J. Dallas, November 16, 1803, MdHS Microfilm 3504.

4. Mary Abigail Willing Coale's notebook, MdHS MS 1530. The notebook is cited by Heather Ersts Venters in "Can the Town Belle Influence Decorative Arts?" (1997) MdHS.

5. Mary Barney, *Biographical Memoir*, 240.

6. MdHS MS 142, box 1.

7. Pichon to Talleyrand, November 3, 1803 in Mitchell, *A Family Lawsuit*, 38.

8. Jerome Bonaparte to Betsy, October 1803, MdHS MS 143.

9. Baltimore County court record, October 29, 1803.

10. "Lifetime" quotation, Didier, 7–8, as well as Masson, *Napoleon et sa famille*, 2:64. On the supporters of the marriage, according to John Quincy Adams, the Pattersons and Smiths were all for it. JQA's *Diary*, January 7, 1804 cited by Mitchell, 44. Smith's ambition: Sam Smith to Thomas Jefferson, November 15, 1801 (Jefferson Papers); Smith to W. C. Nicholas, October 12,

1802 (Nicholas Papers, University of Virginia); Nicholas to Smith (Smith Carter Papers); all cited by Casell, *Merchant Congressman*, 107–9.

11. Madison to Livingston, MdHS MS 142, box 1.

12. Sam Smith to William Patterson, October 26, 1803, MdHS MS 142, box 1.

13. Dallas to Patterson, November 3, 1803, MdHS MS 145.

14. Patterson to Dallas, November 16, 1803, MdHS Microfilm 3504, "Letters and Notes Concerning Elizabeth Patterson Bonaparte."

15. Anonymous letter Patterson marked "Received this letter by the Penny Post, on Saturday, 5th November 1803, at one o'clock P. M." It is found in W. T. R. Saffell, *The Bonaparte-Patterson Marriage in 1803 and the Secret Correspondence on the Subject Never before Made Public* (Philadelphia: privately published, 1873), 29 –30. [Hereinafter, Saffell.] Many of William Patterson's incoming letters have disappeared; Saffell is at present almost our only source for them. He bought them from a scrap-paper dealer who was cleaning out Patterson's old warehouse, where they were found tied in a neat bundle. After Saffell completed his book he gave them to a Patterson descendant, and their location is now unknown. See Saffell's Introduction, 7–8.

16 Callcott, *Mistress of Riversdale*, 62.

17. Betsy to Miss Eliza Monroe, Betsy's letter book, MdHS MS 142, box 1.

18. Most early accounts say the couple arranged for their returns to coincide, but marginal notes made by Betsy in her copy of *Mémoires et Correspondance du Roi Jerome et de La Reine Catherine* (Paris: Librairie de la Société des Gens de Lettres, 1861), contradict this. On page 147 she wrote: "He left New York a week after my return to Baltimore." On page 148 she wrote: "Neither of us wrote to the other one line."

19. Robert Patterson to William Patterson, March 12, 1804, Saffell, 36–8.

20. Marriage Contract, MdHS MS 142, box 12.

Chapter 7

1. Washington to the D.C. Commissioners, November 20, 1791 in Charles Burr Todd, *The Story of Washington* (New York: G. P. Putnam's Sons, 1889), 29–30. Kenneth R. Bowling, *Creating the Federal City, 1774–1800: Potomac Fever* (Washington, D.C.: The American Institute of Architects Press, 1988), 98–102. Ben Perley Poore, *Perley's Reminiscences of Sixty Years in the National Metropolis* (1886; repr., New York: AMS Press, 1971), 54.

2. John Clagett Proctor, "Washington and Environs" (*Washington Sunday Star*, 1928–1949), 58.

3. For the lost congressmen: James Sterling Young, *The Washington Community 1800–1828* (New York: Columbia University Press, 1966), 43. The British attaché was Augustus John Foster, in Todd, *The Story of Washington*, 363. The partridge hunter was Francis J. Jackson, cited in Proctor, "Washington and Environs," 40.

4. Cynthia D. Earman, "Remembering the Ladies: Women, Etiquette, and

Diversions in Washington City, 1800–1814" in Kenneth R. Bowling, *Coming into the City: Essays on Early Washington, D.C.* (Washington: The Historical Society of Washington, D.C.): *Washington History,* Spring–Summer, 2000): 118–21.

5. *Washington History,* 104.

6. Ibid., 111–12.

7. Callcott, *Mistress of Riversdale,* 77.

8. Saffell, 88.

9. Spencer, *History of the United States,* 506–7.

10. Thomas Twining, *Travels in America A Hundred Years Ago* (New York: Harper & Brothers, 1894), 94–7.

11. Regarding Jerome's borrowed carriage, see Callcott, 83.

12. Sam Smith to William Patterson, February 2, 1804, Saffell, 33.

13. Anonymous to William Patterson, January 14, 1804, Saffell, 32.

14. William Patterson to Robert Livingston, February 10, 1804, Saffell, 33–4.

15. Union Tavern, *The WPA Guide to* Washington, D.C. (Washington, D.C.: U.S. Government Printing Office), 720–21.

16. Will and Ariel Durant, *The Age of Napoleon,* 134–5.

17. *Olio,* April 4, 1803.

18. Margaret Bayard Smith, *The First Forty Years of Washington Society,* ed. Gaillard Hunt (1906; repr., New York: Frederick Unger Publishing Company, 1961), 46–7.

19. Callcott, *Mistress of Riversdale,* 77.

20. Paul F. Boller Jr., *Presidential Wives* (New York: Oxford University Press, 1988), 40.

21. *The National Intelligencer,* February 3, 1804. Boller, *Presidential Wives,* 40. Cokie Roberts, *Ladies of Liberty* (New York: William Morrow, 2008), 90–1.

22. Earman, "Remember the Ladies," 108–9.

23. James Thomas Flexner, *Gilbert Stuart: A Great Life in Brief* (New York: Alfred A. Knopf, 1955), 137.

24. Charles Merrill Mount, *Gilbert Stuart, A Biography* (New York: W. W. Norton, 1964), 250–1.

25. William T. Whitley, *Gilbert Stuart* (Cambridge, MA: Harvard University Press, 1932), 123–4. Richard McLanathan, *Gilbert Stuart* (New York: Henry N. Abrams, 1986), 119–20. Patterson's Will, MdHS MS 645.

Chapter 8

1. Robert Patterson to William Patterson, March 12, 1804, Saffell, 36–8.

2. Robert Patterson to William Patterson , March 14, 1804, Saffell, 50–1, with a duplicate sent by a different route on March 16; and Paul Bentalou to William Patterson, March 16, 1804, Saffell, 51–6.

3. Ibid., 62–4.

4. Frank McLynn, *Napoleon: A Biography* (1997; repr., New York: Arcade Publishing Company, 2002), 292–97. David G. Chandler, *Dictionary of the Napoleonic Wars* (New York: Simon & Schuster, 1993), 75–6, 140, 290, 343.

Chapter 9

1. Jerome Bonaparte to Letizia Bonaparte, March 19, 1804, MdHS Microfilm 3504.

2. Robert Livingston to William Patterson, June 20, 1804, Saffell, 85–7.

3. Denis Decrès to Andre Pichon, April 20, 1804, MdHS MS 142, box 1. See also Saffell, 66–79.

4. *The Times* [London], June 4, 1804.

5. Madame Victor Dupont to Madame Mangault, April 2, 1804, and May 6, 1804, Eleutherian Mills Historical Society, Wilmington, Delaware, letters #51 and #52.

6. John Maude, *A Visit to the Falls of Niagara in 1800* (London: Longman, Rees, Orme, Brown & Green, 1826); Robert Sutcliff, *A Visit to Some Parts of North America in the Years 1804, 1805, and 1806* (York, UK: W. Alexander: 1815); Lt. Francis Hall, 14th Light Dragoons, *Travels in Canada and the United States in 1816 and 1817* (London: Longman, Hurst, 1818); Pavel Petrovich Svinin, *Picturesque United States of America, 1811, 1812, 1813* (1818; repr., New York: William Edwin Rudge, 1930). All of these books are in the library of the MdHS.

7. Regarding Chateaubriand: Alexandre Dumas, *The Last Cavalier*, trans. Lauren Yoder (New York: Pegasus Books, 2007), 157.

8. (Boston), *Gazette*, August 13, 1804.

9. Betsy to William Patterson, September 5, 1804, Saffell, 98.

10. Didier, 21–22.

11. *The Times* [London], "Reports from America," November 30 and December 3, 1804.

12. William Patterson to Jonathan Jones, November 11, 1804.

13. William Patterson to Betsy, March 9, 1805, MdHS MS 142, box 1.

14. Betsy's friend Eliza Anderson had been left impoverished by a bad marriage. She tried to make a living as a writer using the pen name *Eleanor Ironside*. Later, she became the wife of architect Maximilian Godefroy (see later chapters) and again wound up impoverished.

15. Journal of Captain William Stevenson, 1805–1806, Library of Congress Manuscript Collection 73-99515. Stevenson kept his journal for the enjoyment of his family at home, but in 1808 the *Erin* sank with all hands. Twenty-six pages of the journal survived in a waterproof container. It was sold at public auction in Philadelphia and eventually acquired by LOC. Two articles appearing in *Maryland Historical Magazine* helped me to decipher Stevenson's faint handwriting: "Jerome and Betsy Cross the Atlantic" by Dorothy M. Quynn and Frank F. White Jr. (vol. 48, 1953, 204–14) and "A Voyage to the East Indies, 1805" by Frank F. White Jr. (vol. 59, 1964, 182–98).

16. Jerome Bonaparte to William Patterson, April 2, 1805, Saffell, 174 and Mitchell, 65.

Chapter 10

1. Robert Patterson to William Patterson, February 16, 1805, Saffell, 153–8.

2. Robert Patterson to William Patterson, March 5, 1805, quoting the French government's official paper, the *Moniteur*, Saffell, 159.

3. Denis Decrès to Louis Andrè Pichon April 20, 1804 [delivery delayed], Saffell, 66–79. Other writers give shortened versions (Masson 3: 88–9; Didier, 13–16, and Mitchell, 52–3). Betsy obtained a copy several years later, which she appears to have translated herself. It can be found in MdHS MS 142, box 1.

4. Robert first learned of the Decrès letters in November 1804 when they were published in the *Halifax Morning Chronicle* and summarized in the November 8, 1804 issue of *Cobbett's Political Register*. According to Saffell, 109–10, Robert thought they were a forgery.

5. Betsy kept this jewelry all her life. These items, along with many others from Betsy's collection, are in the Maryland Historical Society.

6. Betsy often expressed her most emotional moments in French. Her notebooks can be found in MdHS MS 142, boxes 9, 13, and 14.

7. *Memoires de la Madame la Duchesse d'Abrantès*, Paris 1832, 7:107. Also summarized in Mitchell, 66–8.

8. In the various accounts of this meeting, the most reliable appears to be Masson, *Napoléon et sa famille*, 3:94–5. He gives Betsy's reply to Serurier as: "Dites à votre maitre que Madame Bonaparte est ambiteuse et qu'elle réclame ses droits comme membre de la famille impériale."

9. Journal of Captain William Stevenson, 1805–1806.

Chapter 11

1. Jerome to Betsy, April 5, 1805, plus additional undated notes, MdHS MS 143.

2. Jerome to Betsy, April 9, 1805, MdHS MS 143.

3. Jerome to Betsy, April 19, 1805, MdHS MS 143.

4. Jerome to Betsy, May 3, 1805, MdHS MS 143.

5. Napoleon to Mme. Mère, in Mitchell, 65–6.

6. Napoleon to Jerome, Mitchell, 96.

7. Napoleon to Lucien and Lucien's reply, Mitchell, 95–96.

8. Napoleon to Jerome, MdHS MS 141.1 and Didier, 26.

9. Saffell, 218.

10. For Jerome's motivation, see Masson, *Napoléon et sa Famille*, 3:97–8.

11. Napoleon to Mme. Mère, April 21, 1805, in Mitchell 65–6; Napoleon to Fouché, May 13, 1805, and Napoleon to Decrès, May 18, 1805, *Memoires du roi Jerome* 1:299.

12. Napoleon to Pope Pius VII, May 24, 1805, in Didier, 31.

13. Didier, 31 and Mitchell, *A Family Lawsuit*, n 97.

14. Pope Pius VII to Napoleon, June 27, 1805, in Mitchell, 98–100. There is also a translation made by Betsy in her letter book, MdHS MS 142, box 1.

15. Journal of Captain William Stevenson, 1805–1806.

16. (Dover) *Courier*, May 19, 1805.

17. *The Times* [London], May 19, 1805.

18. Journal of Captain William Stevenson, 1805–1806.

19. Mr. Skeffington to William Patterson Jr. and Mme. Bonaparte, May 20, 1805, MdHS MS 142, box 1.

20. *The Times* [London], May 21, 1805.

21. Lady Frances Erskine to Thomas Cadwalader, May 31, 1805. The Thomas Cadwalader Papers, the Historical Society of Pennsylvania, Philadelphia.

22. *The Times* [London], August 14, 1805.

23. *The Times* [London], August 21, 1805.

24. Mitchell, *A Family Lawsuit*, 100.

25. Robert Patterson to William Patterson Sr., Saffell, 200–1.

Chapter 12

1. Alexandre Le Camus to William Patterson, June 12, 1805, Saffell, 195–7.

2. Napoleon to Jerome, June 11, 1805. Eventually Betsy was sent a copy of this letter. It was obtained by her father's business associate R. G. Beasley, who sent it to her from Havre by way of Boston in care of William Patterson & Sons. She received the letter on January 1, 1810. Her copy is in MdHS MS 142, box 1. Napoleon's letter to Jerome is also in the *Mémoires et Correspondance du Roi Jerome* in MdHS MF 179.B712C . This was Betsy's copy and is filled with marginal comments, such as "A tissue of lies! Fudge!" and so on.)

3. Robert finally wrote to his father about this on September 5, 1805. See Saffell, 210–12.

4 . Journal of Paul Bentalou, MdHS MS 125.

5. Jerome's letter of May 16, 1805 arrived in Baltimore September 17, 1808, MdHS MS 142, box 1.

6. Saffell 195, quoting an unnamed London paper of May 30, 1805.

7. *The Times* [London]. Dispatches from Genoa of June 16 and June 23, 1805.

8. Betsy's letter to Paul Bentalou, in her letter book, MdHS MS 142, box 1.

9. Betsy to Eliza Monroe, MdHS MS 142, box 1. Later, Betsy added a note to her copy saying that Miss Monroe had given her enclosure to Hortense.

10. All three draft letters are in the letter book, MdHS MS 142, box 1. Proof that she sent all three is in her letter to her father, September 3, 1805, Saffell, 210.

11. To that December 25, 1803 excuse letter (MdHS MS 42, box 1), Betsy later added the comment: "This letter was written to me the day after my marriage by Dr. Garnier (a contemptible fellow) who has been my constant enemy. E. Bonaparte, July 5th 1813."

12. Regarding this letter, Betsy wrote her father: "As Bonaparte did not write himself, we are disposed to think that Mr. Garnier wrote the letter of his own accord, and indeed the letter bears all the marks of being a deception." Betsy to William Patterson, September 3, 1805, Saffell, 209.

13. Garnier to Betsy as "Mrs. Anderson," July 15, 1805, MdHS MS 142, box 1. A second letter to Betsy at Camberwell from Dr. Garnier, dated August 2, 1805, arrived in Baltimore April 1, 1806. It can now be found in MdHS MS 142, box 1.

14. Alexandre Le Camus to William Patterson, July 29, 1805, Saffell, 202–204.

15. Jerome to Betsy, July 29, 1805, MdHS MS 143. This letter was not received until it was redirected to Baltimore, arriving there April 1, 1806.

16. Mary Berry to Betsy, August 10, 1805, MS 142, box 1.

17. Barbara Donegal to Betsy, August 20, 1805, MS 142, box 1.

18. Letters to William Patterson Sr. from his son Robert and from Betsy, August 15 and 16, 1805, Saffell, 207–8.

19. Paul Bentalou to Robert Patterson, October 9 and 18, 1805, Saffell, 216–20.

20. Jerome to Betsy October 4, 7, 16, 1805, MdHS MS 143. These letters and others written to Betsy by Jerome also appear in *Mémoirs et Correspondance du Roi Jerome*.

21. Bill of Lading sent by Alexandre Le Camus with the boxes given to Lady Elgin.

22. In spite of diplomatic immunity, Lord Elgin was detained in France while on his way home. He was eventually released, in 1806.

23. James McIlheny to William Patterson, October 28, 1805, Saffell, 221.

Chapter 13

1. *Baltimore Federal Gazette*, November 14, 1805.

2. Patterson's Account Books, MdHS MSS 145 and 904; A. J. Dallas to William Patterson, December 23, 1804, MdHS MS 145.

3. Napoleon had taken the money out of his government's Sinking Fund, so he required Jerome to sign a promissory note to repay the loan within one year after starting his reign as king of Westphalia. Unfortunately, when Jerome got to his new kingdom its treasury was already nearly empty. Philip Sergeant, *Jerome Bonaparte, the Burlesque Napoleon* (New York: Brentano's, 1906), 168.

4. Written in Betsy's hand on her copy of Jerome's October 7, 1805 letter from Paris, MdHS MS 143.

5. Lady Elgin to Betsy, November 5, 1805, MdHS MS 142, box 1.

6. Written in one of her notebooks, MdHS MS 142, box 9.

7. Written on her father's letter to her of November 4, 1829, MdHS MS 142, box 5.

8. Jerome to Betsy, November 21, 1805, MdHS MS 143.

9. Jerome to Betsy, May 23, 1806, MdHS MS 143.

10. Jerome's letters to Betsy of October 4 and 16, 1805, MdHS MS 143.

11. William Neilson Jr. to William Patterson, April 21, 1806, Saffell, 223–4.

12. Jerome to Betsy from Martinique, June 20, 1806, MdHS MS 143.

13. Robert Patterson wrote to his father from Boston, September 8, 1806, Saffell, 222.

14. Jerome to Betsy, July 17, 1806, MdHS MS 143.

15. Melish, *Travels in the United States of America*, 1:153

16. Boller, *Presidential Wives*, 45.

17. Dolley Madison to Betsy, November 24, 1813, MdHS MS 142, box 2.

18. Augustus John Foster to his mother, November 27, 1806, Foster Papers, Library of Congress, Manuscripts Division. Foster later returned to Washington as British minister and for several years maintained a warm friendship with Betsy.

19. Brugger, *Maryland, A Middle Temperament*, 176.

20. William Patterson to Wilson Cary Nicholas, November 21, 1806, Saffell, 223.

21. Bernier, *At the Court of Napoleon: Memoirs of the Duchess d'Abrantès*, 323–30.

22. Masson, *Napoleon et sa famille*, 3, 405.

23. Jerome Bonaparte to Lucien Bonaparte, August 26, 1807, Mitchell, *A Family Lawsuit*, 164.

24. Betsy's Notebook, MdHS MS 142, box 9.

Chapter 14

1. Frank McLynn, *Napoleon: A Biography*, 386, and Phillip Sergeant, *The Burlesque Napoleon* (New York: Bretano's, 1906), ch. 6–10 passim. Sergeant's work is based on the eyewitness account of M. J. Norvins, chamberlain to Queen Catherine, and possibly one of Napoleon's spies in Westphalia; H. A. L. Fisher's *Studies in Napoleonic Statesmanship: Germany* (New York: Greenwood Press, 1969); and the works of Baron du Casse, Jerome's biographer and editor of the *Memoires et Correspondance du Roi Jerome*.

2. Sergeant, *The Burlesque Napoleon*, 169–71.

3. Ibid., 191.

4. J. M. Thompson, *Napoleon's Letters*, especially Napoleon to Jerome, March 6 and July 16, 1808.

5. Copy of Joseph Patterson's reply to Count Furstenstein, January 6, 1808, MdHS MS 142, box 1.

6. Auguste Le Camus to Betsy, August 23, 1807, MdHS MS 142, box 1.

7. Jeanne de Volunbrun rented property from William Patterson for several years and was mentioned in his will. Stephen Whitman says she was Baltimore's richest woman, owning twenty-two slaves—ten men, nine women, and three children—who made the cigars she sold in her tobacco shop. Whitman, *Price of Freedom*, 23 and 52n.

8. Bishop John Carroll to Betsy, May 9, 1808. The baptismal documents show

the godparents were Bishop Carroll and Mrs. Caton, daughter of Charles Carroll of Carrollton. Three of Mrs. Caton's daughters signed as witnesses. MdHS MS 142, box 1.

9. Anna Kuhn to Betsy, November 24, 1807, MdHS MS 142, box 1.

10. Eliza Anderson to Betsy, July 2, 1808, MdHS MS 142, box 1.

11. Copy of Betsy's correspondence to Turreau, July 8, 1808, MS 142, box 1. In *A Family Lawsuit*, Mitchell notes that he found the actual letter in Paris at the Archives du Ministère des Affaires Etrangères, correspondances politiques – États-Unis, vol. 61, 299–301.

12. Letters and invitations from Turreau, March 13 and July 7, 1805; March 16, July 13, September 8, and September 15, 1807; September 8 and September 19, 1808, MdHS MS 145 and MS 142, box 1. William Patterson and Betsy dined with him on March 12, 1807, and Miss Spear and Betsy were his guests on September 15, 1807.

13. Timothy Wilson-Smith, *Napoleon: Man of War, Man of Peace* (NY: Carroll & Graf, 2002), 173.

14. Betsy's letter book, MdHS MS 142, box 1.

15. Jerome to Betsy and her father, dated May 16, 1808 but not received until September, MdHS MS 143.

16. Jerome to Betsy, November 22, 1808, MdHS MS 143; Betsy's English translation can be found in MdHS MS 142, box 1.

17. Betsy's letter book, MdHS MS 142, box 1.

18. Copy of Betsy's correspondence to James Monroe, October 15, 1808, MdHS MS 142, box 1.

19. James Monroe to Betsy, November 6, 1808, MdHS MS 142 , box 1.

Chapter 15

1. Reference is made to social events of 1808 in Gaillard Hunt, ed., *The First Forty Years of Washington Society*, 55 and 57.

2. Correspondence between Betsy, Samuel Graves, and his mother: May 16, 1808, MdHS MS 142, box 1; May 14, May 18, July 27, and December 1, 1809; July 10, 1810, in MdHS MS 142, box 2.

3. MdHS has a large collection of books owned by Betsy, and this one is among them.

4. There are six letters from Willink to Betsy between March 2, 1812 and February 27, 1813 in MdHS MS 142, box 2.

5. Lydia Hollingsworth to her cousin, August 12, 1809, MdHS MS 1849.

6. Bishop John Carroll to Elizabeth Brent, August 18, 1809, *The John Carroll Papers*, ed. Thomas O'Brien Henley (Notre Dame, IN: University of Notre Dame Press, 1976).

7. *Diary and Letters of Sir George Jackson 1809–1816* (London, 1873, 2 vols.], cited without specifics in an unpublished typescript by D. M. Quynn, MdHS TS 2194.

8. Napoleon to Minister Champagny, November 18, 1808, Mitchell, *A Family Lawsuit*, 167. Betsy's translation is in MdHS MS 142, box 1.

9. Betsy's notes in her letter book, MdHS MS 142, box 1.

10. Copy of Betsy's letter to Turreau, October 17, 1809, MdHS MS 142, box 1.

11. Letters from Betsy, January 7 and March 17, 1809 to Mme. Volunbrun; Betsy to Auguste Le Camus and General John Armstrong at Paris on March 17, 1809; to Turreau on March 31, 1809; copies in Betsy's letter book, MdHS MS 142, box 1.

12. Turreau to Betsy, September 29 and October 23, 1809 in MdHS MS 142, box 2.

13. Betsy's notes regarding her income are in a notebook in MdHS MS 142, box 9.

14. Turreau's instruction to Tousard, November 24, 1809, and Betsy's translation in her letter book, MdHS MS 142, box 2.

15. Betsy's translation of this dispatch from Napoleon to Minister Champagny is in her letter book, MdHS MS 142, box 2. It is also cited in Mitchell from the Paris Archives in *A Family Lawsuit*, 168.

16. Letter from Lady Jackson in *Diary and Letters of Sir George Jackson*, cited without specifics in D. M. Quynn, MdHS TS 2194.

17. Madame L. Breuil to Betsy, June 20, 1810, MdHS MS 142, box 2.

18. Augustus John Foster, *Jeffersonian America: Notes on the United States of America, Collected in the years 1805–6–7 and 11–12*, ed. Richard Beale Davis. (San Marino, CA: Huntington Library, 1954), 67.

19. Betsy to Consul Beaujour, July 5, 1810, copy in letter book MdHS MS 142, box 2.

20. "Foster's Notes on the United States," *Quarterly Review* 85 (June 1841): 29–31.

21. Foster in *Jeffersonian America*, quoted in Mitchell, *A Family Lawsuit*, 168. On her copy of her letter to Mme. Volunbrun of January 1, 1809, Betsy later added this note: "General Turreau had the audacity subsequently to the above letter, to demand my hand in marriage for himself, a demand answered by myself with all the scorn which it deserved." Betsy's letter book, MdHS MS 142, box 2.

22. Sérurier to the new foreign minister in Paris, the Duc de Bassano, July 14, 1811, Mitchell, *A Family Lawsuit*, 171.

23. Clement Eaton, *Henry Clay and the Art of American Politics* (Glenview, IL: Scott Foresman, 1957), 23.

24. Clay's letter to George Thompson on March 14, 1810, The Papers of Henry Clay, ed. James F. Hopkins (Lexington: University of Kentucky Press, 1959), 1, 458.

25. Senator Gold to Betsy, January 9, 1813, and William Johnson Jr. to Betsy, March 28, 1814; both in MdHS MS 142, box 2.

26. Henry Lee Jr. to Betsy, letters between August 22, 1812 and September 10,

1814, MdHS MS 142, box 2. On one of the letters, Betsy noted that Henry later wrote a biography of Napoleon and died at Paris in 1837.

27. The story of the Washington Irving marriage scheme is from Stanley Williams, *The Life of Washington Irving*, 2 vols. (NY: Oxford University Press, 1935), 134. I am indebted to historian William Dunne for bringing this to my attention in a letter of September 21, 1991.

28. The information about Betsy's friendship with Elbridge Gerry is from Samuel Eliot Morrison's *By Land and by Sea*, cited by D. M. Quynn without specific page numbers. Quynn also mentions the diary of Gerry's son, 150, 167, and 176; and a letter from Gerry to his daughter on July 3, 1813, D. M. Quynn, MdHS TS 2194.

29. Jerome to Betsy and to Bo, February 20, 1812, MdHS MS 143.

30. Joseph Patterson to Betsy, April 25, 1812, MdHS MS 142, Box 2.

31. Information concerning Betsy's investments appears throughout MdHS MS 142: letters, dividend statements, letter book comments, notes made later on transactions, and in her many notebooks in boxes 9, 11, and 13. In regard to her long-term investment practice, the Union Manufacturing Company stock is an example. On an early dividend notice for her ten shares, she noted later, in 1845, that she still owned it and had tripled the number of her shares.

32. Robert Patterson to Betsy, February 25, 1811, regarding the house purchase installments; and on October 31, 1811, saying that "Jas. Jennings charged for plastering your house $191.77"; both can be found in MdHS MS 142, box 2.

33. Jerome's involvement in the march into Russia is described by Wilson-Smith, 67–72.

34. The invasion and retreat from Russia were vividly depicted by French engineer Charles Menard in the extraordinary 1869 chart he drew on a map to show the shrinking of the army as it traveled. It was published by *Forbes Magazine*, May 18, 1987, 121–3.

Chapter 16

1. Francis F. Beirne, *The Amiable Baltimoreans*, 146–7.

2. W. H. Earle, "The Phantom Amendment and the Duchess of Baltimore," *American History Illustrated*, November 1987, 33–9.

3. John Purviance to Betsy, July 16 and July 18, 1811, MdHS MS 142, box 2.

4. Betsy to Baron Lescallier, consul general for France at Philadelphia, October 10, 1811, MdHS MS 142, box 2.

5. Betsy's copy of her letter to the General Assembly, MdHS MS 142, box 2.

6. William Barney to Betsy, December 4, 15, and 16, 1812. The divorce is in Chapter 130 of the Maryland General Assembly's Acts of 1812, No. 8, Folio 470.

7. Jan Willink to Betsy, March 2, 1812, and Elbridge Gerry to Betsy, April 22, 1814, both in MdHS MS 142, box 2.

8. Bo to Betsy, March 5, 1813 and December 7, 14, 18, 26, 1813, all in MdHS MS 144, box 1.

9. Bo to Betsy January 3, 11, 14, 20, and 30, 1814, MdHS MS 144, box 1.

10. Bo to Betsy, February 2, 9, 15, March 18, 28, and April 4, 1814, MdHS MS 144, box 1.

11. Pancake, *Samuel Smith and the Politics of Business*, 102.

12. Betsy kept her financial information in a series of notebooks. Most of them are in MdHS MS 142, box 13, but a few are in boxes 9 and 11. The notebooks mingle various years together and at times the records end in one notebook and take up the next calculations in another one. At other times she filled a notebook, then turned it upside down and filled it up again on the backs of previously used pages.

13. Jonathan Russell to Betsy, February 20, 1815, MdHS MS 142, box 2. The letters of introduction are in the same manuscript.

14. The correspondence regarding attempts made by the Eustis family to get to Europe is dated December 31, 1812, January 17, 1813, November 24, 1813, and December 29, 1814. MdHS put the originals written by Dolley Madison away in safe-keeping, with photocopies stored in MS. 1084. There are also some additional duplicates in MS 142, box 2 with Betsy's other correspondence.

15. Bo to Betsy at Boston, March 30, 1815, MdHS MS 144, box 1.

16. The Maryland involvement in the War of 1812 is described in a number of excellent accounts. Most useful in the present context is Walter Lord, *The Dawn's Early Light* (Baltimore: Johns Hopkins University Press, 1972).

17. D. C. Hollingsworth to Ruth Tobin, September 15, 1814, Hollingsworth Papers, MdHS MS 1849.

18. Harold R. and Beta K. Manakee, *The Star-Spangled Banner* (Baltimore: The Maryland Historical Society, 1954).

19. Patterson death dates were found in the family graveyard on the grounds of their Cold Stream property. The reference to Margaret's artistic ability is in a letter from Eliza Anderson-Godefroy to Betsy, July 2, 1808 in MdHS MS 142, box 2.

20. Mrs. Caton to Betsy, November 7, 1814, MdHS MS 142, box 2; Betsy's note written about Caroline's beauty was written on back of Caroline's letter to her, January 1st, 1814, MdHS MS 142, box 2.

21. Mrs. Caton to Betsy, November 7, 1814, MdHS MS 142, box 2.

22. McLynn, *Napoleon: A Biography*, 630.

23. David Cordingly, *The Billy Ruffian: The Bellepheron and the Downfall of Napoleon* (London: Bloomsbury, 2003), 249.

24. Lydia Hollingsworth to Ruth Tobin, March 27, 1815, MdHS MS 1849.

Chapter 17

1. William Patterson to Betsy, December 13, 1815, Didier, 50.

2. Cordingly, *The Billy Ruffian*, 268.

3. Eliza Godefroy to Betsy, June 8, 1815, MdHS MS 142, box 2.

4. Lydia Russell, letter of recommendation to Benjamin West, n.d., MdHS MS 142, box 2.

5. Mary Caton Patterson to Betsy, July 15, 1815, MdHS MS 142, box 2.

6. William Patterson to Betsy, November 16, 1815, Didier, 46–7. Upon his meeting with Betsy, James McIlhiny repeated Patterson's comments to her.

7. James McIlhiny to Betsy, August 29, 1915, MdHS MS 142, box 2.

8. Betsy to William Patterson, August 22, 1815, Didier, 41–2.

9. *Cheltenham Chronicle*, 1815, British Library Newspapers (Colindale: London).

10. Betsy to William Patterson, September 2, 1815, Didier, 42–45.

11. William Patterson to Betsy, November 16, 1815, Didier, 46–7.

12. Betsy to William Patterson, February 22, 1816, Didier, 52.

13. Betsy to William Patterson, September 23, 1815, Didier, 47–50.

14. John McIlhiny to Betsy, quoting her father's refusal of support, March 8 and April 16, 1816, with Betsy's handwritten note confirming that her father sent her no money from 1805 to 1836, MdHS MS 142, box 3.

15. Charles Carroll of Carrollton to his granddaughters, as reported to Betsy, January 11, 1817, MdHS MS 142, box 3.

16. There are several references to Patterson's mistresses in the correspondence. See Betsy's handwritten comment on a letter she received from James McIlhiny on April 16, 1816, MdHS MS 142, box 3. Her comment reads: "His mistress Nancy Todd was in his house when his wife was on her death bed and when expelled by Edward Patterson was succeeded in the same capacity by Sommers." The latter's first name was Providence. As Miss Spear wrote to Betsy, on November 17, 1815 in MdHS MS 142, box 3: "Things go on as usual in your father's house. Providence is still there." On this letter Betsy added: "the mother of his bastard."

17. William Patterson to Susan Bonaparte, February 16, 1833, MdHS MS 2978.

18. Patterson's financial transactions appear in several manuscript files, including numbers 145, 904, and 1084. Transactions relating to Providence are also summarized in his will and his various amendments to it, in MdHS MS 645.

19. Edward Patterson to Betsy, November 16, 1815, MdHS MS 142, box 3.

20. Dolley Madison to Betsy, November 24, 1813, MdHS MS 142, box 2.

21. Betsy to Mary Caton Patterson, November 7, 1815, *Maryland Historical Magazine* 20 (1925): 125–6.

22. Betsy to John Spear Smith, August 22, 1816, MdHS MS 142, box 3.

23. James Gallatin claimed John Jacob Astor's table manners were so atrocious that he once wiped his hands on young Frances Gallatin's dress, prompting Mrs. Gallatin to ask, "Oh, did we fail to give you a napkin?"

24. Diary of James Gallatin.

25. David Baillie Warden Papers, MdHS MS 871.

26. This story is told in several books about Wellington, and Betsy herself recounted the tale often. The duke's invitations to her are dated December 1 and 29, 1815 and March 30, 1816 in MdHS MS 142, box 3.

27. John Spear Smith to Betsy, March 25, 1816, MdHS MS 142, box 3.

28. John Spear Smith to Betsy, April 18, 1816, MdHS MS 142, box 3.

29. This account appears in several sources, including Didier's *Life and Letters*, 51, and Theo Aronson's *The Golden Bees: the Story of the Bonapartes*, 185. The reference to Napoleon as a blackguard appears only in James Gallatin's account, and doesn't sound like something Betsy would say. We do know that Betsy decided against applying to the new government for an extension of her pension, as the letter written by David Parrish on her behalf to Tallyrand—which includes a detailed justification for the award—was never used. The letter remains in MdHS MS 142, box 2.

30. MdHS MS 142, boxes 3 and 4 show more than two dozen notes from the Marquise de Villette arranging meetings with Betsy.

31. Lady Sydney Morgan's *Memoirs and Correspondence*, ed. W. Hepworth Dixon (Paris: A. and W. Galignani, 1862.) contains letters from Betsy to Sydney. Correspondence from Sydney to Betsy is found in MdHS MS 142, boxes 3, 4, and 5. The confession about Betsy's poverty is reinforced in her letter to Sydney dated March 14, 1849, in the *Memoirs*.

32. Betsy to Sydney Morgan, *Memoirs and Correspondence*.

33. Ibid.

34. Heather Ersts Venters, "Can the Town Belle Influence Decorative Arts?" (1997) MdHS.

35. Sydney Morgan to Betsy, July 29, 1818, MdHS MS 142, box 3.

36. Betsy to Mrs. Caton, February 2, 1816, in *Maryland Historical Magazine*, 20 (1925): 123–4.

37. These books are in the collection from Betsy's library at MdHS. She marked them with her signature, along with the date and place of purchase.

38. Letters to Betsy from John Jacob Astor are found in MdHS MS 142, box 4.

39. Diary of James Gallatin, August 11 and 18.

40. Betsy to David Baillie Warden, April 1816, David Baillie Warden Papers, MdHS MS 871.

41. Betsy to Father John DuBois, June 1816, *Baltimore Sun*, December 8, 1910.

42. Betsy to John Spear Smith, August 22, 1816.

43. Betsy to the Morgans, *Memoirs and Correspondence*.

44. Duke of Wellington to Betsy, January 1817, MdHS MS 142, box 3.

45. Betsy to the Morgans, May 26, 1817, *Memoirs and Correspondence*.

46. Written by Betsy in her copy of *Lettres Chinoises* (La Haye, 1744) in the MdHS collection from her library.

47. Brugger, *Maryland: A Middle Temperament*, 198–9.

48. Sydney Morgan to Betsy, May 26, 1817, MdHS MS 142, box 3.
49. Bo's early notebooks are found in MdHS MS 144, box 1.

Chapter 18

1. Betsy to William Patterson, April 25, 1820, Didier, 73.
2. Bo to William Patterson, n.d., Didier, 67–8.
3. Bo to William Patterson, November 6, 1820, Didier, 73.
4. Betsy to William Patterson, December 11, 1823, Didier, 150.
5. Regarding Joseph Bonaparte's offer, see Betsy to William Patterson, May 22, 1821, Didier, 74–5.
6. Bo to William Patterson, December 21, 1821, Didier, 84.
7. Mme. Mère to Joseph Bonaparte, January 25, 1822, Didier, 108.
8. Bo to William Patterson, n.d., Didier, 74.
9. Bo to William Patterson, December 7, 1822, Didier, 87.
10. Mme. Tousard to William Patterson, Didier, 110.
11. Betsy to William Patterson, August 3, 1822, Didier, 105–6.
12. Betsy to William Patterson May 30, 1828, Didier, 209.
13. Bo to William Patterson, August 16, 1824, Didier, 156.
14. Betsy to William Patterson, June 4, 1825, Didier, 161.
15. Betsy to Sydney Morgan, n.d., Didier, 159–61.
16. Betsy to William Patterson, July 7, 1822, Didier, 101–104.
17. Betsy to D. B. Warden, November 26, 1823, Warden Papers, MdHS MS 871.
18. Betsy to William Patterson, February 1, 1826, Didier, 177.
19. Jerome Bonaparte to Bo, March 6, 1826, Didier, 179.
20. Bo to William Patterson, June 1826, Didier, 184.
21. Bo to William Patterson, January 25, 1827, Didier, 199.
22. Bo to William Patterson, January 7, 1827, Didier, 198.
23. The provisions of the Bonaparte-Williams marriage contract can be found in William Patterson's papers, MdHS MS 145. They are also summarized in Edward Patterson's letter to Betsy of October 28, 1830, MdHS MS 142, box 5.
24. The letters Bo received from the various Bonapartes were saved and eventually submitted as evidence in his 1859 lawsuit for recognition as a legitimate Bonaparte. They were copied by Bo (or his clerk) and are collected in MdHS MS 144, box 8. They also appear in Mitchell, *A Family Lawsuit*.

Chapter 19

1. Edward Patterson to Betsy, October 24, 1829, MdHS MS 142, box 5.
2. Edward Patterson to Betsy, March 5, 1830, MdHS MS 142, box 5.
3. William Patterson to Betsy, November 4, 1829, MdHS MS 145.
4. Betsy to William Patterson, December 4, 1829, Didier, 218–20.
5. Betsy to William Patterson, December 21, 1829, Didier, 220–22.

6. Betsy's house designs, MdHS MS 142, box 11.

7. Bertrand's visit, Didier, 265.

8. Information regarding Alexandre Gortchakoff is found in *The Encyclopedia Britannica, Eleventh ed.* (1910), vol. 12, 246–7 and *Les Familles Princieres de L'Ancien Empire de Russe,* Recueil Génélogique, 2d ed., vol. 2, 223–27, "GORTCHAKOV" (Paris: Jacques Ferrand, 1998). The letters to Betsy from Prince Gortchakoff plus her drafts of replies—almost none of them dated—can be found in MdHS MS 142, boxes 5–9 and 12.

9. William Patterson to Betsy, March 10, 1834, MS 145.

10. Pleasant View and its surrounding property was bought by Patterson in 1779 and eventually deeded to Bo. It later became a school for troubled girls (Montrose), then a National Guard facility, and most recently, headquarters for the Maryland Emergency Management Agency.

11. William Patterson to Betsy, November 27, 1830, MdHS MS 145.

12. Miss Spear to Betsy, November 26, 1823, MdHS MS 142, box 4.

13. William Patterson's will, MdHS MS 645.

Chapter 20

1. Marriage contract, December 24, 1803, MdHS MS 142, box 12.

2. Bo to Betsy, March 31, 1835, MdHS MS 144, box 2.

3. Folder titled "Questions for Lawyers Regarding WP's Will," MdHS MS 142, box 12.

4. William Patterson's will, MdHS MSS 145 and 645.

5. Lawyers' preliminary opinions, MdHS MS 142, box 2; correspondence between Betsy and Roger Brooke Taney, MdHS MS 142, box 6.

6. Bo to Betsy, March 31, 1835, MdHS MS 144, box 2.

7. Horace Binney's opinion, April 4, 1835, MdHS MS 142, box 6.

8. Horace Binney and John Sergeant, joint opinion, April 4, 1835, MdHS MS 142, box 12.

9. Betsy's note stating that Miss Spear sold her letters to Joseph Patterson was written much later on an undated letter from Miss Spear. Betsy had received the letter in 1815 or 1816, MdHS MS 142, box 3. This was repeated on a note in MdHS MS 142, box 12.

10. Betsy to George Patterson, August 12, 1835, MdHS MS 142, box 6.

11. Undated letter from Miss Spear to Betsy, MdHS MS 142, box 9.

12. Betsy's note about Edward was written on an undated letter in MS 142, box 12. Her closeness to Edward is shown in the twenty letters from him, also found in MS 142, box 12. The letter from Betsy to George Patterson describing the correspondence between them is dated August 12, 1835, and is found in MdHS MS 142, box 6.

13. This comment was written on Bo's letter to Betsy of March 31, 1835, MdHS MS 142, box 6.

14. *Baltimore Patriot,* August 10, 1835.

15. Pancake, 195–6; Cassell, *Merchant Congressman*, 262–4.

16. Taney to Sergeant and Binney, May 6, 1835, MdHS MS 142, box 6.

17. Betsy to John Campbell White, June 12, 1830, MdHS White Papers, MS 1005.

18. Betsy to Sydney Morgan, March 14, 1849, Didier, 258–61, and Betsy to J. C. White June 1, 1827, MdHS MS 1005.

19. There is a copy of Cardinal Fesche's will annotated by Bo in MdHS MS 144, box 1; Bo's passport is found in MdHS MS 144, box 2.

20. Roger Price, *A Concise History of France* (Cambridge, England: Cambridge University Press, 1991), 174–7.

21. The seven letters between Lewis Cass and Bo, dated from October 1838 and November 1839, are in MdHS MS 144, box 6.

22. Betsy to David Baillie Warden, August 15, 1839, MdHS MS 871.

23. Betsy to J. C. White, January 20, 1840, MdHS MS 1005.

24. Betsy to J. C. White, January 31, 1832, MdHS MS 1005.

25. Betsy to J. C. White, November 19, 1839, MdHS MS 1005.

26. James Gallatin to Betsy, July 27, 1848, MdHS MS 142, box 7. In reference to Berkeley Springs: this was located in Virginia when Betsy went there in the 1840s and 1850s. The area became part of West Virginia when that state was created, in 1863.

27. Betsy to J. C. White, August 8, 1840, MdHS MS 1005.

28. *Encyclopedia Britannica*, 11th ed. (New York: Cambridge University Press, 1910), vol. 19: 211–16.

29. Dolley Madison to Betsy, February 23, 1842, MdHS MS 142, box 7.

30. Letters from Robert E. Lee to Bo span the years 1846 through 1855 and are in MdHS MS 144, box 2.

31. Price, 177–8.

32. Betsy to Sydney Morgan, March 14, 1849, Didier, 252–4.

33. For Betsy's correspondence about rentals November 1849 see MdHS MS 142, box 7. A guinea was a gold coin worth more than twice the value of a British pound.

34. Sydney Morgan to Betsy, December 1, 1849, MdHS MS 142, box 7.

35. Correspondence between Betsy and George Peabody is dated from November 1849 to May 1, 1850, MdHS MS 142, box 7.

36. Price, 179.

37. Bo to Napoleon III, January 1, 1853; Napoleon III to Bo, February 9, 1853; MdHS MS 144, box 2.

38. Bo's letters to obtain a leave for his son, over several months in 1853, MdHS MS 144, box 2.

39. Bo and his son both wrote to Susan May detailed descriptions of their reception and events throughout their stay in Paris, June 6, 1854 and following months. See MdHS MS 144, box 2, and MdHS MS 2978.

40. Bo Junior's military record can be found in MdHS MS 144, box 4.

41. Letters forwarded by Princess Mathilde, signed by her to Bo as "Your very devoted sister," MdHS MS 144, box 8.

42. Bo to Napoleon III, July 25, 1854, MdHS MS 144, box 2.

43. Minister to Bo and Bo's acknowledgment regarding the 70,000-franc pension, August 2, 1854, MdHS MS 144, box 2. Regarding the dukedom of Sartène, see April 17, 1855, in Mitchell, 146.

44. Citation under Bonaparte-Patterson name, Didier, 257 and Mitchell, 151.

45. Decision of the Family Council, July 5, 1856, Mitchell 148–50; Napoleon III's added note, Didier, 258.

46. Bo to Napoleon III, July 28, 1856, Mitchell, 151–2.

47. Betsy to James Gallatin, May 4 and November 3, 1852, MdHS MS 142, box 7. A partial record of Betsy's payments to her elder grandson is in MdHS MS 142, box 7.

48. Letters between Betsy and Berryer, December 1857 through January 1859, MdHS MS 142, box 7.

49. Bo Junior to Bo, letter of July 4, 1860, states that after he had put in a request to Grand Master of Ceremonies Cambacères, he was informed that a place would be reserved for him, MdHS MS 144, box 8.

Chapter 21

1. *Harper's Weekly*, March 9, 1861.

2. Betsy to Berryer, Dec. 3, 1857, MdHS MS 142, box 7.

3. Berryer to Betsy, January 19, 1858, MdHS MS 142, box 7.

4. Prince Napoleon to Bo, September 5, 1840, Mitchell, 139.

5. The letters Bo gathered are in several large ledgers, with an index in a clerk's hand, MdHS MS 144, box 8.

6. Mitchell, 72.

7. Jerome Junior to Bo, July 11, 1860, MdHS MS 144, box 8.

8. The *Exposé des Faits* was translated by Mitchell and appears in full in A *Family Lawsuit*, 77–153. The original French was published as a pamphlet entitled *Exposé des Faits: Demande a fin de compt, liquidation et partage de la Succession de S. A. I. Le Prince Jérôme par son fils Jérôme-Napoléon Bonaparte et Madame Elisabeth Patterson, épouse divorcée et veuve de Son Altesse Imperiale,* Tribunal de Premiere Instance de la Seine, Prémière Chambre. It can be found in MdHS MS 142, box 12.

9. *The Illustrated London News*, February 9, 1861.

10. Didier, 259–60.

11. *The London Examiner*, February 9 and 16, 1861.

12. The report in the *New York Express* was quoted in the *Baltimore Sun* on July 20, 1861.

13. *The Atheneum* (London), August 31, 1861.

14. Betsy to Bo, July 18, 1861, MdHS MS 144, box 9.

15. Betsy to Berryer, August 15, 1861.

16. Betsy's unsent letter to Gortchakoff is in MdHS MS 142, box 7.

17. Gortchakoff to Betsy, February 19, 1861, MdHS MS 142, box 8.

18. Brugger, *Maryland: A Middle Temperament*, 248, 274–80.

19. Bo's Civil War letters to Jerome Junior, January 18, 1862, February 8 and May 19, 1863, MdHS MS 144, box 9.

20. Susan May Bonaparte to Major General Banks, in Scharf, 652–3.

21. Betsy's Baltimore agent, William Mentzel to Betsy, ca. 1860, 1861, MdHS MS 142, box 7.

22. Bo to Jerome Junior, n.d., MdHS MS 144, box 9. According to *The Random House Historical Dictionary of American Slang*, to "suck the monkey" meant to drink hard liquor from a bottle or direct from the keg.

23. This proposed deal was reported in local newspapers. If true, it may have been a conversation, since there is no written record of it.

24. All of these letters are in MdHS MS 142, boxes 7 and 8.

25. *New York Herald*, January 17, 1873 in Saffell, 133–4.

26. Betsy's will can be found in MdHS MS 142, box 12.

27. George Eliot, *Daniel Deronda* (New York: Harper & Bros., 1961), 474.

Afterword

1. Letter to the author from Jerome Napoleon Bonaparte, August 26, 1995.

2. Chestnut Hill eventually became part of the Roland Park Country Day School campus.

3. The correspondence and memoirs can be found in MdHS MS 142, box 11.

4. "Proceedings of the Society," *Maryland Historical Magazine* 17 (1922): 89, 94–7.

5. Procedures for the archival organization of manuscripts have changed over the years, as is evident in MdHS Manuscript Collection 142. Betsy's correspondence was rearranged during the collection's early years at the society. On one occasion, all of her incoming letters were removed from their envelopes, and the envelopes were filed in a separate folder. This made dating the letters more difficult. The January 8, 1922, note was among these rearranged folders. Later curators, following National Archives procedures for organizing and describing manuscripts, did a much better job putting the letters in order, creating a complete inventory of the collection, and making the information more accessible to researchers.

SELECTED BIBLIOGRAPHY

Abrantès, Laure Junot, Duchesse d'. *At the Court of Napoleon: Memoirs of the Duchesse d'Abrantès.* New York: Doubleday, 1989.

Adams, Henry. *Life of Albert Gallatin.* Philadelphia: J. B. Lippincott, 1879.

Asprey, Robert. *The Rise of Napoleon Bonaparte.* New York: Basic Books, 2000.

Bailyn, Bernard. *The Peopling of British North America: An Introduction.* New York: Alfred A. Knopf, 1986.

———. *Voyagers to the West.* New York: Alfred A. Knopf, 1986.

Barnes, Robert. *Maryland Marriages 1801–1820.* Baltimore: Genealogical Publishing Co., 1993.

Barney, Mary. A *Biographical Memoir of the Late Commodore Joshua Barney from Autobiographical Notes and Journals in the Possession of His Family and Other Authentic Sources.* Boston: Gray and Bowen, 1932.

Beirne, Francis F. *The Amiable Baltimoreans.* Baltimore: Johns Hopkins University Press, 1984. First published 1951 by E. P. Dutton.

Boller, Paul F., Jr. *Presidential Wives.* New York: Oxford University Press, 1988.

Bowling, Kenneth R., ed. *Creating the Federal City, 1774 – 1800: Potomac Fever.* Washington, D.C. : The American Institute of Architects Press, 1988.

Bowling, Kenneth R., ed. "Coming into the City: Essays on Early Washington, D. C." *Washington History* (Spring–Summer, 2000). Washington, D.C: The Historical Society of Washington, D. C., 2000.

Brodie, Fawn M. *Thomas Jefferson: An Intimate History.* New York: Norton, 1974.

Brugger, Robert J. *Maryland: A Middle Temperament, 1634–1980*. Baltimore: Johns Hopkins University Press, 1988.

Callcott, Margaret Law. *Mistress of Riversdale: The Plantation Letters of Rosalie Stier Calvert*. Baltimore: Johns Hopkins University Press, 1991.

Cassell, Frank A. *Merchant Congressman in the Young Republic: Samuel Smith of Maryland 1752–1829*. Madison: University of Wisconsin Press, 1971.

Cerami, Charles A. *Jefferson's Great Gamble*. Naperville, IL: Source Books, 2003.

Chandler, David G. *Dictionary of the Napoleonic Wars*. New York: Simon & Schuster, 1993.

Clay, Henry. *The Papers of Henry Clay*. Edited by James F. Hopkins. Lexington, KY: University of Kentucky Press, 1959.

Cordingly, David. *The Billy Ruffian: The Bellerophon and the Downfall of Napoleon*. London: Bloomsbury, 2003.

Demidoff, Alexandre Tissot. "Bonaparte and Demidoff: A Tale of Two Family Dynasties." *The European Royal Family History Journal* (April 2003): 8–15.

Didier, Eugene L. *The Life and Letters of Madame Bonaparte*. New York: Charles Scribner's Sons, 1879.

Dollarhide, William. *Map Guide to American Migration Routes, 1736–1815*. Bountiful, UT: Heritage Quest, 1997.

Dumas, Alexandre. *The Last Cavalier*. Translated by Lauren Yoder. New York: Pegasus Books, 2007.

Durant, Will and Ariel. *The Age of Napoleon: A History of European Civilization from 1789 to 1815*. New York: Simon and Schuster, 1975.

Eaton, Clement. *Henry Clay and the Art of American Politics*. Glenview, IL: Scott Foresman, 1957.

Les Familles Princieres de l'Ancien Empire de Russe. Recueil Généalogique, 2nd ed. 2 vols. Paris: Jacques Ferrand, 1998.

Fischer, David Hackett. *Albion's Seed: Four British Folkways in America.* New York: Oxford University Press, 1989.

Flexner, James Thomas. *Gilbert Stuart: A Great Life in Brief.* New York: Alfred A. Knopf, 1955.

Footner, Hulbert. *Sailor of Fortune: The Life and Adventures of Commodore Joshua Barney, U.S.N.* New York: Harper & Brothers, 1940.

Foster, Augustus John. *Jeffersonian America: Notes on the United States of America, Collected in the Years 1805–6–7 and 11–12.* Edited by Richard Beale Davis. San Marino, CA: Huntington Library, 1954.

Gallatin, James. *A Great Peacemaker: The Diary of James Gallatin.* New York: Scribner's Sons, 1960.

Hall, Francis. *Travels in Canada and the United States in 1816 and 1817.* London: Longman, Hurst, Rees, Orme, & Brown, 1818.

Heilbrun, Carolyn. *Writing a Woman's Life.* New York: Ballantine, 1989.

Hungerford, Edward. *The Story of the Baltimore and Ohio Railroad 1827–1927.* 2 vols. New York: Arno Press, 1973.

Hunter, Robert, Jr. *Quebec to North Carolina in 1785–1786: Being the Travel Diary and Observations of Robert Hunter, Jr., a Young Merchant of London.* Edited by Louis B. Wright and Marion Tinling. San Marino, CA: Huntington Library, 1943.

Leyburn, James G. *The Scotch-Irish: A Social History.* Chapel Hill: University of North Carolina Press, 1962.

Lord, Walter. *The Dawn's Early Light.* Baltimore: Johns Hopkins University Press, 1972.

Ludwig, Emil. *Napoleon.* Translated by Eden and Cedar Paul. New York: Boni & Liveright, 1926.

Manakee, Harold R. and Beta K. *The Star-Spangled Banner.* Baltimore: Maryland Historical Society, 1954.

Masson, Frédéric. *Napoléon et sa Famille,* 13 vols. Paris: P. Ollendorff, 1900–1919.

Maude, John. *A Visit to the Falls of Niagara in 1800*. London: Longman, Rees, Orme, Brown & Green, 1826.

McCusker, John J. *How Much Is That in Real Money?* American Antiquarian Society: Worcester, MA, 1992.

McLanathan, Richard B. *Gilbert Stuart*. New York: Henry N. Abrams and National Museum of American Art, Smithsonian Institution, 1986.

McLynn, Frank. *Napoleon: A Biography*. New York: Arcade Publishing Company, 2002. First published 1997 by Jonathan Cape.

Melish, John. *Travels in the United States of America in the Years 1806 and 1807, and 1809, 1810, & 1811*. 2 vols. Philadelphia: printed by the author, 1812.

Mitchell, Sidney. *A Family Lawsuit: The Story of Elizabeth Patterson and Jerome Bonaparte*. New York: Farrar, Straus and Cudahy, 1958.

Moreau de St. Méry's American Journey 1793–1798. Translated and edited by Kenneth Roberts and Anna M. Roberts. Garden City, NY: Doubleday, 1947.

Morgan, Sydney. *Memoirs and Correspondence*. Edited by W. Hepworth Dixon. London: W. H. Allen, 1862.

Mount, Charles Merrill. *Gilbert Stuart, A Biography*. New York: W. W. Norton, 1964.

Pancake, John S. *Sam Smith and the Politics of Business: 1752–1839*. University, AL: The University of Alabama Press, 1972.

Poore, Ben Perley. *Perley's Reminiscences of Sixty Years in the National Metropolis*. New York: AMS Press, 1971.

Price, Roger. *A Concise History of France*. Cambridge, UK: Cambridge University Press, 1991.

Proctor, John Clagett. "Washington and Environs." *Washington Sunday Star*, 1928–1949.

Quynn, Dorothy Mackay. "Jérôme Bonaparte aux Antilles, 1801–1803." *Revue de Institute Napoléon*. 60 (Juillet 1956).

———. "Maximilian and Elizabeth Godefroy." *Maryland Historical Magazine* (March 1957). Typescript, MdHS MS 2194.

Roberts, Cokie. *Ladies of Liberty.* New York: William Morrow, 2008.

W. T. R. Saffell, *The Bonaparte-Patterson Marriage in 1803 and the Secret Correspondence on the Subject Never before Made Public* (Philadelphia: privately published, 1873), 29–30.

Scharf, John Thomas. *Chronicles of Baltimore, Being a Complete History of "Baltimore Town" and Baltimore City from the Earliest Period to the Present Time.* Baltimore: Turnbull Brothers, 1874.

Sergeant, Philip. *Jerome Bonaparte: The Burlesque Napoleon.* New York: Brentano's, 1906.

Sioussat, Annie L. *Old Baltimore.* New York: Macmillan, 1931.

Spencer, J. A. *The History of the United States from the Earliest Period to the Administration of James Buchanan,* 3vols. New York: Johnson, Fry & Co. 1858.

Sutcliff, Robert. *A Visit to Some Parts of North America in the Years 1804, 1805, and 1806.* York, UK: W. Alexander, 1815.

Svinin, Pavel Petrovich. *Picturesque United States of America.* New York: William Edwin Rudge, 1930. First published 1818, Petersburg.

Thompson and Walker. *Baltimore Town and Fell's Point Directory of 1796.* Reprint, Silver Spring, MD: Family Line Publications, 1983.

Thompson, J. M. *Napoleon Bonaparte.* Cambridge, MA: Harvard University Press, 1990.

———. *Napoleon's Letters Selected, Translated, and Edited by J. M. Thompson.* London: Prion, 1934, 1998.

Todd, Charles Burr. *The Story of Washington: The National Capital.* New York: G. P. Putnam's Sons, 1889.

Tuchman, Barbara W. *The First Salute: A View of the American Revolution.* New York: Ballantine Books, 1988.

Twining, Thomas. *Travels in America: A Hundred Years Ago.* New York: Harper & Brothers, 1894.

Whitley, William T. *Gilbert Stuart.* Cambridge, MA: Harvard University Press, 1932.

Whitman, T. Stephen. *The Price of Freedom: Slavery and Manumission in Baltimore and Early National Maryland.* Lexington, KY: University Press of Kentucky, 1997.

Williams, Stanley. *The Life of Washington Irving.* 2 vols. New York: Oxford University Press, 1935.

Wilson-Smith, Timothy. *Napoleon: Man of War, Man of Peace.* New York: Carroll & Graf, 2002.

Young, James Sterling. *The Washington Community 1800–1828.* New York: Columbia University Press, 1966.

INDEX